In exploring the ethical dimension of political life, the contributors discuss the basic moral principles and their important relationship to the political order. They examine this linkage between ethics and order with relation to coercion, liberalism, violence, foreign policy, and related themes. Particular issues discussed include: biocultural evolution and political ethics; ideology, technology, and truth; the genesis of Americanism; the theological basis for ethical judgments in the political sphere; and the relationship between history and the moral order.

The Ethical Dimension of Political Life

Essays in Honor of
John H. Hallowell

Edited by Francis Canavan

Duke University Press *Durham, N.C.* 1983

Printed in the United States of America on acid-free paper

Library of Congress Cataloging in Publication Data
Main entry under title:

The Ethical dimension of political life.

"Publications of John H. Hallowell": p. 247.
Includes bibliographical references and index.
1. Political ethics—Addresses, essays, lectures.
2. Hallowell, John H. (John Hamilton), 1913–
I. Hallowell, John H. (John Hamilton), 1913–
II. Canavan, Francis, 1917–
JA79.E818 1983 172 83-1772
ISBN 0-8223-0490-2

Contents

Editor's Preface

These essays are published in honor of John H. Hallowell on his retirement from Duke University where he taught for forty years, most recently as a James B. Duke Professor of Political Science. John Hallowell was born in Spokane, Washington, on August 19, 1913, the son of Harold A. Hallowell and Anna Blanche (Williams) Hallowell. He attended the public schools of Philadelphia, Pennsylvania. In 1935 he graduated from Harvard College, A.B. cum laude. After a year of study in Germany he pursued his graduate studies at Duke University under the tutelage of R. Taylor Cole and received the M.A. degree in 1937, having written a Master's thesis on the Nazi Chamber of Culture. He then transferred to Princeton University where he received the Ph.D. degree in 1939 for which he wrote a dissertation on *The Decline of Liberalism in Germany*. His first teaching position was at the University of California at Los Angeles.

Since throughout his academic career Dr. Hallowell sang outside the chorus of twentieth-century American political science, he has often felt himself to be a voice crying in the wilderness. He has made his voice heard nonetheless through his *Decline of Liberalism as an Ideology*, *Main Currents in Modern Political Thought*, *The Moral Foundation of Democracy*, numerous articles, book reviews, and published talks. The present collection of essays testifies in a small way to how many have heard him and to what effect.

Among the contributors is Gerhart Niemeyer, who taught John at Princeton University and directed his doctoral dissertation. Others are longtime friends and associates who have come to know him through his service in such posts as president of the Southern Political Science Association, editor of the *Journal of Politics*, member of the Council of the American Political Science Association, director of the Lilly Endowment Research Program in Christianity and Politics, and a member of the editorial boards of *The Political Science Reviewer*, *Journal of Church and State*, *Interpretation*, and *Zeitschrift für Politik*. These friends include Professors William C. Havard, Claes G. Ryn, Ellis Sandoz, Mulford Q. Sibley, and

Kenneth W. Thompson. The remainder of the contributors are among Professor Hallowell's former graduate students.

As the range of views here represented shows, John Hallowell has not made disciples or formed a school. But he has, in the words of the citation which accompanied the Litt.D. degree conferred upon him by the College of the Holy Cross (1963), been "a teacher's teacher" who "inspired by precept and example a whole generation of scholars which has found in his person and accomplishments the inspiration and resolution for their own endeavors." These essays reveal how effective he has been in that role. Not all who studied under him have subscribed to his thesis that a revival of political philosophy in the West will require a return to that ancient tradition which synthesized the wisdom of Plato and Aristotle with the Christian revelation. But it is clear that he has confronted us with the basic issues of ethics and politics and made us think about them seriously and deeply. We have gone forth from Duke to carry into a broader academic world, if not always his message, at least his intense concern with questions that will not go away.

From one angle or another, these essays all focus on this concern with the ethical dimension of political life. Some do it by treating the thought of a particular writer—Plato, Hume, or Rousseau—others by dealing with a particular topic. Some write from a philosophical, others from a theological, still others from a scientific point of view. But all are aware of the epistemological, metaphysical, and theological issues that are raised by political theory, and strive to throw light on these issues. The result is a volume that enjoys the unity of a discussion, at times of an argument, centering on a common theme. If it arouses discussion or, better yet, argument, it will have honored John Hallowell by doing what he himself does best.

William C. Havard opens the discussion, in "Policy Sciences, the Humanities, and Political Coherence," with an analysis of a recent development in American political science. The emergence within the discipline of the study of public policy, he points out, has raised to the surface issues which were submerged by the tide of behavioralism that ran so strongly for a generation or more of political scientists. Yet our continuing faith in the problem-solving capacity of science and technology has kept us from squarely facing these issues because it still concentrates our attention on the means, rather than the ends, of public policy. In order adequately to consider the ends of policy, we need a revival of the study of the humanities, including philosophy.

Kenneth W. Thompson develops this theme in "Ethics and Foreign Policy," an essay whose scope is broader than its title indicates. No issue in political theory, he says, is more fundamental than the relationship between ethics and politics (which involves the relationship between political ends and means). American and Western thought generally on this topic has drawn historically on Judeo-Christian, classical, and modern philosophy. Thompson reviews the strengths and deficiencies of each of these traditions and shows why all of them have been weakened by developments in modern history. But with the raising of the political stakes, particularly in relations among nations armed with nuclear weapons, we need a kind of guidance that we can get only by rediscovering ancient truths, and especially those contained in classical and Christian ideas of prudence.

The main political expression of what Thompson calls modern philosophy is liberalism. R. Bruce Douglass makes it the object of a slashing criticism in "Liberalism as a Threat to Democracy." Far from being the essential principle of democratic government, he says, liberalism undermines democracy and ultimately paralyzes it. This is seen with particular clarity in the theory of the "open society" as the democratic ideal. By persuading democratic societies that they can and should be neutral in regard to metaphysics and ethics, Douglass argues, open-society theorists destroy the necessary conditions for democracy's survival.

Francis Canavan pursues this theme in "Liberalism in Root and Flower." Liberalism's intellectual and moral impotence derives, he claims, from its utilitarian hedonism. This in turn he traces back to its roots in the late medieval school of nominalist philosophy, which has made us incapable of recognizing natural wholes and, consequently, of acknowledging natural goods.

The first great thinker of the opposing realist school of philosophy was, of course, Plato (or, if you insist, Socrates—but Plato's Socrates). In "The Force of Reason" James L. Wiser analyzes the argument in Plato's *Gorgias*. In the dialogue between Socrates and his opponents, he shows, two metaphysics are in conflict, one of which leads to hedonism as an ethic, the other to an ethic founded on a natural hierarchy of goods. Yet each view has its own internal consistency which renders it nearly invulnerable to the impact of adverse evidence presented by the other side. The basic issue is the nature and status of "the good," and men's views on that are strongly influenced by what they love. In ethical discourse reason encounters limits because only an *eros* that is responsive to the attraction of transcendent reality can achieve wisdom and a knowledge of what is truly good.

Walter B. Mead replies in "Will as Moral Faculty" that the classical conception of eros did not furnish an adequate understanding of the human will as free and self-determining. Classical philosophy, identifying virtue with knowledge, could not account for man as a free and responsible moral agent. Mead has no desire to emancipate will from the normative direction of reason—quite the contrary—but he insists that it is the very ability of the will to choose the opposite of what reason commends that manifests its radical freedom. We must therefore go beyond the classics' reliance on reason and knowledge to provide the foundations of ethics and politics.

J. M. Porter continues the examination of the will as a fundamental element of political theory in "Democracy and Autonomy in Rousseau." In Rousseau's writings will becomes the essence of personality: one is free, and therefore human, to the extent that he obeys no will that is not his own. This idea flowers, as is well known, in the theory of the General Will by which liberty and law are reconciled in civil society. Porter defends this theory against the charge of internal inconsistency but concludes that Rousseau understands neither will nor reason, and achieves his regime of democratic freedom only by abolishing politics.

In "History and the Moral Order" Claes G. Ryn addresses the question of the roles of reason and will in formulating ethical and political principles from still another angle. There has been a reaction in recent decades against relativism in social and political thought. We cannot, however, he maintains, simply return to an earlier doctrine of natural law, because it was too rigid and static. A way of reconciling universality and flexibility in our ethical judgments might be found, he suggests, in a "value-centered historicism." This would yield us a morality dependent not on precepts of reason but on the ultimacy of will, a higher will that is saved from arbitrariness by its set purpose of achieving goodness amid constantly varying circumstances.

Another effort to present the idea of an objectively valid moral norm in terms acceptable to modern man is made by Thomas A. Spragens, Jr., in "David Hume's 'Experimental' Science of Morals and the Natural Law Tradition." Spragens argues persuasively that Hume, the intellectual father of modern empiricism, emotivism, and ethical relativism, was in fact trying to base moral standards on our common human nature. Hume admittedly denied the moral competence of reason—but of reason in the truncated form in which his century understood it. On the other hand, he believed that the social feelings, or "sympathy," of the mass of mankind revealed the real needs and natural ends of human beings and sufficed to furnish us with moral precepts subject to empirical (or "experimental") validation. Hume's theory has its very real problems, which Spragens points out, but they are not, he feels, beyond solution, and their solution might enable us to speak to positivists and skeptics about a modern equivalent of natural law.

In a more radical effort to set political ethics on an empirical foundation, Fred H. Willhoite, Jr., presents "Biocultural Evolution and Political Ethics." Contemporary theories of biological and cultural evolution, he says, show how and why human beings, striving to assure the propagation of their own and their kinsmen's genes, moved from the family to government and the state. This application of Darwinian natural selection to social and political evolution reveals man as naturally competitive, a being who submits to political authority, when it eventually emerges, for the sake of protection but feels the need for protection against the abuses of authority. It is a view of man, Willhoite maintains, that should inoculate us against the utopian but murderous dreams of twentieth-century ideology, and will provide us with a realistic basis for the political ethic of prudential moderation on which constitutional democracy depends.

In "Ideology, Technology, and Truth" Barry Cooper explains how the disappearance from the modern mind of the idea of nature as a norm has removed from our thinking the notion of limits on what we are permitted to do. The limits to our desires that we encounter are now only problems to be solved, "challenges to the will, not mysteries to be respected." Consequently, for most of us today, "the highest political good is the creation of the technological society." Theory can no longer control practice because technique is our theory, and political philosophy has been replaced by ideology. We move, therefore, toward the universal and homogeneous state. There is, however, no prospect of reversing that movement by a revival of Greek philosophy or biblical religion, still less by contemporary chatter about "values." The reader must decide for himself whether the essay ends with an affirmation, a question, or a sigh. He will in any case find it fascinating.

The most powerful of the modern ideologies that have replaced philosophy and religion is Marxism. Gerhart Niemeyer addresses himself to the Marxist-Leninist answer to the perennial question of the nature of "the good" in "Communism and the Notion of the Good." That communism contains a strong moral element is clear, and this is a large part of its appeal. But, says Niemeyer, it rests on nothing other than a radical negation, the rejection of present and past society as evil. The good is merely the opposite of what now exists, a contentless promise of what will emerge once evil is done away with. Communist thought has no room for such constants as gods, essences, nature, being. It offers us not even the blueprint of a utopian future, but only the "coming to be" of that which is "not yet" as the measure of good and evil. We thus arrive at a point 180 degrees removed from Plato and the Idea of the Good.

The other main strand in John Hallowell's thought has been the Christian revelation. James W. Skillen draws on it for his answer to the question he raises in "Societal Pluralism: Blessing or Curse for the Public Good?" The created universe, he says, is complex and pluriform, not uniform and homogeneous. Human society, too, reflecting the order of creation, is inherently pluralistic. The public order that unifies it must therefore recognize society's pluralistic character and respect the supreme authority of the Creator from whom it ultimately derives its character. Any political ideology that suppresses societal pluralism for the sake of a univocal social goal—even of freedom, as in Rousseau—is totalitarian and idolatrous.

Political authority has often been identified with the ability to exercise coercive force. In "The Problem of Coercion" Mulford Q. Sibley says that the justification of violent coercion, and of war in particular, came into Christian thought with St. Augustine and the doctrine of original sin. A more positive view of the function of political authority as social coordinator and promoter of distributive justice would be, he feels, more compatible with Christianity. Followed through, it would lead us to the renunciation of violent coercion, therefore to the abolition of capital punishment, unilateral disarmament, and refusal to offer armed resistance to tyranny. But a people imbued with the Christian ethic of love and willing to put up an organized, nonviolent resistance to oppression could effectively withstand tyranny and would be more disposed than we have been to pursue just social goals.

Clarke E. Cochran takes a somewhat different view of the political consequences of Christian faith in "The Radical Gospel and Christian Prudence." The demands of Jesus in the Gospel are indeed radical, he says, and we must not diminish them. But they stand side by side in the Gospel with the refusal of Jesus to enunciate a political or economic theory or to preach a program of social change. One risks turning the Gospel into an ideology when one derives a political program from it. The application of the Gospel to politics therefore requires the exercise of a genuinely Christian prudence. There are a lower and a higher Christian prudence, both found in the Gospel and harmonized in the concept of stewardship as a guide to Christian political action.

Ellis Sandoz analyzes the "founding myth" of the American republic in "Power and Spirit in the Founding." The generation that won American independence and set up the republic, he argues with ample documentation, had a high and noble conception of their enterprise and based it on not merely secular but explicitly Christian beliefs. They knew that good government presupposes good people, and they did not expect people to be good without religion. They disestablished religion and established religious liberty, it is true, but, Sandoz concludes, they did so "on the understanding that basic agreement on the principles of Christianity is an essential element of the moral foundation of the society."

We end with William R. Marty's "The Search for Realism in Politics and Ethics." This is the only essay in the volume that was previously published elsewhere, in vol. 1 of *Logos* (University of Santa Clara). It is republished here, in revised form and with the permission of the editor, because of John Hallowell's known admiration for it as a statement on what has been the major theme of his own thought. The trouble with ideologists, it has been remarked, is that they have not yet noticed the twentieth century. Marty vigorously directs our attention to what has happened in this century because of ideological dreams and argues trenchantly that a return to political realism will require an admission that the religious assessment of human nature was the right one. It is a fitting conclusion to a volume dedicated to John Hallowell.

In closing, I must express my deep appreciation for the generous help I have received from another of my former teachers at Duke University, R. Taylor Cole, in preparing this volume for publication. Its publication has been substantially aided by a grant from the Earhart Foundation, which I here gratefully acknowledge. I also want to add another word of thanks. Like so many of John Hallowell's students and friends, I have been a frequent visitor in his home. I am sure that I speak for all of them in thanking his wife, Sally Hallowell, for the gracious hospitality with which she has on so many occasions brightened the lives of graduate students and even (if this be possible) of professors of political science.

Francis Canavan, S.J.

The Ethical Dimension of Political Life

William C. Havard · *Policy Sciences, the Humanities, and Political Coherence*

In little more than a decade (dating its early visibility from approximately the mid-1960s) the formal study of public policy moved from a peripheral place in the concerns of American political science to a central position in the discipline. To be sure, political science has always paid attention to what was once referred to as "the functions of government." The emphasis on policy was strengthened in the New Deal period, when American political scientists were reassessing the role of government, especially the central government, in response to, first, the economic crisis and, later, the movement away from isolationism to activism in the face of the international disorders leading to World War II. The New Deal also greatly increased the connection between research in the social sciences and active participation in politics and administration on the part of social scientists. Scores of social scientists enthusiastically went to work on the expansive agencies of the Roosevelt administration, buoyed up by a newfound confidence in the practical applicability of the knowledge generated by social science to the social problems at hand, and an urge to be a part of the Baconian translation of knowledge (especially technical knowledge) into power.

But today the effect of the study of public policy on the curricula of political science (and other social science) departments, and perhaps even on the renewed efforts to find some way to reintegrate knowledge within a liberal educational context, far outstrips anything that occurred in any earlier period. Policy studies are surely the growth enterprise not only in the social sciences, but in higher education generally today. There is an expanded production not only in courses and areas of concentration, but in the establishment of research institutes of public policy, the organization of professional associations of policy study "specialists," and the enlistment in the cause of scholars in various subfields who want to be on the "cutting edge" of knowledge (being at the "forefront" is apparently passé as old fads give way to new ones).

For purposes of advancing the argument rather than attempting to provide a definitive explanation, it may be suggested that two interconnected developments (each in its respective way the product of a disenchanting or disillusioning tendency) affected the shift of attention to public policy as a (possibly *the*) major object of inquiry in political science (and the other social sciences as well).

The first was essentially epistemological: behavioralism, rooted in positivism and its promise of a cumulative theoretical advancement to a teleological culmination in a "predictive science" of politics, had been the dominant mode of the discipline for the preceding generation. Not only did behavioralism fail to fulfill its progressivist promises, but its exponents concentrated so much on political processes and so narrowed the range of problems studied (apparently in the interest of relying on method to subsume the substance of politics) that the very nature of politics as a human activity could hardly be discerned in most of what one read in the professional journals.

The second contributing factor was directly political, and it came in the form of the latest crisis (or series of crises) in American society and government. One need not recite in detail the complex course of events over the past two decades to recall the increasing social disruption and individual anomie, the limited effects of the Great Society programs in meeting even basic physical needs (let alone those of a moral and spiritual nature) of large segments of the society, the adverse effects of the Vietnam venture on both foreign and domestic policy, and the threatened breakdown of the constitutional order posed by Watergate and its aftermath. It became increasingly clear that policy issues could no longer be resolved by the application of social technologies (usually in the form of additives) to isolable issues. Some of the symptoms might be relieved, but the basic problems of social cohesion, adaptation of a traditional order to new challenges to its coherence, and confusion in the meaning of the symbols through which the identity of the society as a polity was expressed, seemed to demand reexamination by modes of analysis that went beyond instrumental rationality.

Some of the new or revitalized policy institutes, centers, and publication outlets for policy-oriented study placed some emphasis on the nature of the values that informed policy decisions rather than treating the issues as questions of process involving the authoritative allocation of goods ("goods" being defined *via negativa* as utilitarian). But most of the public policy analysts in political science wanted to transfer their behavioral mode and methods from the "science" of politics (i.e., politics as formal processes) to the "policy sciences."[1] In other words, while the problems confronted defied, or seemed to defy, the ingenuity of instrumental reason, and to demand a rational reexamination of the human needs and purposes served by the public order within the context of the limits and possibilities inherent in the practice of politics as this particular society had experienced it, the epistemic foundations of the social sciences were so deeply grounded in the scientistic faith that the change in focus from formal political processes to policy formation and implementation was made without any alteration in the expectation that steady accumulation of positive results to the point of definitive knowledge would result from the proper application of methods to particular problems perceived by the analyst.

The core of the problem, then, is that the eighteenth-century bifurcation of knowledge into the Kantian "pure" and "practical" reason, followed by the appropriation of the grounds of truth by the methods of the mathematized sciences of external phenomena, and the relegation of the classical rational sciences of man and society to the realms of relativity, subjectivity, and emotive drives or "sentiments" (as in the ethics of *Ressentiment* of the French Encyclopaedists, or the natural moral sentiments of Hume) have been slavishly adhered to by the general run of the social sciences in the twentieth century. And this trend continues even as the underpinning secular faith in progress through the mediating grace of science and technology is undermined by the historical disorders of the twentieth century.

The new emphasis on policy studies thus grew out of a latent crisis of confidence in the continuing capacity of our public institutions, through their systemically perceived processes, to formulate, enact, and implement policies that are capable of satisfying both the symbolic and utilitarian expectations of the society at large. But this shift did not alter the direction of inquiry from the phenomenal to the noetic basis of the processes and issues under examination. As a friendly British critic—Bernard Crick—pointed out more than twenty years ago with specific reference to the theoretical weaknesses of American political science, the historic success of the American political experience resulted in our placing so much faith in the problem-solving capacity of science and technology, on the one hand, and reposing so much confidence in the strength and stability of our democratic institutions, on the other, that we tend to ignore the need to confront those persisting, fundamental issues of politics that have been constants in most political societies.[2]

In many respects the academic problems of the humanities that have also clearly emerged in recent years have their earlier origins in the same set of misplaced confidences. When Baconian methods and Newtonian advancements in the sciences were translated by the Encyclopaedists into a division of all knowledge into the useful sciences and the study of arcane subjects, the prestige of the classical disciplines in the humanities began to decline by comparison with the scientific and applied scientific ones. Consequently, the place of the former in the understanding of and influence on the affective areas of both private and public human concerns also began a long process of erosion and displacement by the latter.[3] Obviously these changes have not been complete—the humanities have not disappeared either from the academies or from the bases of individual ethical and collective political actions of the public. But the universalization and democratization of higher education, with the subsequent focus on vocational objectives aimed at the fulfillment of tabulated manpower and womanpower "needs," placed the very conception of an integrative liberal education, and especially those components drawn from the humanities, on the defensive. It is appropriate, if ironic, that this development coincided in time with the beginning of the recognition of the massive public issues that so obviously required reexamination from historical and philosophical perspectives. One might even go so far as to say that the organization of the National Endowment for the Humanities had as one of its implicit (later explicit) motive forces not only the revival of the status of the humanities in academia but also the promotion of an active role for the humanities in the understanding of public problems and the limitations and possibilities in politics as a basic human activity.

Despite its long-range dissociative effect on our understanding of human reason and its reductive consequences for epistemology, the division between "pure" and "practical" reason has a certain heuristic value. In the application of this dichotomy to the objects of knowledge, politics seems to me clearly to belong to that class of phenomenological experience that has to be dealt with by the practical reason. I am acutely conscious of the fact that some of my colleagues insist on scientific purity as a condition of being recognized as a professional by one's fellows, and I think that some behavioral attributes of humans that we consider political can be quantified and described in terms of empirically testable propositions or hypotheses. But I also think that, quite apart from its practice, the study of politics reveals serious reductionist problems if the underlying assumptions of the inquiry are rigidly tied to the epistemology and methods of the natural sciences. Only the more superficial aspects of political activity exhibit the regularity and conformity to deterministic "laws" of action and reaction supposedly characteristic of the phenomena of the natural, or external, world. And even those quantifiable, structured, and presumably predictive aspects of politics are rarely, if ever, universal; their uniformities are the results of habits or traditions of behavior whose meanings are rooted in a particular societal context or even a civilization that has been formed out of its own historical experience and is open to further alteration through conscious adaptation to changing circumstances. I am not, of course, suggesting that either the ends sought through political action or the means through which a political entity conducts its public life are totally derivative or relative. Politics is a ubiquitous human activity, with its elaborate permutations reflecting choices and adaptations that run the full gamut of human ingenuity in the application of the practical reason. The meaning of politics is discovered in the nature of man writ large, and is thus an activity that exemplifies Eric Voegelin's profound observation that man is a participant in the structure of reality of which he is a part.[4]

Perhaps the biggest giveaway on the part of those who hold a firmly positivist view about the study of politics is the way they act when they remove themselves from the detached posture of the scholar and become political participants. Rarely, if ever, do they insist on or apply their own articulated canons of science to their judgments on the practical activities that engage them in the real political world, or even to the discourse by means of which these engagements are pursued collectively. One of the most implacable logical positivists I know as a scholar is also in his practical life the most opinionated man I have ever encountered. He never hesitates to assert the most sweeping categorical moral imperatives; his judgments on the character and fitness of individuals and national states are as unequivocal as his expressions of taste in relation to all forms of art, and he shows little evidence of having reduced either his ego or his considerable mental power to mere objects of analysis. In fact, he might, in the conduct of his practical life—i.e., in his ethics, politics, and all activities other than purely intellectual pursuits—be taken to represent the very antithesis of what he professes to perceive as objective reality. When one observes such obvious discrepancies between the behavior of an individual as a practitioner of value-free science, on the one hand, and as an active participant in the phenomena he studies, on the other, one can hardly avoid entertaining doubts about the extent to which the positive theory is sufficiently encompassing to describe, let alone explain, political experience.

But even if one presupposes that the study of politics may be cumulatively transformed into a "pure" science, the practice of politics can hardly be said to conform to the specifications of an applied science of humanity in the manner in which technology translates the results of natural science into a utilitarian control over natural phenomena. For the practice of politics is purposive and creative; it is a matter of choice and of interest, one's own or that of others, and is, therefore, more fraught with moral than with technical difficulties, although there are decision makers who try to turn all problems into questions of technique. The very language of politics is, as Michael Oakeshott tells us, "the language of desire and aversion, of preference and choice, of approval and disapproval, of praise and blame, of persuasion, injunction, accusation and treat [*sic*]. It is the language in which we make promises, ask for support, recommend beliefs and actions, devise and commend administrative expedients and organize the beliefs and opinions of others in such a manner that policy may be effectively and economically executed: in short, it is the language of everyday, practical life."[5]

At this point the general objects of inquiry and methods of the humanities seem to me to come into full congruence with the practice of politics in ways that may inform that practice so it can be enhanced rather than perverted. The humanities are concerned precisely with those aspects of life identified as belonging peculiarly or particularly to human beings, but not to human beings conceived simply as objects, or as the mere cumulative results of discreetly analyzable properties. We are speaking of human beings considered as a whole and as having certain unique characteristics, characteristics that both define them and make it possible for them to understand themselves. So far as we are aware, humans are the only creatures who have a self-conscious relation both to themselves as individuals and to things external to them. They are the only creatures who reason both instrumentally and axiomatically; who distinguish between good and evil, abstractly and pragmatically; who attempt to establish standards of truth, beauty, and justice; who discern intimations of transcendence; who have inherited and constantly embellish the elaborate logical and affective structures known as languages; who create myths through which they symbolize the meaning of their existence; and who have enough awareness of the past and sense of identity with membership in a tribe, polis, state or empire to have generated an intelligible history. Without drawing the obvious connections, I submit that these unique qualities are the most generalized objects that the disciplines in the humanities seek to comprehend in whole or in part. And it is because of these qualities, and by means of their mediation, that man is able to conduct his practical life, with the result that the humanities, if they are true to themselves, cannot avoid or ignore the practical realms of morals and politics.

It is true that there are purists who argue that the humanities have to do solely with an aesthetic mode of experience complete in itself, and that its devotees should not grub around in anything so mundane as the practical arts of morals and politics which, by contrast with the absolute ideas of the idealized humanities, are subject to so many contingencies. But I submit that the humanities, if they are not to abstract themselves from the human experience they are seeking to symbolize and explain, must cope with the practical in its own terms because its terms are so much at one with those of the humanities.

One may, of course, admit that all of this high-blown rhetoric does say something about the connection between the objectives and pursuits of the humanities and those of practical life, and still ask the question, "What, if anything, can the scholar in the humanities do specifically that will contribute to a more effective resolution of public issues?" The answer is both positive and negative. In a positive sense, the humanities can bring special understanding to bear on political questions in a way that clarifies the grounds on which choices are made and refines the manner in which the advocate of a particular position presents his conclusions and supporting arguments. On the negative side, the student of the humanities can warn and constrain because he knows the limits imposed on any form of human activity by what is so often referred to in a shorthand way as the human condition itself. And in the process the scholar may learn some things about the nature of human experience and the way human beings express their understandings of experience that the literature of his discipline has not sufficiently illustrated.

In the matter of clarifying the grounds on which choices are made, those engaged primarily with the humanities are accustomed to bringing a holistic perspective to bear on human concerns. Certainly analysis of political issues is important, but so is the reintegration of all the specifics disclosed by analysis. Politics does not take place in a vacuum; it is integrally related to nearly all other forms of human activity, and man has a need to explain his actions to himself so that they appear to be internally consistent. The student of literature has a trained awareness of this necessity because it is implicit in the very form of literature, with its ultimate reconciliation, or denouement, of the complex characters and events on which a play or story turns. And it is worth noting that literature is a refinement and extension of the primitive mythic symbols by which man first demonstrated his need to integrate the confusing and conflicting experiences confronting his consciousness.

The historian has a similar unifying point of view to bring to bear on issues. Out of a vast agglomeration of historical facts the historian is constrained to select those events and personalities through which the past becomes a connected or continuing account of human experience right into the present, and even into the as yet unexperienced, but anticipated, future. A political order cannot long survive without an awareness that its very existence is a matter of historical interpretation, and it needs to bring the implications of the experience of its own past way of doing things to bear on the problems of the present. Societies and governments are held together by a set of common beliefs, habits, and traditions. Historians are concerned with the critical elucidation of these socially binding forces as part of their connective account of the past. How are the society's successes and failures related to these agents of cohesion? How have they changed, and how adaptable are they to the threats of social dissolution? Such considerations are as crucial to the intelligent discussion of public issues as they eventually are to the survival of a working political system.

In an address delivered at an early meeting of members of the committees of an NEH program in the humanities and public policy, the late Charles Frankel noted that philosophy has been, above all, a discipline that looks into the coherence of our working assumptions. Others have projected more grandiose ends of philosophy by suggesting that it aims at reconciling at the highest level the apparent contradictions or contingencies in the more specialized intellectual pursuits, or even that its function is to come to terms with experience as a whole. If philosophy's function is to seek coherence, to reconcile seemingly conflicting objects of knowledge and to unify the whole range of experience, and if it assimilates both observed phenomena and introspection into its conclusions, it may be said to be the most comprehensive of the humanities in the application to problems of public policy. In this respect all of those engaged with the humanities may be said to be philosophers manqué when they turn their attention to the practical life. Philosophy, then, is not one way of attempting to deal with the existential, moral, and aesthetic realities of public affairs; it is the ultimate way of dealing with it as a fully developed human being.

In all this discussion of applications of the humanities to public affairs, one should not neglect the implications of language as the medium through which issues are articulated and eventually resolved. And as students of the languages clearly know, language is not a simple thing in either the structural or the symbolic sense. Since ordinary language is our means of communicating about politics, it behooves us to understand that its uses in this context can be so diversified that only its most astute students can classify its intentions and effects. It can be used analytically or hortatorily, creatively or destructively; it can be designed to clarify or confuse, placate or incite, motivate or inhibit, and it can be an instrument of freedom or of repression. Surely we cannot consider any effort to offer a forum to the public for articulating its views on issues to be a success unless it seeks to exercise some influence on the improvement of the association between reality and its expression through the written or spoken word. Oakeshott wisely reminds us, and not in a derogatory sense, that politics has always been three-quarters talk, and if we do not know how to use the current vocabulary of politics we are seriously hampered in our wish to participate.[6] In a democracy, where it is assumed that everyone may, and should, participate in politics, students of language have a special obligation to provide assistance in the developing of the essential tools of political action.

Perhaps I can illustrate by an example from the real world how some or all of these possible roles of the humanities need to be applied to the discussion of a social issue. For this purpose I choose a homey, localized incident that is universal in its implications. A few years ago a controversy raged in parts of West Virginia, and in some places in southwest Virginia, over the reading materials used in English courses in the public high schools. The dispute was acrimonious and soon debouched into direct political action in the form of strikes and picketing against use of school buses and school attendance. Individuals were arrested for creating disturbances, property was damaged, and it was even reported that physical harm was inflicted on a few persons. Certainly real or perceived damage was done to the human spirit and to the social harmony of the affected communities.

On the surface the issue may appear simple to the putative man in the street, especially if the adjective "enlightened" can be applied to him. The parents who demanded replacement of the reading series then in use presented their arguments in the form of fundamentalist religious doctrines: the literature was said to be full of obscene expressions; it was designed to tear down belief in God; it was anti-Christian; it was atheistic, Marxist, antipatriotic; amoral or immoral, disruptive of parental and other authority, etc., etc. As one of the presumably enlightened men in the street, my first reaction to the protesting parents and their supporters was extremely negative. As one who thinks that his basic religious and social values may be expressed with some degree of logical and linguistic refinement, I tended to deplore the simplistic views expressed by the antitextbook crowd. As one whose value system is impregnated with the ideals expressed in the first amendment to the constitution, I looked on the efforts of the parents and their ministerial spokesman as attempts at censorship in its most blatant form. And as a longtime member of the academic fraternity, I had a conditioned reaction against those who wished to override the judgments of professional educators about what should be taught and how it should be taught.

But as I followed the events reported in the newspapers, I reached a point at which I realized that the issues were far more complex than the overt representations of the disputants made them appear. In fact, they now seem to me to have reached toward certain basic human concerns that may be merely prefigured or inadequately symbolized by the specific texts around which the controversy revolved. Certainly values, interests, and choices were at stake. So were questions of citizenship, social organization, and political power. The parents obviously felt that, as measured by the standards they had adopted or been socialized to, the texts had a corrupting influence on both individuals and society. Patterns of authority were also being called into question. The authority of parents in a family-oriented society seemed to have been threatened by educational institutions whose socialization processes differed markedly from traditional ones, and the schools appeared to be part of a monolithic rather than a customary pluralistic governmental system. Perhaps the parents heard echoes of the counterculture of the sixties whose spokesmen threatened to take over their children. Considered from the latter perspective, the confrontation may be perceived to have been directed against an impersonal, unmalleable, and unresponsive educational bureaucracy bent on changing man and society without let or hindrance. To those involved, the replacement of the books under attack was apparently not a matter of censorship but of removing an absolute and irresponsible public authority from control over the ends of education, especially as these related to its moral and social content.

Here, then, was a controversy over a literature that had been selected by public employees and made required reading in a state school system. It was a literature, furthermore, that was apparently perceived by all parties to the controversy as having historical and philosophic content that in its own way interpreted reality and influenced practical—i.e., moral, social, and political—existence.[7]

What was most disheartening was the rhetorical and evidential inadequacy of the debate because one set of protagonists, and perhaps both, lacked a sufficiently developed political vocabulary to carry on the type of discussion that is at the heart of all effective resolution of issues by ameliorative politics; one based on a publicly oriented, classical dialectical exchange, as opposed to persuasion by demagoguery and action through physical force.[8] As long as the concerns over values, power, social stability, tradition, and change remain inchoate because the means of expressing them in ways that can be understood by all affected parties is not available to the participants in a controversy, unrelieved frustrations will drive some beyond the limits of political endurance and restraint, and others are likely to respond in kind. And I am afraid that this breakdown of normal politics is becoming too ubiquitous for comfort. I am reminded by the behavior of the more adamant parties in the textbook confrontation of the statement that was so often made about erstwhile rebellious college youth: "They are trying to tell us something, and we had better listen." To which I would like to add: "We had better find out how we can assist our contesting publics and their ostensible representatives to express their concerns by means of an adequate political vocabulary, and help resolve the issues raised through the application of the perspective of the humanities to their discussions."

I have argued here, in an obviously general way, that the objects of study, methods of analysis, and theoretical integration of knowledge constituting the substance of the academic disciplines in the humanities have a unique connection with the modes of human experience—particularly morals and politics—apprehended by the practical reason. And in the course of that argument I have implied that students of the humanities have an obligation to assume an active role in shaping the world of experience embraced by morals and politics. Indeed, the connections are so inseparable that even the refusal to consider the problems of politics and public policy as objects of inquiry appropriate to scholarship in the humanities has major practical effects on both the humanities and politics.

In the first place, the world of politics constitutes the most important conditioning environment within which students of the humanities pursue their particular activities as scholars and teachers. Freedom of inquiry and the dissemination of its results in all areas of scholarship are dependent on the nature of the political regime and its policies, and the humanities may be more vulnerable to the vagaries and exploitative tendencies of politics than the sciences. In the second place, even if scholarship in the humanities remains "pure" and cloistered, the minds and characters of the students taught in humanities courses will be affected by their exposure to the contents of these disciplines. Ever since the emergence of the academy in ancient Greece, the mission of the university has included as its main purpose the shaping of the Aristotelian *spoudaios*, the fully formed person; and the identification of the spoudaios with the good citizen in a properly constituted polity has always been an integral part of the higher educational objective.

The restoration or revival of an appropriate role for the humanities in the public arena naturally involves risks. The cultivation of the classical virtue of prudence has been, and remains, critical to the enterprise. Students of the humanities are as susceptible to ideological traps as other people (including "scientists"), despite their presumed grasp of the subtleties of human nature as explored in their respective literatures. The romantic subjectivism that seems so pervasive in both literature and life today, for instance, seems to be the most frequent answer offered by the humanities to the critical issues of our times. And that response is a final demonstrated capitulation to the instrumentalist's rejection of the essential unity of reason, and thus the abandonment of the quest for a rational foundation for moral, political, and aesthetic values. At the other extreme, the centrality of the critical spirit in the makeup of the scholar in the humanities has often led to an excessive cynicism about the existential world, and a retreat into the "Republic of Letters," from which idealized sanctuary the total critique of society can emanate without the need to assume responsibility for what goes on in the workaday world.

The challenge is to find a way between the extremes of activism aimed at complete transformation of a practical world that is less tractable than we would like it to be and the passivity that can render us powerless to effect even the incremental change needed to avert disaster or to arrest decay. The humanities, like it or not, are the main carriers of the symbols by which we express our experience as a civilized society. They are thus the conservators of tradition. But they are also the constant reinterpreters and even modifiers of those symbols as experience unfolds through history. Neither preservation nor change is a given, although paradoxically each may be a necessity for man's continuing participation in the structure of things of which he is a part. For as Edmund Burke has noted, perhaps out of the personal paradox of having been a conservative Whig, "A state without the means of some change is without the means of its conservation."

Kenneth W. Thompson · *Ethics and Foreign Policy*

No issue is more fundamental in political theory than that of the relationship between ethics and politics. Not surprisingly, the debate has resumed in discussions by contemporary thinkers of politics and international politics. Is politics a branch of ethics or is ethics an aspect of politics and foreign policy, as Mr. Cyrus Vance declared in an interview in late 1976 on his appointment as secretary of state?

The wellsprings of American and Western thought on ethics and politics are Judeo-Christian, classical, and modern political philosophy. The great merit of Christian thought for international politics was its linking of the vision of the universal brotherhood of man deriving from mankind's common ancestry with the Christian view of man as being both good and evil. Individual Jewish and Christian thinkers have tended to emphasize one or the other side of Judeo-Christian thought, the idea of brotherhood or the idea of man's imperfectibility. Both are recurrent themes in tension with one another and neither has been set aside. The message of Christian thought for Americans who seek to interpret American values to the world, therefore, is that because all men are God's children, the American dream has relevance for others, but because Americans have shaped that dream with selfishness as much as with vision, it has at best limited relevance. The Christian perspective, therefore, helps men to understand the dilemmas which confront groups and nations in relating ethics and politics. The great merit of classical political philosophy derives from its emphasis on reason and virtue. While acknowledging the limitations of imperfect man, it places stress on the possibilities of relating ethics and politics. Political philosophy has the responsibility of throwing light on what is good, better, and best in politics. It is not enough to point the finger at imperfect and sinful man. The philosopher, who enjoys man's highest possibility of political contemplation, must reflect on what is "simply good" and on what is good or best under the circumstances. Christian thought falls prey, according to classical philosophers, to overemphasizing the difficulties and ambiguities of politics. The good man who seeks what is good in politics is more likely to realize the good regime. A good regime finds a way of bringing together good men. Individual and collective virtue are related. Man has the ability through reason to achieve good government. His task is not only to perceive the limitations of politics but also its possibilities for good. Moreover, because man is a social animal he realizes his highest potential through participating in politics. Politics in the final analysis is part of ethics.

Christian thinkers in the tradition of Aquinas and some Jewish philosophers with a passion for justice seek to appropriate and adapt classical thought. In so doing, they and classical political philosophers run the risk of casting political virtue in abstract moral categories. Natural law is tempted to propound fixed moral principles that, being rigid, may thwart the search for what is right in given political circumstances. (The most noteworthy example is the absolute view of birth control and abortion which can clash with social and economic realities and lead to injustice in particular cultures.)

The great merit of modern political philosophy has been to concentrate on the actual conditions of political life. Whereas Christian and classical thought both helped men to understand the ends of politics, modern political thought, in centering on means and excluding the transcendent realm, has focused attention on the social and political order. Of all the great political traditions, it has had most to say about contemporary political arrangements. Its contributions have been noteworthy in providing guides to political action. Its failures are most striking in the breakdown of its prescriptions for the good political society and improved systems of governance. Modern political thought too readily assumes that civilization is on the march, that strengthening one institution of government or another guarantees progress, and that earlier political traditions are irrelevant to contemporary life. Its tendency has been to select from a multitude of urgent social needs a particular reform promising utopia. In the nineteenth and early twentieth centuries prison reform, free trade, or the long ballot were social and political reforms heralded as announcing the dawn of a new era. In the 1980s tax reform and military preparedness are being offered as panaceas to all the disorders of national and international life. Some seek the good society through an expansion of executive power and others through its contraction. By singling out some plausible and defensible reform and offering it as the one route to a new and better world, modern political thinkers become ideologues rather than philosophers. They depart from the ancient vision of political contemplation as the highest order of human life.

The Nation and Political Values

Each of the great political traditions has its own conception of human values and the good life. For the Christian belief in God and serving one's fellow man is uppermost in the Christian hierarchy of values. For the disciple of classical political thought the search for virtue in society is the highest calling. For modern political thinkers, the establishment of the best social and constitutional arrangements within existing societies is the foremost objective. The Christian and the classical traditions depend on certain objective values and standards above and outside the social and political order. Modern political thought depends for the most part on values and standards within society and the political process. The values of the two older traditions are ultimately transcendent while those of modern political thought are immanent. Contemporary exceptions include those political theories for which the earlier traditions have residual importance, such as those of the founding fathers of the American constitutional and political system.

The prospects of all three political traditions have been diminished, however, by certain forces at work within the present-day nation-state. Christian thought from its beginnings assumed that man necessarily and inevitably lived in two worlds, the city of man and the city of God. The former was the temporary realm of contingencies, imperfection, and sin; the latter was the enduring realm of certainty, perfection, and the good. The one was realizable here and now, the other in eternity. The social and political order was structured to reflect, partially at least, the reality of the two worlds. The Christian vision provided for both a horizontal and vertical dimension in human life, with men reaching out to one another in the social order and seeking to know God in the spiritual order. Government was the custodian of the social and political order and citizens were enjoined to give to Caesar what was Caesar's. The church was the custodian of the spiritual order and believers were enjoined to serve God with what was God's.

The rise of the modern nation-state and the breakdown of the Corpus Christianum diminished, if it did not destroy, the vision of the two cities. The authority of the one universal church was undermined by the Reformation and the Renaissance. The religion of the prince within emerging political societies determined the religion of the people. Religion and patriotism tended to reenforce one another whereas they had earlier constituted a system of checks and balances interacting with one another. If the universal Catholic church was in part responsible for the union of the two because of its tendency to equate and make itself coextensive with the city of God, the embryonic nation-state was also responsible by becoming the repository of individual and group morality in order to assure political cohesion. Whereas the church had taught believers the commandment "Thou shalt not kill," princes and rulers taught "Thou shalt kill to preserve the nation-state."

Moreover, other forces were at work weakening the hold of the Christian tradition. The Christian tradition in its historical formulation presupposed a world of sheep and shepherd. The modern era has witnessed the growth of ever more complex societies in which the individual to whom Christianity ministered was further and further removed from primary human relations with his fellow men. The great society supplanted the good Samaritan. Furthermore, Christianity itself became more and more fragmented. In America a great Civil War found men praying to the same God and justifying their acts from the same Scriptures. During the conflict President Abraham Lincoln wrote that "each party claims to act in accordance with the will of God. Both *may* be, and one *must* be wrong. God can not be *for*, and *against* the same thing at the same time." In recent days Martin Luther King and Jerry Falwell invoked the Scriptures to defend actions affecting millions of people in diametrically opposite ways. Maintaining a universal Christian tradition is complicated by the rise of sovereign nation-states. "The nation fills the minds and hearts of men everywhere with particular experiences and, derived from them, with particular concepts of political philosophy, particular standards of political morality, and particular goals of political action."[1]

If the Christian tradition has been challenged by the circumstances surrounding the modern nation-state, the classical tradition was threatened in a similar way. Modernity has brought about a shift, it is argued, from discussions of the good man and the good state to discourse on political power and political tactics. Classical political philosophy was not unaware of the realities of good and evil in human nature. The Platonic dialogues are filled with examples of cynical and selfish men overriding reason and virtue in their political attitudes and conduct. Yet for the philosopher, contemplating the human drama as a whole, reason was superior to the irrational and virtue was the standard by which cynicism and selfishness were judged. Man approached his true and best nature in participating in the social and political order. He realized himself as a social animal.

Classicists maintained, however, that man's fulfillment was most attainable within the polity, a small-sized political community in which face-to-face political discourse occurred. By contrast, the citizen in the larger nation-states has little, if any, contact with his rulers. He is remote from the scene of urgent problems and unable to comprehend the complex issues on which he must decide. The closest aide to President Lyndon B. Johnson once observed that nuclear questions escaped him no matter how faithfully he studied them. He was forced to find scientists he could trust. Comprehension required scientific and technical knowledge which only scientific specialists possessed.

The history of modern times throws a cloud over the case that classicists make for reason and virtue. Wise students of political history such as Reinhold Niebuhr, Herbert Butterfield, and Hans J. Morgenthau have traced the influence of the irrational in politics. The German people, whose culture matched any in Europe, followed a fanatical leader, Hitler, who stirred popular emotions with slogans depicting the Germans as racially superior. Legislative assemblies, intended for prudent deliberation, become the scene of chauvinist and bellicose debate. National self-determination, which had promised satisfaction and peace to the world's people, was successfully invoked by Hitler for the annexation of the Sudetenland. Reason proved defective in anticipating the consequences of thousands of apparently reasonable acts. Unintended and unforeseen consequences of reasonable historical acts outweighed the expected or intended results. Thus the Protestant Reformation rested on the proposition that individuals should be free to read and interpret the Bible, but by strengthening nationalism, it caused a weakening of individualism. The French Revolution, which promised liberty, equality, and fraternity, led to the submergence of liberty and equality in the Napoleonic Empire.

To recite a litany of individual virtues when individuals are swallowed up in big government, big labor, or big management seems less relevant in the modern world. More germane are discussions of the problems of hard-pressed individuals seeking to reconcile competing virtues. The busy executive, for whom long hours and neglect of family are sometimes required to assure profits and livelihood, struggles to be a good father. For the devoted parent caring for children may necessitate overlooking his own parents. Being a man of virtue and principle may not be enough under these circumstances. The truly virtuous man has to find his way through a maze of conflicting principles.

If Christian and classical thought are criticized for too much opposition to modernity and too great a faith in historical political values, modern political thought links modernity with progress. Whereas the older traditions stand in opposition to present trends, modern political theory tends to sanctify them. It glorifies the state and, more particularly, certain branches of government which it favors one after the other as the cycle turns. Transposed to the international scene, modern thought manifests an exaggerated confidence in institutions as instruments for transforming international realities. It has viewed the United Nations, the World Bank, and the U.N. specialized agencies as answers to all the difficult problems of international politics. The rise and fall of popular enthusiasm for each of these institutions in turn has thrown into question the judgment of modern thought. It has also led some contemporary thinkers to reopen the question of the relevance of Christian and classical thought to present-day problems.

International Politics and Values

Not only has the rise of the nation-state profoundly affected the relation of the great political traditions to politics but so have the changing patterns of international politics and diplomacy. Historically, the Christian and classical political traditions assumed a consensus on values within the Christian and classical worlds. Four developments have altered the political world within which any of the historic traditions must operate. First, a worldwide system of political ideologies and conflicting religious faiths has replaced the Christian Europe of which historians like Christopher Dawson wrote in tracing the formation of Western Christendom.[2] Universal Christendom lost out to a pluralistic international system of competing nation-states and cultures. Second, the political faiths which inspired men took on the characteristics of the terrestrial world rather than the adornments of the heavenly city. To the extent the latter existed at all it was a "this worldly" utopia. Carl Becker described the heavenly city of the eighteenth-century philosophers; Marx and Lenin elaborated a creed that identified the end of history with the Marxist classless society. Salvation was achievable here and now and its standards were not outside, but within, history. The direct application to international problems of the Christian tradition was undermined by the breakdown of a consensus on values and the disappearance of faith in effective objective moral principles outside history.

Two other developments coincided with and reenforced the afore-mentioned changes. They profoundly affected the relevance of the classical tradition. One of these was a consequence of the vast increase in the size of viable political units. The movement from city-states to nation-states culminated in the postwar emergence of the superpowers. That good men would create good regimes became a difficult proposition to sustain. Good and bad men alike seized power in large collective states claiming that only they were capable of solving the momentous social problems of great masses of people. Events that good men had prophesied were rationally impossible, such as global depressions, world wars, and totalitarianism, followed one another in rapid succession. Large populations responded to programs whose defenders argued that they served all the people. If Americans had any doubts concerning the far-reaching effects of this third development, they had only to compare the deliberative processes of leaders addressing the New England town meeting with Mussolini or Hitler haranguing the German and Italian people with the claim, "forty million Italians (Germans) can't be wrong." In short, the concept of popular sovereignty replaced that of personal virtue.

A fourth development was the radical transformation of political communication. Classical political thought had maintained that personal and collective morality were indivisible. In the modern era not only totalitarian rulers but democratic leaders determined what was moral and right in terms of the interests of states. While certain moral principles applicable to individuals survived in the eighteenth-century idea of raison d'état, as Machiavelli had clung to the concept of virtue, contemporary rulers maintained that whatever their personal moral standards on war or slavery, national unity and preserving the state took precedence and were controlling. Thus both Christian and classical thought lost a large measure of their force in the face of far-reaching historical changes.

Modern political thought appeared to offer an alternative to the decline of the ancient traditions. Especially liberalism held out the promise to the great mass of the people of human improvement through universal public education. Today's pressing problems would yield to the workings of free society. Individuals, ever more enlightened by science and reason, would throw off human traits and archaic political ideas and institutions that had led throughout history to conflict and war. Individual man pursuing his selfish interests would be guided nationally and internationally as if by a hidden hand to act for the common good. Nationally the process would operate in free-market economies guaranteed to serve the general welfare. ("What is good for General Motors is good for the country," a cabinet member in the Eisenhower administration prophesied.) Internationally, Woodrow Wilson proclaimed that national self-determination would lead to a peaceful world, never dreaming that Hitler would invoke a Wilsonian principle to justify his expansionist policies. Moreover, national and international economic stagnation in the 1930s led millions of people to turn to new and more dynamic collectivist solutions.

Not only did the four developments sound the death knell for the effectiveness and coherence of the three great political traditions; another factor sped the disintegration of the international political order. The values which had introduced a limited degree of stability within single political communities proved ineffective on the international stage. The standards that had assured relative peace within nations proved ineffectual or largely irrelevant in international affairs. What was disallowed or dealt with as an exception to the normal processes of national societies was accepted as inevitable in international society. While civil war represented the breakdown of the political order within nations, war was accepted as the continuation of diplomacy by other means in relations among nation-states.

The problem, as Reinhold Niebuhr discussed it in a succession of treatises on foreign policy, was that in international politics no single moral principle existed for ordering all other separate moral principles.[3] In international politics, rough-and-ready norms such as "damage limitation" became the overarching principles rather than such benign standards as the quest for the good society or for communities aimed at human self-fulfillment. In the end modern political thought which had promised a new and better world became an even more tragic victim to history than Christian or classical thought.

Rediscovering Ancient Truths

For these reasons the culmination of history on the international stage was not the heavenly city but the nuclear age. The end of warfare which liberal political thinkers had predicted yielded to the specter of warfare as universal human destruction. Ironically, human advancement and progress led not to the refutation of ancient political truths but to their rediscovery. Prudence has once more become the master virtue in international politics at a moment in time when anything less is a threat to human existence. But political prudence was an idea that Aristotle set forth as a guide for political practice as distinct from political contemplation. From Aristotle and Augustine through Edmund Burke to Niebuhr and John Courtney Murray, prudence as an operative political principle was kept alive not as any rigid formulation or precise definition of what was right or wrong but as a concept of practical morality. Leaders embracing prudence are enjoined not to think of what is invariant in human relations but what practical reason may dictate under a given set of circumstances. Practical morality involves the reconciliation of what is morally desirable and politically possible. It offers few absolutes but many practical possibilities. Prudence is the central precept in the ancient tradition of moral reasoning. It recognizes the need for the moral man in an immoral world to find his way through "a maze of conflicting moral principles" no one of which reigns supreme.

Thus justice is a moral objective in international politics but so is international peace. Freedom is a value which must compete with national security. In the same way that the Supreme Court within the United States declared that freedom doesn't give men the right to cry fire in a crowded theater, so internationally the establishment of free states everywhere cannot justify overriding the necessity for order or survival in the newer and poorer nation-states. Resistance to the spread of communism, which is a clear objective of Americans, may clash with the realities of communist societies that are unlikely to change except through the historic processes of nations like China and Yugoslavia that must work their way through to their own "best possible regimes." Indiscriminate anti-communism can no more be equated with political prudence as a coherent foreign policy for Americans than indiscriminate world revolution can for the Soviet Union.

National interest as a guide to foreign policy may at first glance seem remote from the ancient ideas of prudence of Christian and classical writers. Yet what political realism and practical reason have in common is acceptance of the best solution appropriate to particular circumstances. Philosophers and reformers may offer more glittering answers to the world's problems, but it is unlikely any other approach can come closer to a practical way of thinking. Every foreign policy decision presently has its military, political, and Soviet-American dimension. Too often policymakers choose policies that apply exclusively to one or the other dimension. Prudence requires attention to all three dimensions and an attempt to find best possible solutions after giving weight to all three. Tragically, the political process by which men come to office in the United States is unlikely to elect men with the capacity to think clearly in all three dimensions at once. Yet anything less will likely lead to disaster in American foreign policy.

Ethics and foreign policy require a summoning of the great political traditions and both ancient and modern political wisdom. Foreign policy is doomed if it lacks experimentation and innovation. In equal measure it demands the learning of the lessons of the past, from political thought as well as from history. In this respect John Hallowell's life and work, which has had its greatest influence on political theory, is ultimately relevant to ethics and foreign policy. To the extent that he has called up the wisdom of the past he also speaks to the present. Because he has been impatient with anything less than the fundamental questions of political science, his work has enduring value for the diverse sectors of the discipline. When foreign policy studies or any other political science studies move away from the essential truths about which he has written, they run the risk of becoming no more than passing fads and fashions. Not all great universities or popular departments understand this, and those who give them support may understand it even less. The lure of false promises and faulty prophecies is as strong now as it has been throughout history. Sophistry is not dead. In such a world we can all be grateful that Professor Hallowell has remained faithful to what he has conceived to be his vocation: the search for truth and the love of wisdom, never abandoning his belief in Christian ideals and democratic principles. Whatever our personal intellectual journey, those of us he has influenced owe him an immense debt. He inspired us more than he will ever know.

R. Bruce Douglass · *Liberalism as a Threat to Democracy*

It is common today to speak of democracy as it has come to be understood and practiced in the West as "liberal democracy." Exactly what this means is rarely specified very clearly, but generally it may be taken to mean that liberalism as an ideology is the foundation of democracy in the Western sense. This in turn may be interpreted in at least three different ways: (1) as an historical statement, to the effect that liberalism played a key role in bringing the distinctive institutions of Western democracy into being; (2) as a descriptive statement about the political culture of Western societies today; or (3) as a normative statement, to the effect that liberalism is the natural, or ideal, complement to Western democracy, the set of beliefs most likely to provide effective support for the functioning of democratic institutions.

My concern here is primarily with the relationship between liberalism and democracy in principle. This is the aspect which is most important to the defense of liberalism, and it is also the most debatable. Both the historic contribution of liberalism to the development of democratic institutions in the West and its current influence are reasonably well established facts, and they are likely to be conceded by those who have no particular commitment to liberalism. They do not, however, establish the strong linkage between liberalism and democracy intended by liberal apologists. What they have in mind, typically, when they speak of liberal democracy is that liberalism embodies a set of beliefs that are somehow essential to the survival of democratic government. They mean to suggest that the political institutions of the Western democracies are liberal not only in the sense that liberalism contributed significantly to their development, but also—and more important—that a liberal political culture is a necessary condition of their health, if not of their very existence.

I propose here to criticize this claim, focusing in particular on one of the more popular forms liberalism has assumed in this century—the theory of the "open society" as developed by such figures as Karl Popper and F. A. Hayek.[1] The hallmark of liberalism is, of course, its emphasis on liberty, and the thrust of the argument of its apologists is that liberalism is uniquely suited to support the institutions of constitutional democracy by virtue of this fact. It is precisely the liberal emphasis on liberty, they say, which has protected constitutional democracy, in the countries where it has succeeded, from the perversions to which democratic politics is otherwise vulnerable. The problem, however, is that constitutional democracy has to do with much more than simply liberty, and it takes more than simply an appreciation of liberty to make it work. What the functioning of democracy requires, in fact, is a whole set of virtues, and the danger liberalism has always posed is that civic virtue will be subverted by excessive preoccupation with liberty.

That danger, I shall argue, is realized in the theory of the open society. Before the twentieth century, liberal theorists generally balanced their concern for liberty with at least an equal concern for education of the citizenry in virtue.[2] They sought to avoid the degeneration of liberty into license by relying, in one way or another, on what Sheldon Wolin has aptly characterized the "socialization of conscience."[3] But in this century, in large part because of the influence of ethical relativism, liberals have been increasingly inclined to interpret the demands of freedom differently. Freedom has come to be associated with the absence of any philosophical or moral orthodoxy, and freedom in cultural affairs has been interpreted to mean a policy of laissez faire. A free society, it is said, is an "open" society in the sense that it does not prejudge the question of what citizens ought to be, do, or believe; therefore anything remotely approximating a common philosophical and moral formation is inadmissible.

The open society thus understood is presented as the operative ideal of the Western democracies, and the success of constitutional democracy in the countries where it has prevailed is attributed to approximation to this ideal. In point of fact, the opposite is the case. The idea of a society that is neutral with respect to metaphysics and ethics is an innovation, which if seriously pursued would radically alter the political culture of these societies, probably in ways that would subvert the health and vitality of their political institutions. Unless one is willing to make highly optimistic assumptions about human nature for which no persuasive reasons are given, I shall argue, it is reasonable to conclude that the likely consequence of actually realizing the ideal of the open society would be a combination of reduced civic virtue and increased political conflict such as to make effective democratic government impossible. Far from capturing the essence of constitutional democracy, therefore, open-society liberalism badly distorts its character; and to the extent it succeeds in capturing the imagination of Western peoples, it is likely to undermine the very institutions it is meant to defend.

I

The ideal of the open society is liberal individualism carried to its logical conclusion. In particular it is J. S. Mill's argument in *On Liberty* carried to its logical conclusion. Its basis is a particular attitude toward liberty. Liberty is defined as autonomy, being left alone to pursue, as Mill put it, "our own good in our own way."[4] It is being able to think for one's self and to act on the basis of one's own decisions without being required to submit to the ideas and plans of others. The good society is one which maximizes liberty defined in these terms. Because liberty is the preeminent social and political good, the primary criterion for evaluating social institutions is the extent to which they promote freedom of thought and action for both individuals and groups.

Liberty is valued both as an end in itself and as a means to other goods. Liberals of this type typically argue that it is intrinsically good for people to be free, but at the same time, from the exercise of freedom will come a variety of other benefits. Individual happiness and well-being will be enhanced; the general welfare will be promoted; above all, the progress of civilization, both material and spiritual, will be fostered. An open society, it is said, is a dynamic society, and from its dynamism come all sorts of benefits that would otherwise not be available.

As Mill argued, the only legitimate reason for curtailing liberty is to prevent violation of the freedom and well-being of others. People are to be left alone unless what they do inflicts harm on others. As much as possible they should be left to their own devices. In particular, they should be left to think and to define "the good" for themselves. Except for the principle of freedom itself—

i.e., liberalism—a free society is neutral in matters of philosophy and morals. It has no orthodoxy, but is open to as many different "experiments of living" as people care to explore.[5]

Mill, however, was not consistent on this matter. He personally did not in fact believe that all possible definitions of human good were equally defensible. Some pleasures (and, implicitly, ways of life) were more appropriate to human beings than others. Nor was he content simply to leave the choice to chance. On the crucial matter of education he was not willing to follow the logic of laissez faire. He advocated compulsory education of the whole citizenry—"the uncultivated cannot be competent judges of cultivation"[6]—and he expected education to have a moral dimension.[7] The principle of utility would be actively promoted, and the result he expected was a certain moral attitude and a certain level of sophistication in the way people used their freedom.

The theory of the open society does away with this inconsistency. It assumes that the distinction which Mill drew cannot and should not be made. "It is one of the characteristics of a free society," observes Hayek, "that men's goals are open."[8] People differ as to what is good and beautiful; opinions change; and there is not any way rationally to determine who is correct. So without qualification people should be left to think and act as they choose. The course of societal development should be left up to "natural" evolution. "The ultimate decisions about what is good or bad will be made not by individual human wisdom," says Hayek, "but by the decline of the groups that have adhered to the 'wrong' beliefs."[9]

II

How in fact would the democratic process work in such a society? It is almost part of the definition of an "open" society in this sense that there would be much potential for conflict. There would be, presumably, a wide variety of different groups, each with a distinctive set of beliefs and values. One can imagine that, indeed, there might well be a whole potpourri of different ways of living existing side by side and interacting with one another. The increased variety would significantly enhance the likelihood of conflict, much of it on matters of importance. For, to some extent at least, these different beliefs and values would inevitably contradict one another. What was sacred to one group (e.g., religious observances) would be unimportant and even absurd to others; what was moral to one (e.g., abortion) would be positively immoral to others; what was in good taste to some (e.g., casual dress) would be offensive to others; etc.

Some of the differences could perhaps be interpreted as being of no real importance, and people would learn to tolerate them. ("They have their ways, and we have ours.") But presumably there would be other differences that would not easily lend themselves to this sort of interpretation. Some differences (abortion is a current example) would be seen by almost everybody to be more than mere matters of personal taste. Presumably even on these issues the prevailing ethos would encourage as much toleration as possible. But even if people generally adhered to the principle of toleration, there still unavoidably would be moments at which the differences would have to be addressed. Those moments would come, in particular, whenever the different groups entered the public realm and had to confront one another in discussion of what public policy ought to be.

Even the minimal state, which is generally favored by proponents of this kind of liberalism, requires some definition of the public good. Even in an open society some projects (foreign policy, defense, law enforcement, etc.) have to be undertaken in common, and the moment discussions began concerning what policies ought to be adopted, the likelihood is that the philosophical and moral differences separating the various groups would quickly come into play. Some groups would favor a foreign policy of Realpolitik; others would want to take into account moral principles of various kinds. Some would favor a national security policy entailing vast peacetime military expenditures; others would favor minimal military preparedness. In the treatment of criminals some would favor rehabilitation, others retribution. In tax policy some would favor progressive schemes while others would argue for the opposite. There would be serious disagreements as well about what should be counted as crime; some, for example, would almost certainly feel compelled to try to make abortion a form of murder, while others would feel just as strongly that any such law would be unfair.

The room for debate would greatly expand, moreover, if the state were to take on welfare functions. Which benefits should be provided? To whom? Funded how? There almost certainly would be deep disagreements, reflecting underlying differences of opinion about the nature and purposes of government. Some, at least, of the differences in outlook among the various groups would inevitably translate into differences in political philosophy.

The political task would then consist in attempting to achieve workable compromises among the various competing positions. For the good (indeed, survival) of society it would be essential to arrive at policies on most of these issues which a majority, if not all, of the citizenry could accept as legitimate and which were also workable. Somehow the conflict would have to be resolved, and in a manner which did not undermine the legitimacy of the political system. The principal dangers threatening such a society, in turn, would be: (1) a paralysis of the policy-making process through an inability to achieve workable compromises; or (2) withdrawal of support from the political system by one or more significant groups as a result of having their desires thwarted on issues of major importance.

The ability to achieve such compromises on a consistent basis would depend heavily on the attitude with which citizens approached public affairs. Would they exercise self-discipline in making demands on government, or would they instead try to grab for themselves as much as they possibly could? Would they be willing to bear burdens and accept sacrifices for the good of society, or would they try whenever possible to pass the burdens and sacrifices off on others? Would they be willing to compromise, or would they instead assume that their views were the only right ones? Would they respect the rights of minorities, or would they assume that all that matters is the might of numbers?

It is arguable that in any sort of democracy an ethic of civility and fairness is important. But in a society with such an enormous potential for conflict, it would be essential. The political system simply could not function for long without it. If even a significant minority lacked self-discipline and self-restraint, it would pose serious problems for the whole polity. The search for compromise would probably break down, and even if somehow that were avoided, the likelihood of truly workable policies being adopted on a consistent basis would be very small. At best, government would limp along from one ill-designed compromise to the next;

at worst, it would be paralyzed. It simply would not function. The probable consequences for social order do not need to be spelled out.

III

The question, then, is whether it makes sense to expect that such an ethic would prevail in an open society of the kind advocated by contemporary liberals. Is it likely that in a society which is, for all practical purposes, agnostic on the question of what constitutes virtue, most citizens would conform on a regular basis to the democratic ethic? More directly to the point, is it realistic to think that amidst all the various philosophies and "outlooks" that would arise, most of the population would find their way to positions that provided sufficient reason to discipline their selfishness (and self-righteousness) so as to cooperate fairly in the conduct of public affairs?

In the past, indeed, in every known society to date, the inducement to act virtuously has come primarily from tradition and religion. Most people have accepted moral discipline primarily out of a respect for established ways of life and/or a fear/love of the Lord. A minority, especially those with advanced education, may have had more reasoned or pragmatic motives for acting morally, but these have been unknown or unimportant in the lives of the many.

In a society of the kind Popper and Hayek envision, this would change. The whole ethos of such a society would promote change. Skeptical questioning of inherited beliefs would be encouraged, and the greater the pluralism, the more the effects would be felt.[10] Presumably not everyone would succumb. But it is reasonable to expect that large numbers would no longer find the traditional beliefs plausible. They would have to find a new basis on which to orient their lives. They would need to go "shopping," so to speak, in the "marketplace of ideas" to find a point of view with which to identify.

In order for this sort of liberalism to be persuasive, one must assume that most of those confronted with this choice would make it in a way that would provide an effective substitute for the moral discipline provided in the past by tradition and/or religion. The standard liberal answer to the vacuum created by the decline of tradition and religion has been, of course, reason—or, more precisely, reason as developed through education. Today the same claim is repeated: an educated citizenry will find in its developed intellectual capabilities an adequate basis on which to handle the problem of moral choice.

But as we have noted, education means something different today in liberal theory from what it used to mean. No longer is it appropriate to think of education as though it were intended to be a common, uniform experience. A consistent proponent of the open society argument has to allow for freedom of choice in education. Indeed, there is a sense in which freedom of choice in education is the crucial issue in the design of such a society. The pluralism which is expected would be severely compromised if the state (or any other institution) were to assume the power to decide what and how all citizens must learn. Even if we say that the state has a right to make a certain number of years of formal education mandatory and to insist that a few basic skills be mastered, it would not follow that the general design of education should then become a matter of public policy. Precisely because education is so inextricably bound up with philosophical and moral commitments, the content of education would need to be left as much as possible up to the free choice of providers and purchasers.

Presumably, therefore, an open society would provide as many different kinds of education as alternative philosophies. There would be Catholic schools, fundamentalist schools, Quaker schools, Jewish schools, "progressive" schools, "free" schools, and on and on. Each would promote values in one way or another, but they would define goodness in different—and sometimes contradictory—ways. Each would have its own distinctive pedagogy, and in that respect, too, they could well be at cross-purposes. Probably they would also differ, sometimes widely, in their ability to achieve their objectives.

The question now becomes: In this situation, with no mode of education any more preferred than any other, is it realistic to think that most of the population would choose the kind of education that would be needed to insure responsible democratic citizenship? Is it realistic to think that most of the population would voluntarily select, for themselves and for their children, that kind of education that would in fact promote the degree of moral discipline that democratic politics requires?

IV

To answer in the affirmative, it is necessary to make some very optimistic assumptions about human nature. One must assume, first, that virtue is somehow automatic—that most people, at least, have a natural tendency to seek the good of others, and that this tendency can be expected to prevail over competing contrary inclinations. But—no less important—one must also assume that good judgment somehow comes naturally—that most people, confronted with the choices we have just reviewed, would be able to choose wisely. It is necessary to assume a generalized ability to separate the wheat from the chaff on matters no less fundamental than philosophies of life and education.

If either of these assumptions is mistaken, then the prospects for durable democratic government in such a society are not good. Even if we concede that virtue is a natural inclination but deny that good judgment comes naturally, there is a serious problem. Well-meaning people who lack the inclination or ability to reason effectively can make mistakes which are every bit as harmful as acts which derive from bad motives. One can well imagine all sorts of well-intentioned people choosing philosophies for themselves and modes of education for their children that would in fact turn out to have pernicious consequences they could or would not foresee. To take two obvious examples, one can imagine that some people would be attracted to ways of thinking and educating that encouraged indifference to the well-being of others, while others would be drawn toward various kinds of moral and religious fanaticism. Both, in quite different ways, would be directly subversive of the democratic ethic.

The problem would be greatly compounded, of course, if virtue turned out not to be a natural inclination. If the truth about human nature is better captured by the more pessimistic theories, then the increased freedom afforded by the open society would simply provide more of an opportunity for greed, bigotry, sloth, and other of our less admirable qualities to flourish. Education could well be used to promote—consciously or unconsciously—these very qualities. The net effect would be a sharp increase in antisocial attitudes and behavior, with obvious implications for the health of democratic institutions.

Rarely are the assumptions about human nature which the theory of the open society entails seriously discussed by its proponents, much less defended. Usually the closest approximation is a vague reference to the "basic goodness and rationality" of human beings. Popper, for example, waxes eloquent about the importance of having "faith in man and in human reason,"[11] but the assumptions about human nature which such a faith entails he does not carefully discuss. The key assumption would appear to be the indeterminacy of human nature.[12] It is characteristic of this kind of liberalism to resist any sort of final statement about human nature. Because human nature is open and developing, what human beings have been in the past does not foreclose what they can be in the future. Even Hayek, who at one moment affirms the "fallibility and sinfulness of man,"[13] characterizes the history of civilization as the unfolding progress of human powers into an indeterminate future.

The problem is that this begs the very questions which need to be discussed. Is human nature in fact so indeterminate? And if it is not, what is to prevent the "fallibility and sinfulness of man" from flourishing in an open society? What is to prevent the new freedoms from degenerating into antisocial license? Or, alternatively, if human nature is not fixed, why should we assume that change will be progressive? Why in particular should we assume that from greater freedom will come progress? The notion that human nature can be changed for the better is disputable in any form, but it would seem to be especially dubious in a form which suggests that progress somehow occurs spontaneously, without any conscious effort beyond the expansion of the realm of free choice.

The theory of the open society carries to its logical conclusion the recurring liberal idea that there is a natural harmony between self-interest and the general welfare which can be realized if only society is liberated from the interference of political authority. But in earlier liberalism this "touching faith," as Reinhold Niebuhr aptly characterized it,[14] was made at least plausible by the assumption that society would educate its members, in one way or another, to share a common outlook. Once this assumption is set aside, the argument is reduced to the bare claim that there is literally a "self-generating or spontaneous order in social affairs."[15]

On its face such a claim is preposterous. The only way it can be taken seriously is if one assumes the very thing which is denied—i.e., a process of acculturation in which certain moral standards come to be taken as self-evident. This, of course, is what has made liberalism plausible in the West: certain assumptions about human nature could be taken for granted because of the civilizational history of the West. But what is likely to occur if the process of acculturation changes? What would happen if, as the proponents of the open society propose, there were less and less of a common culture?

V

Constitutional democracy as we know it derives from a cultural heritage that is anything but neutral with respect to metaphysics and ethics. That heritage, a product of several different religious and philosophical influences, some ancient and some modern, entails a distinctive way of viewing the world which is congenial to the characteristic institutions of constitutional democracy.[16] It has proved to be especially congenial to constitutional democracy in the form it has taken in Anglo-Saxon culture. In turn, democratic institutions have been able to take root and thrive in the countries where constitutional democracy has succeeded largely because of this cultural inheritance. Far from being the ideological potpourri the theory of the open society would suggest, most of these societies have been culturally homogeneous. They have been characterized by a high degree of consensus on the more fundamental philosophical and moral questions, and this homogeneity is not at all accidental. It is a result, in country after country, of deliberate efforts to insure the unity of culture and its transmission from one generation to the next.

The real meaning of the theory of the open society is that constitutional democracy can survive the abandonment of this cultural inheritance and its replacement by something altogether new and different. The claim is not simply that constitutional democracy can be separated from its original cultural foundation, but that it can somehow survive in a society which, in large measure, has no common culture.

The claim is utterly implausible. A society without a consensus about first principles is no society at all, and the consensus must go deeper than the mere design of political institutions. Citizens can be relied upon consistently to do what is necessary to nurture and support a regime only if they share, to some extent at least, common beliefs about the nature and purpose of human existence and a common way of life. Any successful political regime is in fact a reflection of a certain way of life, and especially is this the case with democracies. In a democracy in particular what the citizenry do and do not do, what habits they acquire, is critically important to the health of the regime, and it is simply an illusion to think that democratic institutions can somehow endure, much less prosper, in the absence of a common culture.

"Any polis which is truly so called, and is not merely one in name, must devote itself to the end of encouraging goodness," said Aristotle.[17] The point is unavoidable. Any politics worth the name is inevitably soulcraft. Liberalism, to the extent that it ignores this fact or tries to deny it, is a subversive doctrine which will destroy the very things it claims to protect. It is the enemy of constitutional democracy and even of freedom itself.

Francis Canavan · *Liberalism in Root and Flower*

Pornography has become the hallmark of liberal democracy. When General Franco died and democracy returned to Spain, pornographic establishments blossomed all over Madrid, heralding the dawn of liberty. But the phenomenon was not a unique or peculiarly Spanish one. Throughout the democratic world pornography is the external sign of that bland, permissive tolerance which is now liberalism's sole remaining inward grace.

It may appear strange that liberal democrats should have come to accept mass pandering to a degraded taste as the symbol of their regime, but that they have done so is clear. Why they have done so, however, is a question that invites inquiry. The reason, upon inquiry, will turn out to have little to do with sex but much to do with the subjectivism that is the essence of liberalism.

John H. Hallowell described, over forty years ago, the original or "integral" liberalism of the seventeenth century in his *The Decline of Liberalism as an Ideology*.[1] It was based, he said, on a concept of individuality which emphasized "the inherent moral worth and spiritual equality of each individual, the dignity of human personality, the autonomy of individual will, and the essential rationality of men." Because of the importance attached to both autonomy and rationality, "two essential elements are found in liberalism in its integral form: first, the belief that society is composed of atomic, autonomous individuals; and, second, the belief that there are certain eternal truths transcending individuals and independent of either individual will or desire." Consequently, integral liberalism blended two different theories of law: "On the one hand, there is the notion that law is the product of individual wills and the embodiment of individual interests; on the other hand, there is the notion that law is the embodiment of eternal and absolute truths independent of either individual will or interest."[2]

The foundation of integral liberalism, therefore, is a merging of "the two concepts, despite their logical inconsistency and respective self-sufficiency, into one theory." The cement that held the two concepts together was conscience, conceived of as each individual's share of human reason. Integral liberalism, Hallowell explains,

> espoused freedom for the individual under the impersonal authority of law. It conceived of the law as being eternal, universal, and rational, and as containing substantive limitations upon subjective interest and will. To an anarchic conception of society as composed of autonomous individual units, liberalism opposed the conception of an order transcending individuals, and placed the responsibility for realizing this order, potentially embodied in eternal truths, upon individual reason and conscience. The link between the subjective will of the individual and the objective order was reason and conscience.[3]

The greater part of Hallowell's book is devoted to showing how the liberal synthesis fell apart under the impact of historicism and positivism. As people lost confidence in their ability, through reason, to know truths that transcend sense experience, reason became increasingly individualized and moral judgment turned into the mere expression of individual preference. The disintegration of the liberal synthesis paved the way in Germany, he argues, for the triumph of Hitlerism. But (as Hallowell, of course, is well aware) the liberal conception of reason contained within itself the seeds of this disintegration from the beginning. The subjective will of the individual eventually prevailed over the objective moral order because of the way in which liberals understood reason and its capacities.

Liberal rationalism has always contained a strong streak of hedonism.[4] We may cite a few well-known English writers in the liberal tradition for illustration. The view of Thomas Hobbes as the author of that tradition is recent and admittedly controversial, but it is held by eminent scholars.[5] John Locke, too, is the subject of endless controversy, but Sheldon Wolin expresses a common opinion when he says, "To the extent that modern liberalism can be said to be inspired by any one writer, Locke is undoubtedly the leading candidate."[6] Jeremy Bentham brought into bold relief the utilitarianism that was implicit in liberalism. His somewhat recalcitrant disciple, John Stuart Mill, was the nineteenth-century liberal par excellence.

These writers began their moral reasoning by reducing "the good" to pleasure. Thus Hobbes: "*Good*, and *evil*, are names that signify our appetites, and aversions. . . ."[7] Locke agrees:

> Things then are good or evil only in reference to pleasure or pain. That we call good, which is apt to cause or increase pleasure or diminish pain in us; or else to procure or preserve us the possession of any other good, or absence of any evil. And, on the contrary, we name that evil which is apt to produce or increase any pain or diminish any pleasure in us; or else to procure us any evil, or deprive us of any good.[8]

Bentham repeats the theme in these words: "Nature has placed mankind under the governance of two sovereign masters, *pain* and *pleasure*. It is for them alone to point out what we ought to do, as well as to determine what we shall do."[9] John Stuart Mill strove to free utilitarianism from the crudity of Bentham's quantitative analysis of pleasure and pain, and maintained in his *Utilitarianism* that pleasures differ in quality as well as in quantity. But he did not break with Bentham's thesis that pleasure and pain are the only springs of human action. He devoted chapter 4 of *Utilitarianism* to showing that "happiness is a good," that "there is in reality nothing desired except happiness," and that happiness is pleasure or the absence of pain, so that "to desire anything except in proportion as the idea of it is pleasant is a physical and metaphysical impossibility."[10]

It is important to notice at this point the effect that hedonism has upon rationalism. A philosophy which equates the good with pleasure severely limits the scope of reason. The whole realm of judgment on what is good or bad for human beings, therefore of normative ethical and political judgment, is closed to reason. This explains why Hobbes's laws of nature are only "conclusions, or theorems" of enlightened self-interest,[11] why Locke's efforts to set his law of nature on a firm rational foundation were unsuccessful,[12] and why Bentham declared that talk of natural rights was "simply nonsense . . . nonsense upon stilts."[13]

It also explains why Mill's *On Liberty*, although it is premised upon a theory of human development and progress, nonetheless insists on identifying development with the cultivation of individuality. For if the good is reducible to pleasure, and pleasure is a subjective and individual experience, then all judgments about the good must ultimately be felt preferences or aversions that are beyond the criticism of reason and intellect.

A more recent writer than any previously mentioned, Robert A. Dahl, rejects the idea of natural rights, on which he says James Madison's theory of the constitutional republic in *Federalist No. 10* is based, because natural rights have no operational definition and are therefore unacceptable to "anyone of positivist or skeptical predispositions." "The other alternative"—and the one which Dahl proposes to follow in his theory of democracy—"is to lay down political equality as an end to be maximized, that is, to postulate that the goals of every adult citizen are to be accorded equal value in determining government policies."[14] This is to say that, since the relative worth of different goals cannot be discerned by reason, the political system must postulate the equal worth of all adult citizens' desires. Thus political equality comes to be founded, by default, so to speak, on the subjectivity of all values. This is the direction in which the inner dynamism of liberal thought has moved it from the beginning. The substantive limitations upon subjective interest and will, which Hallowell pointed out in integral liberalism, broke down under the pressure of liberal hedonism.

Underlying the hedonism and subjectivism of the liberal mind is its individualism, and this in turn springs from its nominalism. Michael Oakeshott explains:

> Individualism as a gospel has drawn its inspiration from many sources, but as a reasoned theory of society it has its roots in the so-called nominalism of late medieval scholasticism, with its doctrines that the reality of a thing is its individuality, that which makes it *this* thing, and that in both God and man will is precedent to reason. Hobbes inherited this tradition of nominalism, and more than any other writer passed it on to the modern world. His civil philosophy is based, not on any vague belief in the value or sanctity of the individual man, but on a philosophy for which the world is composed of *individuae substantiae*.[15]

Locke's nominalism runs throughout his *Essay concerning Human Understanding*. The object of our knowledge, he holds, is our own ideas, and these are either sensations caused from without or our interior reflection on the operations of our own minds. From these elementary building blocks we compose the ideas that constitute our knowledge of the world. Consequently, we never know the real essence of a thing, but only its nominal essence, which is a mental construct that we make up for the sake of convenience in dealing with the world. Besides, the real essence of any substance, could we know it, would be its particular and individual constitution, that which makes it this thing and no other.[16] Locke's world, as much as Hobbes's, is a world of individual substances, known to us only in the sensations they cause in us.

Concerning Bentham, Crane Brinton remarks, "It may seem no small violence to Bentham's memory to describe him in a term drawn from those Middle Ages he so disliked, but he really is the perfect nominalist. The individual, John Doe, is for him an ultimate reality."[17] Mill's theory of knowledge is a more mixed bag, on the contents of which there are widely varying views among scholars. R. P. Anschutz, who has written an extended analysis of Mill's epistemology, sees him as oscillating between nominalism and realism, but coming down on the side of realism where science was concerned. "He was always a realist when he was in earnest about science: . . . and there are few philosophers who have been more thoroughly in earnest about science than Mill," says Anschutz. Mill could therefore hold a deterministic view of man in "the heavier treatises on scientific method like the *Logic*." But in "the more popular essays on ethics like the essay on *Liberty*," he could espouse "the romantic or self-formative view."[18] It is in his highly individualistic ethics that Mill's nominalism comes into play. The individual must decide upon his own good because it is so thoroughly his.

A few references to a few writers prove very little, of course. But one may venture the suggestion that the nominalist view of the world, which reduced it to a collection of individual substances only externally related to each other, furnishes a key to understanding what has happened to the liberal tradition. It explains, for one thing, why the idea of a moral law of nature, which still persisted in Hobbes and Locke (in however withered a form), was abandoned and replaced by scientific laws of nature of the sort that Bentham and Mill believed in.

For if, in our ignorance of the nature of anything, we cannot know its natural good, we may yet observe and apprehend the relations of efficient causality that obtain among things. And if, instructed by David Hume, we learn to doubt even our ability to know causality, we may yet perceive patterns among the data of the senses, patterns which can be expressed in statistical "laws" and may be explained by hypotheses that are at least conditionally valid. Our knowledge of the real, therefore, insofar as we have genuine knowledge, is simply knowledge of those aspects of reality that are quantifiable.

Such a view of the world has a tendency to make substances themselves disappear, because it depends on a particular method of analysis and synthesis. Just as we understand a clock when we can take it apart and put it together again, so we understand any other thing in particular and all things in general. As the Enlightenment *philosophe*, Jean le Rond d'Alembert, put it, "we can hope to know nature . . . by thoughtful study of phenomena, by the comparison we make among them, by the art of reducing, as much as that may be possible, a large number of phenomena to a single one that can be regarded as their principle."[19] The synthesis or reconstitution of the object analyzed shows how the subsidiary phenomena follow from the one or few basic phenomena which are the principles from which the whole ensemble flows. This way of understanding things creates at least a temptation to regard the parts as more real than the whole because it is they that "explain" the whole: we understand something when we can reduce it, if only in thought, to its elements and see how they fit together again.

Michael Polanyi describes this view of scientific understanding in these words:

> The paradigm of a conception of science pursuing the ideal of absolute detachment by representing the world in terms of its exactly determined particulars was formulated by Laplace. An intelligence which knew at one moment of time—wrote Laplace —"all the forces by which nature is animated and the respective positions of the entities which compose it . . . would embrace in the same formula the movements of the largest bodies in the universe and those of the lightest atom: nothing would be uncertain for it, and the future, like the past, would be present to its eyes." Such a mind would possess a complete knowledge of the universe.[20]

On the contrary, however, far from revealing the whole history of the world, Laplace's theory would not let us know that there was a world at all. As Polanyi says, Laplace assumes that "we should explain *all* kinds of experience *in terms of atomic data*." Once you refuse to make this fallacious assumption, however, "you immediately see that Laplacean mind understands precisely nothing and that whatever it knows means precisely nothing."[21]

Yet it is this type of thinking that makes the community a collection of individuals, the living body a collection of cells, and the cell a collection of atoms. It is capable of regarding a human being as nothing more than a highly complicated chemical compound and the human mind as a mere sum total of its contents. Nominalism does not stop with the individual substance but goes on to dissolve it, too. Its urge to analyze and to synthesize mechanically reduces a substance to its elementary components which it never succeeds in putting together again in their original form because it sees the whole only as an assembly of parts.

The nominalist mind therefore cannot understand a natural whole or appreciate a natural good. To illustrate what is meant by this, let us make an assertion: the life of the mosquito is a good to the mosquito. But of course; the mosquito has a subjective urge that makes it fly away when it sees a hand raised to swat it. Very well, let us substitute another proposition: the life of a tree is a good to the tree.

The tree has no subjective urges, so far as we can tell. It feels neither pleasure nor pain and makes no resistance to the woodsman when he cuts it down. But it is a single, unified organism, all of whose functions serve its life as this unfolds itself in a process of growth, development, and eventual reproduction. Although the tree knows nothing of good or evil, its life is its good because its being and its intelligibility consist in its life. The tree cannot be understood, simply as a fact, unless it is understood as an organic whole, organized for life and growth, not for disease and death.

That all trees eventually die is irrelevant, since a tree cannot be said for that reason to be intrinsically indifferent to life and death. Like all material and composite things, it will finally decompose. But what makes it a tree, so long as it remains one, is its unifying inner thrust toward living, not the fact that it will some day die. Nor does one dispose of the organic unity of a tree by asserting that trees are the products of a blind, mechanical evolution. What evolves is more significant than how it evolves, and the "how" does not explain away the "what."[22] No matter how they came to be here, while there are trees on earth, they are living organisms whose life is the end which their intrinsic functions serve.

That is why it is possible to speak of a particular tree as deformed, diseased, or dying. The being of a tree is a standard by which its good or ill can be judged. The good spoken of here is not a moral but an ontological one. But it is a true, objective, and intellectually knowable good, founded in the recognition of a tree as a natural whole. When we turn our attention to those natural wholes called human beings, we may recognize that they, too, have a premoral and ontological good proper to their nature. It is this premoral good that makes moral judgments by and about human beings possible.

All of this is difficult for the nominalist mind to grasp because it seeks to understand and explain everything in terms of its parts and therefore overlooks the priority of the whole of which they are parts. Because it is antipathetic to the idea of natural wholes, such a mind also finds it hard to entertain the notion of relations as natural. For it, relations are external, accidental, and adventitious, not consequences of the natures of things. Reality is made up of individual things which collide with one another to form more or less lasting patterns. These patterns are the only order of nature that there is.

This conception of reality has led to the understanding of relations among human beings as external and voluntary. The individual human being is an atom, motivated by self-interest, to whom violence is done if he is subjected to a relationship with other humans whom he has not chosen. It is no accident that this mentality thinks of civil society as essentially contractual, that its corrosive view of community is now affecting marriage and the family (to the point of contractualizing the relations among parents and children), and that it seeks to reduce the two sexes so far as possible into one, relations among whose members will be a matter of freely chosen lifestyles.

It is understandable, therefore, that thinkers infected or affected by nominalism should regard all goods as subjective, that is as objects of desires or as what positivism calls "values." One may not know whether the cause of pleasure or pain is objectively good or evil. One may doubt whether objective good and evil are meaningful terms at all. But one can be certain of pleasure and pain precisely because they are so totally subjective; one feels them or one does not.

A politics based upon the pleasure-pain principle must be one that seeks to satisfy the most basic human drives. (Whether they will be the desires of the ruling few or of the democratic many then becomes the primary issue of politics.) The early modern period took greed and the desire for power as the strongest of these drives. "Men pursue their ends, which are wealth and power," as Machiavelli almost casually remarked.[23] Hobbes for his part took as "a general inclination of all mankind, a perpetual and restless desire of power after power, that ceaseth only in death."[24] But these writers did not see what was lacking in their view of the moving forces of human nature.

One of our own contemporaries has pointed it out. "If a leading insight of modernity was that men do badly so long as they try to stifle rather than to compound with the passions," says Joseph Cropsey, "then surely the modern project must be said to have lain in a state of incipience until the sexual appetite, as well as those more visibly political ones disencumbered by Machiavelli and Hobbes, was itself at last reported on the surface."[25]

Now that it has been reported on the surface, our nominalism forbids us to think of it in terms of natural purpose and function, and our individualistic hedonism compels us to leave the judgment on satisfying it to each man's taste, "so long as he doesn't hurt anyone else." Hence follow a number of contemporary trends, one of which is public tolerance of pornography as the sign by which one may know that he is in a liberal democracy. The reader may decide for himself whether this situation represents liberalism's finest hour or its most fetid flower.

Even if it is the flower, however, it is only the flower and not the root. It is worth calling attention to merely because its odor may cause people to wonder about its root. Then they may address themselves to the more serious matter of how long a society and a culture can maintain themselves on the basis of the subjectivity of values.

James L. Wiser · *The Force of Reason: On Reading Plato's* Gorgias

Introduction: Nature of the Gorgias

Although at first it may appear that the *Gorgias* is essentially an investigation of the claims and character of rhetoric, it is, in fact, primarily a political and ethical treatise. Its political character is evident in its concern for the fundamental political question, Who should rule? Given the Socratic expectation that a "true politician" is one who attempts to make the citizens under his care as good as possible, Plato denies that such traditional Athenian heroes as Pericles, Cimon, Miltiades, and Themistocles were actually good citizens. In spite of their popularity, these leaders failed because they lacked both the knowledge and intention necessary for true statesmanship. According to Socrates the politician is a moral artist and, as such, he should never forget the task which is at hand:

> Then it is these qualities [justice and self-control] which the moral artist, the true orator, will have in view in applying to men's souls whatever speech he may use; to these he will apply absolutely every one of his actions. Whether he bestows a benefit or takes one away, he will always fix his mind upon his aim: the engendering of justice in the souls of his fellow citizens and the eradication of injustice, the planting of self-control and the uprooting of uncontrol, the entrance of virtue and the exit of vice.[1]

Socrates' condemnation of Athenian politics was not intended to apply simply to the past. As educators of the new commercial classes, the sophists and rhetoricians of Plato's own day claimed to be able to teach the knowledge and skills that were necessary for successful political rule. According to the rhetorician an essential strength for any politician was the ability to please the people by telling them what they wanted to hear and thereby gaining their favor. Thus by appearing to serve the people the politician would actually become their master. According to Socrates, however, this was precisely what such traditional leaders as Pericles and Cimon had attempted to do in their own time. By giving Athens "ships, walls, and docks,"[2] they sought to serve rather than transform the people's desires and, as such, functioned essentially as flatterers. Thus in condemning the practices of the traditional Athenian heroes Socrates was, at the same time, condemning his contemporaries. Consequently, whereas in the *Apology* Socrates was judged by Athens, in the *Gorgias* the roles are reversed. Athens and its representatives stand condemned in the eyes of philosophy and Socrates offers himself as the only living true politician: "In my opinion I am one of the few Athenians (not to say the only one) who has attempted the true art of politics, and the only one alive to put it into practice."[3] As Eric Voegelin's analysis makes clear, Socrates is calling for a revolution[4] and thus the charges brought against him during his trial have a certain prima facie validity and the anger showed him by the politically ambitious Callicles is well founded.

As was the political, so, too, is the ethical nature of the *Gorgias* revealed by the quality of the questions being asked. In particular the dialogue is concerned with two problems: What is real happiness? How should one live? Indeed for Socrates knowledge of the correct answers to these two questions is a prerequisite for one who would claim the right to rule. Ultimately such an ability to judge the quality of life actually belongs to the sons of Zeus who sit in judgment over men at their death according to the myth that ends the dialogue. Yet during life those who are most like the gods in their ability to judge are the philosophers; for they alone have learned the art of dying and thus are able to experience the true happiness of noetic participation within the *Agathon* (the Good).

A modern reader of the *Gorgias* may be struck by the easy blending of ethical and political concerns within a single Platonic dialogue. Yet such a characteristic is a central feature of the Platonic tradition. For Plato no discussion of human happiness could be complete without a consideration of the intimate relationship that exists between man's psychic and political needs. As medicine cares for the health of the body, politics cares for the health of the soul. Thus to speak of psychic fulfillment one must necessarily speak of the political art which makes such a fulfillment possible.

Inasmuch as the human soul is a complex reality which is capable of assuming a variety of qualities, its proper order is not a given but rather an achievement. In view of this, man's psychic health is dependent upon a proper exercise of the appropriate art. In particular it is the art of ruling which is capable of creating a true harmony among the otherwise diverse elements of man's nature. Thus for Plato the nurturing of human excellence is the very purpose of political order: "The excellence of each thing whether of utensil or of body or (to extend the definition) of soul or of any living thing—this excellence surely cannot be best acquired by mere chance, but by correct arrangement and by an art which is peculiar to each class individually . . . the excellence of each thing [is] produced by order and arrangement."[5]

The Structure and Argument of the Gorgias

For our purposes the *Gorgias* may be divided into three parts, each of which is characterized by Socrates' confrontation with a particular protagonist: (1) Socrates–Gorgias, 447–61; (2) Socrates–Polus, 461–81; (3) Socrates–Callicles, 481–527.

Socrates' debate with Gorgias is more serious than it may appear at first because it is not simply an attempt to define the rhetorician's art. Indeed, Socrates' understanding of an art (*techne*) includes his belief that the performance of an art has a necessary existential effect upon the one who practices it.[6] This being the case, Socrates' attempt to understand the nature of rhetoric is, in effect, an attempt to understand the character of Gorgias as a rhetorician. Thus he suggests that the first question Gorgias answers should be, "Who are you?" As the dialogue progresses it is clear that Socrates wishes to discover if one of the attributes of a man like Gorgias is that he is necessarily just. Indeed, the logical inconsistency of Gorgias' claiming to teach justice after having earlier denied doing so is of a secondary importance compared with what one learns of his character. Rather than being a just man who acknowledges a need for some form of equality, Gorgias is exposed as one who is motivated by an inordinate desire for personal pleasure and power over others. Thus in praising rhetoric he speaks of the rhetorician's power over other men and his ability to use their labor for his own personal benefit.[7]

This revelation moves the argument to Socrates' encounter with

Polus. While admitting that Gorgias may have made a logical error in presenting his case, Polus insists that Gorgias' fundamental position is still sound. Indeed for Polus, the life described by Gorgias, i.e., the life which violates the norms of conventional justice, is, in fact, the happiest of possible lives. Appealing to mass opinion and citing the example of Archelaus of Macedonia, Polus insists that the deepest desire of all men is to live a life of unrestrained pleasure. Socrates' argument to the contrary is dismissed as being simply incomprehensible: "Just exactly as though you, Socrates, would not choose to have the power to do what you thought best rather than not to have it! Just as though you wouldn't feel envy if you saw another man who killed anyone he pleased, or robbed him, or put him in prison."[8] It is obvious, of course, that Polus' intuition regarding Socrates' deepest desires is, in fact, essentially a revelation of his own.

In arguing for the life of moderation and self-control, Socrates reverses the hierarchy of goods as originally presented by Polus. Whereas Polus praises the life of injustice, Socrates condemns it as the most miserable of all possible conditions. Indeed, for Socrates it is better to suffer injustice than to do it; and if one nonetheless commits an injustice, it is better to be punished for it than not. From the perspective of Polus the Socratic alternative represents nothing less than a radical denial of the natural order of the passions, and thus Callicles is driven to comment: "For if you're serious and what you say is really true, won't human life have to be turned completely upside down? Everything we do, it seems, is the exact opposite of what we ought to do."[9]

The real tension underlying this argument is not that which is between custom and nature; but rather one which is due to two differing views of nature itself. Polus' man of injustice is admittedly in violation of Athenian custom and therefore he is offered as an example of what everyman would naturally do if he could be freed from the limitations imposed by convention and tradition. Socrates, on the other hand, argues that the life of harmony and moderation is naturally better and that only it allows the soul to achieve those ends for which it is naturally suited. Such an achievement in turn produces true human happiness and thus becomes the standard by which all other activities must be measured.

Although it is not fully developed, this argument in the *Gorgias* clearly prefigures the comparison of the philosopher and the tyrant as presented in Plato's *Republic*. There the question is whether justice is a natural good and thus whether it would be desired by a truly natural man. In order to answer this question it is necessary first to discover who the natural man is—Thrasymachus' tyrant or Socrates' philosopher. This discovery, in turn, presupposes that one can distinguish between the truly natural and the merely actual, and thus a philosophy of nature or a metaphysics must be developed before a decision can be given. Is nature only known in its perfected form or in its minimal form? If the former, the philosopher is the truly natural man and thus the only one capable of determining whether justice is desirable or not. If the latter, then the tyrant must be allowed to decide, for the tyrant is natural man inasmuch as he is a man who is reduced to his most fundamental or base elements, i.e., the passions. The metaphysics of the *Republic*, therefore is the completion of the philosophical anthropology of the *Gorgias*.

Like Gorgias, Polus ultimately is forced to contradict himself when, in tune with the standards of conventional morality, he admits that doing wrong is "uglier" than suffering it. This admission, in turn, is inconsistent with his earlier argument that the happiest life is the one of unrestrained pleasure. Yet as in the case of Gorgias, Polus' fundamental point is still untouched by these logical errors. Indeed, as Callicles himself argues, the logical difficulties which ensnared Gorgias and Polus arose because both speakers failed to consistently state their case in its own terms. Both Gorgias and Polus spoke on behalf of that happiness which is associated with the natural life of pleasure and power. Their arguments became confused, however, when they allowed themselves to be judged by the standards of conventional morality. Thus the contradictions which emerged were not caused by a fundamental inconsistency within the naturalistic perspective, but rather by the real contradictions which exist between nature and convention itself. According to Callicles, nature and convention "are for the most part opposed to each other; so that if a man is timid and doesn't have the courage to speak his mind, he must necessarily contradict himself."[10]

Thus the arguments of Callicles represent a continuation of the central theme of the earlier debates, i.e., How should man live if he is to be happy? Like Gorgias and Polus, Callicles advocates a life of luxury, license, and liberty[11] and justifies such a choice in strictly naturalistic terms. According to Callicles, nature intends that man serve rather than repress his passions and thus that the pursuit of one's advantage is both proper and good.

Given the assumption that man is to pursue his advantage, the question arises as to what skills are necessary if such a pursuit is to be successful. For his part, Callicles argues that rhetoric is the most important skill because an individual's advantage is best served by gaining political distinction. Not only is rhetoric a means of gaining honor and, perhaps, wealth, but it is also a necessary skill if a man is going to be able to defend himself when being judged by his peers. The philosopher, on the other hand, is truly helpless in such a situation:

> For as the situation is now, if anyone were to arrest you or any of your kind and drag you off to prison, declaring that you'd broken the law though you hadn't done a thing, you know perfectly well that you wouldn't be able to help yourself. You'd stand there, reeling and gaping and not have a thing to say. If the fellow hales you into court, though his accusations are never so unproven and false, you'll die the death if he chooses to claim the death penalty.[12]

In response Socrates does not deny the validity of Callicles' argument. Indeed, given Callicles' assumptions about the value of life and the role of human judgment, rhetoric does function as "the art which renders us immune from suffering unjustly."[13] Yet if life, as understood by Callicles, is truly death for the soul, and if human judgment is itself being judged by the gods who only consider the health of the soul, then rhetoric itself appears truly useless and philosophy becomes the most important of the arts. Thus, just as Socrates rejected Polus' understanding of nature, so, too, does he reject Callicles' experience of death and judgment. Having learned to die and standing under constant judgment, the philosopher alone practices that art which avoids the greatest evil, i.e., the doing of injustice.

As the readers of the *Gorgias* know, Callicles, too, eventually contradicts himself and thus withdraws from the argument. At this time, however, it is important to examine this final contradiction more carefully. For, indeed, like the others, it appears to have been both unnecessary and the result of once again deferring to the standards of conventional morality.

The source of Callicles' contradiction rests in his accepting a ranking among the virtues. In accepting the superiority of intelligence, courage, and spiritedness, Callicles is soon led to a position in which he is forced to admit that some pleasures are better than others. Once this has been admitted, he can no longer consistently argue for the superiority of the life of undifferentiated passion and as a consequence withdraws from the discussion. Yet Callicles' original acceptance of a ranking among the virtues was a concession to conventional morality and as such it was not required by his original naturalism. Indeed, even Socrates himself had admitted that such a ranking was impossible in a natural order as conceived by the rhetoricians. According to Socrates, the true natural order was composed of heaven and earth, gods and men.[14] As such it contained both a divine and a corporal principle and thereby allowed for a ranking of activities according to the standards of a natural hierarchy. In nature as understood by the rhetoricians no such hierarchy is apparent. The natural world was conceived of as simply the world of the flesh and as such contained no principle by which the passions or virtues could be differentiated. Indeed, not only would it be impossible to differentiate among the passions but the very notion of high and low or good and evil would be inappropriate. In referring to such a one-dimensional view of nature Socrates says: "In fact, if the soul were not in charge of the body, if the body were in its own charge and not monitored by the soul to distinguish cookery and medicine, if it were left by itself to estimate them by the gratification provided, the dictum of Anaxagoras would prevail far and wide, my dear Polus . . . everything would be jumbled together and we should not be able to distinguish medicinal and healthy concoctions from those of cookery."[15]

In this quotation the soul is the symbol of the spiritual while the body represents the mundane. Thus in a purely mundane world the absence of a spiritual principle means that it would be impossible to distinguish between the good (served by medicine) and the pleasant (served by cookery). Without a difference of kind in nature there can be no true difference in quality. Given this, all qualities would be equal and Callicles' attempt to argue for the superiority of courage to cowardice would be unfounded. It would appear then that, like Gorgias and Polus, Callicles refused to follow the full logic of his own argument. If he had, the results would have been similar to those achieved by Hobbes.

In my review of the *Gorgias*, I have attempted to focus upon the major sources which provide the thematic unity for each side of the debate. More importantly, I have suggested that there is a certain logical coherence to each of the contending positions. If one were to adopt a one-dimensional metaphysics, then the life of pleasure and power would be the most natural, and thus rhetoric would be the most appropriate technique for true happiness. If, however, one were to adopt an understanding of nature as both spiritual and material, then a life which orders the lower for the sake of the higher would be the best and, as a consequence, philosophy would be the most important of the arts. In both cases, however, the arguments appear to be internally consistent. At the same time this consistency contributes toward the stability of the viewpoints under review. Inasmuch as each side can account for the errors of the other in its own terms, neither perspective is particularly vulnerable to the impact of adverse evidence. From the perspective of Polus and Callicles, Socrates' arguments appear to be fanciful because they are not based in the life experience of the rhetorician. For example, Socrates' appeal to the myth of the last judgment seems as irrelevant to Callicles as Polus' appeal to the example of Archelaus seems to Socrates. For Callicles the arguments of the rhetorician are simply commonsensical, while to Socrates the arguments of philosophy appear to be accurate expressions of his own lived experience. In both cases, then, it would appear that the ideas which one holds are ultimately dependent upon the personality of the knower. If this is correct, then, before there can be a true exchange at the level of ideas, there must first be a real encounter at the level of existence. In other words, it would appear that for Plato intellectual persuasion presupposes an existential conversion.

One of the most striking features of the *Gorgias* is that, given the standards of the text itself, neither side wins the debate. As Socrates repeats on several occasions, the purpose of the debate is to persuade one's opponent.[16] Thus, although Socrates may be able to trap his counterparts in certain logical inconsistencies, he never succeeds in convincing them of his own position. As a consequence Socrates fails to meet his own self-set standard of success. Although Gorgias, Polus, and Callicles are forced to make certain concessions, they simply withdraw from the debate without ever admitting the inadequacy of their own fundamental position. The reason for this, I believe, is clear. Although they may have experienced a certain difficulty in defending their viewpoint, they remain nonetheless existentially committed to its correctness. As such the ideas of Socrates may be formally irrefutable but they, nonetheless, appear as artificial and meaningless. Thus in leaving the debate Polus admits: "Well, Socrates, it seems quite absurd to me; yet it does, no doubt, agree with what you said before."[17]

In analyzing the reason for his own difficulty in persuading his opponents, Socrates suggests the following:

> Callicles, if human beings did not have certain feelings in common (though they may vary a bit from man to man), if each of us had merely his own private sensations unshared by the rest, it would not be very easy to demonstrate to another what one feels. I say this with reference to the fact that at the moment you and I are both experiencing somewhat the same emotion and each of us has two objects of his love: I Alcibiades, the son of Clinias, and philosophy; you the Athenian Demos [people] and the son of Pyrilampes.[18]

Here it seems we are at the heart of Socrates' message. As we know from his *Republic*, Socrates differentiates among men in terms of the objects of love which dominate their souls. Accordingly, in the *Republic* he distinguishes among lovers of wisdom, lovers of honor, lovers of wealth, lovers of freedom, and lovers of order. In the *Gorgias*, however, the differences are reduced to two: the lover of wisdom and the lover of power. Socrates, as the philosopher, is the lover of wisdom. Gorgias, Polus, and Callicles, on the other hand, identify themselves as lovers of power. Indeed, while Gorgias defines rhetoric in terms of its contribution to his quest for mastery,[19] Polus admits to admiring tyrannical power precisely because it is the means for human happiness as he understands it.[20] At the same time Callicles argues that by flattering the masses in a democracy, i.e., the Athenian Demos, he is securing for himself the power he needs to enjoy the life he seeks.[21]

In suggesting that true communication between himself and Callicles will be difficult, Socrates is thereby acknowledging the existential roots of intellectual persuasion. As a lover of power Callicles is predisposed toward a certain understanding of the world. Ideas which reflect this understanding are therefore commonsensical and those which challenge it lack a basis in experience. For his part Socrates is equally disposed toward a particular view of reality. He knows what he does because of who he is and, in order to share that knowledge with others, he must first convert them to his form of existence. Thus, in explaining to Callicles why he cannot really appreciate the philosopher's argument, Socrates says: "It is because the love of Demos dwells in your soul, Callicles, and resists me."[22] Thus it would appear that unless Socrates can convert Callicles into a lover of wisdom he will not be able to demonstrate the truth of his own ideas.

It is interesting to note that the debate in the *Gorgias* fails on at least two levels. Each failure, however, is due to the same cause. First, at the level of argumentation, Gorgias, Polus, and Callicles fail to argue their case consistently. Each in his own way forsakes the realm of nature by appealing to a conventional moral standard and thereby becomes entrapped in a logical contradiction. As mentioned earlier, such errors were not necessary. The naturalist position of the rhetoricians itself did not require that Gorgias claim to teach justice, that Polus consider the doing of injustice uglier than the suffering of it, or that Callicles attempt to rank the virtues. Indeed, as Socrates himself shows, a consistent materialism would be indifferent to such distinctions. Why then, did the rhetoricians make such a mistake? The answer can be found in the very nature of their personalities. As rhetoricians they sought to please their audience and thus acceded to the traditions and principles of their time. By saying what they believed their audience wanted to hear the rhetoricians were simply being true to their calling.[23] As flatterers they sought to flatter and thus did not wish to question the fundamental assumptions of their peers. Thus, even at the level of mere argumentation, the failure of the debate within the *Gorgias* can be traced to the peculiarities of the rhetorical personality.

Similarly, at the higher level of existential confrontation the debate fails for the same reasons. Because they are lovers of power the rhetoricians lack the necessary existential prerequisites which would allow them to understand the arguments of Socrates. As lovers of power they are locked into an intellectual system which is both internally coherent and existentially persuasive to those who are of a similar disposition. Thus at the level of existential confrontation Socrates fails to achieve his goal because of his inability to bring about a psychic conversion. Once again the debate fails because the rhetoricians are who they are.

Conclusion: The Limit of Reason

If we assume that the *Gorgias* is essentially an ethical and political dialogue, then the failure of either side to persuade the other implies that there are certain limitations to ethical-political discourse as such. Inasmuch as knowledge is virtue, it is apparent to Plato that the intellect cannot be abstracted from man's existential condition. Unlike rationalism's faith in the power of an abstract and universal mind, Platonism acknowledges the concrete existential realities which condition man's search for truth. In short, who one is determines what he can know, and as a result man's escape from the cave of opinion presupposes his prior existential conversion.

If this interpretation is correct, it would appear that one of the prerequisites for meaningful ethical and political discourse is that men become like philosophers. But philosophy for Plato is not defined by a particular set of doctrines. To become like a philosopher is to assume a certain attitude toward reality. As the whole body of Platonic dialogues shows, this necessarily includes an attitude of radical openness toward its transcendent ground. Such an attitude in turn can only be maintained against the forces of closure by the strength of an erotic commitment. The philosopher is first of all one who loves the divine; yet to seek the transcendent is at the same time to reject the mundane. Thus it would appear that one of the prerequisites for practical discourse is a certain disregard for the pleasures and goods of the world. According to Plato, one must learn to take pleasure in the right things and in the right way. This, in turn, is a matter of training and therefore presupposes the existence of a well-ordered community and a properly functioning authority. Thus one must first be taught to live philosophically before he can actually do philosophy.

A second consequence of Plato's emphasis upon the intellectual consequences of particular erotic orientations concerns the issue of conversion. Assuming that an existential conversion is necessary and assuming that eros is the ordering source of the soul, it is obvious that a true conversion cannot be compelled. One cannot be forced to love something. Similarly, one cannot force another to abandon that which he truly loves the most. Persuasion therefore depends upon an erotic appeal. Socrates must somehow show Callicles that the love of wisdom is a more satisfying experience than the love of pleasure. To make his appeal, however, he must first lead Callicles to become dissatisfied with that which he already loves. This, I believe, is the true purpose behind Socrates' consistent questioning and probing of his opponents' beliefs. Socrates is not simply attempting to trap his colleagues in logical inconsistencies. Rather he is trying to demonstrate to them the true insufficiency and lack of substance in those things which they hold most dear. Only by demonstrating the relative shallowness of their prior commitments could Socrates hope to persuade the rhetoricians that a richer and fuller object for their love is available to them. His inability to do so in the *Gorgias*, however, indicates the inevitable limitations in any attempt at conversion. How is it possible to engage one in a quest for an object whose very desirability is not yet apparent? The answer, perhaps, is to be found by appealing to the attractiveness of those who have undertaken such a quest for themselves. Thus it is that the ultimate confrontation in the *Gorgias* is that which is between the person of Socrates and that of Callicles.

Walter B. Mead · *Will as Moral Faculty*

My initial observation in this essay is that both classical and modern philosophy fail to provide us with a concept of human volition, or will, adequate to support an understanding of man as moral agent. My main effort then is to suggest some beginning considerations in the development of a moral philosophy of will.

I

Morality, as the concept has emerged in the context of Jewish and Christian thought, is concerned with attributing not only degrees of "right" and "wrong" to human action, of "good" and "bad" to human character, but also accountability and responsibility to the individual as moral agent. Indeed, any concept of moral character that does not assume responsibility on behalf of the moral agent must appear somewhat superficial.

To speak of morality in terms of responsibility requires that we view the moral agent, or that part of his *psyche* which is of central moral significance, as essentially autoinductive—that is, not essentially determined by factors external to its own decision-making activity. In other words, we must be able to identify a faculty or function of mind that is essentially voluntaristic, or perhaps better, volitional, a term that is meant to include both freedom (voluntarism) and intentionality. Such a mental faculty has traditionally been referred to as "will." However, to address the question of will as specifically moral, or accountable, requires still more: an understanding of will as operative within a normatively rational context, or a special relationship of will to the noetic function of judgment.[1]

Although it is not fair to charge Nietzsche with ignoring this relationship, since he does repeatedly insist that the will-to-power receive its proper form through reason, his identification of will with power and the preeminence he assigns to the dionysian life-forces, shorn of even subsidiary rational constraints, have become paradigmatic of a major current in modernity and a rationalization of some of its most unconscionable political movements: nazism, fascism, and even some of the essentially "willful" movements of the 1960s in the United States ostensibly and ironically directed against fascism. Here we encounter the consequences of rationality so submerged in will, that will is in no way answerable to reason or judgment; truly autonomous, it lacks the credentials of a moral faculty.

Similar "demoralization" of will, but in this instance as a consequence of its loss of volitional capacity, has provided the conceptual foundation for the rise of positivism and at least the Marxist forms of extremist-left ideologies in this century. Here we find that will has been so submerged in reason, and reason itself so eviscerated of all nonspecifiable, nonformalistic, nonscientific elements, that deterministic explanations are viewed as sufficient accounts of human activity and historical event. Just as Nietzsche opened the way for the eventual demoralization of will through a deemphasis of the crucial guidance provided will by reason, it appears that at least equally influential in this demoralization process has been a fundamental failure on the part of the ancient Greek philosophers to conceive of will as essentially autoinductive, or self-determining.

The mental faculty which both Plato and Aristotle call the "volitional" or the "spirited" part (*thumos*), clearly comes closer to our concept of will than do either of the other faculties they designate (*logistikon*, or intellect; and the "appetitive" faculty, or bodily passions and drives). They see this spirited part as the soul's capacity for experiencing and expressing a fervor for the good, even before the good is rationally conceived. It is the soul's striving to do what is just and noble. Yet, while dependent—as we conceive will to be—upon intellect for its proper guidance, thumos, as these classical philosophers represented it, displays at best limited qualities of either freedom or intentionality. Plato makes it clear that the spirited part is incapable—indeed, by definition—of allying with the bodily desires against reason.[2]

An examination of those conditions which do allow the thumos to serve irrationality and evil underscores further the obstacles that lie in the path of any effort to identify this faculty with will, at least moral will. According to both Plato and Aristotle:

1. Requiring rigorous discipline and gradual "habituation" (*sunetheia*) over a period of years for its proper development, which

occurs in the young earlier than the development of the rational faculty,[3] the thumos, when deficient in such development, perhaps even in the course of such development, will lack the strength and courage necessary for keeping in check overly developed bodily passions and desires. When the soul comes to be dominated by these appetitive drives, even clever men can be "forcibly enlisted in the service of evil."[4]

2. When the logistikon, or intellect, functions badly, unlike the spirited part and the appetitive faculty, it does so not so much because of weakness (or excess) as improper orientation.[5] Although the spirited part in youth depends for its proper guidance virtually entirely upon nonrational habituation, for its full maturation it eventually depends also upon the proper development and orientation of the intellect.[6] When intellect, out of ignorance, focuses upon the illusory, the irrational, the evil (*doxa*), rather than upon the good and the true (*episteme*), this then is what the spirited part is unwittingly led to serve.

3. Precisely the same results come from the excessive eagerness of a well-intending spirit in its earlier, prerational stage of development,[7] which, as a result of not yet being fully matured by the influence of reason,[8] "mishears" and mistakes the directive orders of reason.

One would ordinarily expect to find precisely in those instances where will acts in a manner contrary to rational or moral directive the most radical evidence of its voluntaristic (free) and intentional (volitional), that is, self-chosen (autoinductive), or moral, character. Yet we do not find such evidence in the explanations of such contrariety provided by the classical philosophers. In the first condition, just described, wrong and irrational action is explained not in terms of either freedom or intentionality but in terms of the domination of appetitive drives. This domination itself is not a result of willing choice (thumos, we noted, is incapable of siding with desire against reason) but of deficiency, weakness, and default, in turn—a product not of self-choice but of improper habituation.

In the second condition, because the spirited part does not include within itself the capacity to judge critically, at its best it can only ultimately, when confronted with intellect (even if this means having its habituated affections overruled), submit to the guidance of intellect. If intellect offers false directive, thumos only performs its proper function in acting upon this directive. We might say (admittedly paraphrasing Socrates) that from the perspective of thumos "to know . . . is to do . . . whether what we 'know' is, in fact, right or wrong." The intentionality of thumos, as we have noted, is defined only in the most abstract terms: "to do good." Any specification of what is meant by the "good," and therefore intentionality itself, practically speaking, can be provided only by the intellect. The spirited part, improperly guided, can act only unwittingly—not perversely. Further, because it is not within the capacity of thumos actively to resist its higher source of directives, we find, again, no evidence of real freedom.

In the third condition, where the spirited part is guided only by impulsive and habituated (even though properly habituated) affection, the action cannot be said to be free. And because, once again, its intentionality is only of the most general kind, bereft of any attunement to reason, intentionality is inefficacious, and action unwitting.

What we discover in the classical writings is a persistent ambiguity on the matter of will, representing a mixture of innate desire, habituated affection, and feeble approximations of volition. Because volition in the classical understanding is barely distinguishable from habituated affection, and the latter from appetition or desire, all emerge as essentially efficient causes, even when guided by the final causes represented by the objects of the intellect: the Good, the True, and the Beautiful. Aristotle probably struggled more than did Plato to make room for a self-determining "affectional" faculty. However, his clearest definition of "choice" (*prohairesis*)—"desire guided by deliberation"[9]—hardly takes us beyond the Platonic offering, which either brings the affectations of thumos dangerously close to appetition or, on other occasions, seems to leave all judgment and choice to intellect, where volition is essentially as extraneous as it is to desire.

To his credit Aristotle puzzled over the strange but familiar phenomenon where one intentionally chooses that which he knows or believes to be the worse course of action when he could choose the better course.[10] But the very term he uses to describe this, *akrasia*, connotes no more than weakness of will, inconsistency, or incontinence, and hardly allows for a fully volitional will—one capable of rebellion (itself certainly not an act of weakness) or moral perversity. Thumos appears to be fully spirited from birth. Its strength is really its attunement to the proper affections. Both Plato's and Aristotle's emphasis upon habituation suggests that whatever strength comes to characterize this spirited part is a product more of proper conditioning and practice than of moral struggle. Therefore Plato advises, for establishing the just *polis*, that children in their precognitive developmental period be isolated from all others in society (over the age of ten), except for the few philosophers, and be reared in an idyllic, controlled environment.[11] In the ideal society, where one's earliest formative years are protected from adverse influence, where one does not have to experience agonizing struggle and exercise willful resistance to negative affection, where education consists primarily of exposure to the proper harmonies and rhythms of poetry and music, presumably strength of character will emerge.

Even beyond the early years, as we trace the classical account of the soul's migration into the higher stages of its noetic development, as represented in Plato's famous Allegory of the Cave,[12] this entire odyssey is conspicuously lacking in willful effort, much less moral anguish. This allegory does not even assume the pristine beginning of an idyllic childhood. Rather, it starts with a psyche whose affective and intellectual orientations are misdirected. What is called for is a radical conversion (*periagoge*) of the entire psyche. Plato presents us with a prisoner who, apparently through no effort of his own, finds himself freed of his chains. Even at this point the prisoner does not opt to redirect his gaze from that to which he has been habituated all of his life. Instead, he is "*forced* suddenly to stand up, turn his head, and walk with eyes lifted to the light." Furthermore, "someone . . . *drags* him away forcibly up the steep and rugged ascent and does not let him go until he has hauled him out into the sunlight."[13]

Obviously there is no self-motivation, no cooperative will in this ascent. Indeed, the thumos, improperly habituated in its affections, combined with a wrongly oriented logistikon, and overwhelmed by the bodily passions (i.e., conditions 1 and 2 described above), represents a highly obstinate psyche that has to be forced every step along the way. Although Plato insists that the conversion experience cannot be forced, that the philosopher-teacher can only attempt to persuade, and even that a beneficent outcome of this educative effort cannot be guaranteed, it appears that until the captive soul is finally brought into the full light of day, the prior attachments have such a hold that both volitional and intellectual appeals are likely to be without success and society must forcefully intervene (compulsory education?). Until the psyche virtually attains the actual conversion itself, there is no evidence of a thumos courageously and agonizingly asserting itself in the face of pain from the brightening light. The ascent is completely without will, except for whatever volition can be identified with a misdirected and therefore resistive thumos. In other places Plato does allow that, in a carefully structured and prolonged educative process (*paideia*), even "true opinion" (*doxa alethes*) can assist in the journey toward episteme, or wisdom.[14] But true opinion is an object of intellect, not a factor of will. It represents not an efficient but a final (guiding, directing) cause; it can only persuade, not compel. Its attractiveness, in fact, presupposes properly habituated affections.

Because of the incredible tenacity of improper affections, it appears that it is virtually not until the psyche has been grudgingly and painfully dragged to the threshold of truth (episteme) that the spirited part becomes cooperative, presumably rehabituated with proper affections, and joins in the effort; but even then thumos offers no semblance of willful, least of all anguished, assertion. The irony is: just as thumos, for all practical purposes, appears to have been inefficacious in the ascent toward episteme, now in the full illumination of episteme, thumos appears superfluous. Truth, finally held in clear view, appears, in itself, sufficient for effecting proper action. It is at the pinnacle of the noetic ascent that the Socratic formula, "To know the good is to do the good," finally becomes relevant. In Plato's words, "A man whose thoughts are fixed on true reality . . . cannot fail to fashion himself in its likeness."[15] The intellect, finally rightly oriented and made fully conscious of its innate affinity with the Truth it now perceives, attends—on its own—to its proper object. The highest virtue, wisdom, once attained—unlike courage, temperance, justice, etc., Plato informs us, does not depend upon habituation.[16] Proper affections that may have served to pave the way are not dispensed with. They merely do not have to be separately inculcated through habituation; the truth itself supplies them. Although at the height of noetic fulfillment thumos is present, this still must not be confused with will. For Plato as well as for Aristotle, the enjoyment of the highest Truth, like the ascent to it, is essentially a "will-less" activity.

Our conclusion remains unchallenged even when we consider the role of *eros*, which, according to the classical account, plays a prominent part in the psyche's attaining and attending to the Good, the True, and the Beautiful. By no means confined to the spirited part, but taking its various, both proper and improper, forms in all three faculties, eros is essentially a felt, innate affinity for its sought objects. Although "intentional" in the sense of having an objective, eros is not intentional in the narrower sense of being self-determined, or autoinductive; therefore, it is not a willful activity. Further, the account of the genesis of eros as the motivational force behind intellect, provided in Plato's Myth of the Charioteer,[17] indicates that eros has for its own driving force the soul's recollection (*anamnesis*) of its previous conversancy with the Forms. In other words, eros receives its own very existence from a prior, essentially cognitive experience, however deeply buried in the intellectual recesses of the soul. Whatever limited semblance of will some might wish to attribute to eros, by the Platonic account, this affective impulse itself is ultimately absorbed in the noetic.

We have suggested that, according to the Allegory of the Cave, intellect at its highest ascent seems to provide its own motivation and proper affections. Yet these affections seem to be adequate only in regard to providing for the continued excellence of intellect itself—or to serving the self-interests only of the class of philosophers. That which is deemed to be for the good of the entire psyche, or in the interest of the whole society, finds no assured support within the motivational resources of intellect—or even from the philosophers themselves. One would think that if there was ever an appropriate time for an identifiable moral will or conscience to emerge within the classical schema, this would be it. Yet it does not. Astonishingly, Plato tells us that even the philosophers will probably have to be compelled to depart from their contemplative existence and return into the cave to provide leadership (through a combination of persuasion and, again, compulsion) for their fellowmen.[18]

Perhaps it is not so astonishing that philosophers should have to be compelled to perform their civic duty when we consider that this is perfectly consistent with what we have seen to be the classical depiction of the relationship between intellect and thumos, where intellect for its efficacy is largely dependent upon thumos, and thumos itself is not self-determining but mostly a product of external, efficient causes. The classical philosophers do offer an insightful portrayal of man's existential tension. But this existential tension is not adequately translated, by the classical thinkers, into a concept of will that takes seriously the inherent egocentricity of infancy and the reoccurring internal struggles of will that confront even the most enlightened of men—in short, man's experience of what Christianity refers to as "original sin."

Any systematic effort to treat more adequately this human experience and condition must not only perceive the psyche as willful, but will as specifically moral. This entails an understanding of will as intentional, anguishing ("reflexive"), radically free, and therefore potentially perverse. It also requires an understanding of the relation that exists between judgment and will, which, in turn, presupposes a thorough treatment of judgment itself. Space does not allow me even to touch upon the last two matters. Indeed, I can offer only some beginning suggestions relative to the other concerns.

II

When we engage in willing, we propose that a certain thing, event, condition, or truth exist (or that it not exist). Willing is self-chosen purposefulness, intentionality. It ought not to be confused with the act of distinguishing between greater and lesser realities, or of responding to the truth by way of acknowledging it as truth and drawing out its logical implications, which is an integral part of all rational thinking. Reason—most conspicuously in the act of judging—has its own power to respond to truth (to the extent that it finds the truth compelling), to say yes to truth and no to untruth; but it is a "yes, that is the way it is," or a "no, that is not the way it is" (what we might call a "deciding about"), which is quite different from saying "yes, that is the way I propose it to be," or "no, that is not the way I propose it to be" (what we might call a "deciding for or against"). The latter, which is the expression of will, is even different from asserting "this is the way it should be," that is, "I judge this to be good" (or "I judge this to be true" or ". . . beautiful"). For willing moves beyond the objective assessment of facts and values as they are, to a first-person endorsement; it involves an act of personal approbation—or disapprobation.

Yet will, as purposefulness and intentionality, is still more than mere preference. Whereas we can prefer something that we know cannot be ("That is the way I would have it be"), we cannot logically will something (propose it to be) that we know cannot possibly be. (Even though we may assume that which we will is unlikely to be, willing assumes some possibility of its being efficacious.) There is an earnestness, an active intentionality, a seriousness of commitment to willing that need not exist in an expression of preference. This is what gives will, unlike intellect and judgment, its special moral character. In those instances where the object of our willing does not presently exist (or exists only partially), then to the extent that we truly will, we are impelled to act in any way that we reasonably can to bring it into full existence. The will in these instances must seek to be effective. To will the good is, in this sense, to do the good. We cannot be said truly to will (or to love) justice if we do not make every reasonable effort to be just and to encourage actions consistent with justice.

Since judging is partially free of the bonds of formal rules, it is reflexive and dialectical in contrast to the more formal, direct, and linear processes of cognition. But even in judging, the intellect does not experience the same kind of division and reflexivity as the will. This becomes evident in the fact that our willing always includes an awareness of the subjective self—that is, of the self as the one who does the willing. In the "I will" the emphasis is as much upon the subject, "I," as it is upon the predicate, "will," or that which is willed. In the "I think" the consciousness is not of the thinker, as such, but of that which is thought. It is in this sense that Martin Heidegger suggests that in thinking, man is totally absorbed in the object of his thinking.[19] Even if the thinking self is part of that object, it is so only as object. This total absorption, however, does not characterize man in the act of willing. In willing we are as conscious of ourselves, as willing-egos, as we are of our willed objects.

Willing is reflexive also in the sense that—like judging—its activity is characterized by an internal contest within its own divided mind, but—unlike judging—a contest in which each contestant has considerable autonomy, that is, virtually takes on a life of its own. In the dialectics of rational reflection the relationship between position and counterposition is essentially convivial; the representation of the respective positions is more or less in the form of a devil's advocacy—essentially hypothetical and within the context of agreed-upon rules of combat. The positioning and counterpositioning of the will, on the other hand, is nothing less than a dead-earnest, all-out, no-holds-barred struggle between the two components of the will standing in adversarial relationship to each other, in which only one can emerge victor, and in which the goal is the spirit, or the soul, of man himself. Hannah Arendt, among others, has in fact spoken of the existence in every person of a will and a counterwill. The experiencing of this dual character of will underlies our occasional confession that even while we want the good, we fail to do it. We acknowledge the presence of a counterwill when we defiantly assert that just because we know something to be right or just, we don't have to like it. In fact, it is not so much the ability of the will to approve of truth and goodness and to disapprove of falsehood and evil as it is this capacity of will to disassociate itself from and to resist the true and the good and to affirm falsehood and evil that provides us with an indication of the true nature and measure of man's freedom.

The question of whether or not our will is a free will is one that cannot be resolved by any logical or systematic form of demonstration. No matter what premises we start with in our reasoning, it can be argued that these premises themselves are not freely chosen. Any effort to provide a logical proof of our freedom is destined to turn out circular. In other words, if freedom of the will is to be acknowledged, it must be assumed or—more accurately—discovered as a primal experience, quite independent of any part of a line of reasoning, and presupposed by the very nature of reasoning rather than sought as a logical conclusion.

In judging, we are involved in the making of decisions for which we are not provided with clear and specifiable intimations or, at least, not with clear criteria by which we can choose among intimations. Therefore our judging is a free activity. Willing, if we view it only in terms of its rational expression and therefore strictly guided and compelled in its approbations and disapprobations by the decisions of judgment (themselves, as we have observed, not strictly compelled), does not itself share in the freedom that characterizes judgment—what we might call intellectual freedom. The will's freedom is of a far more radical and far-reaching nature. There are, of course, ample demonstrations of the ability of will to resist the irrational drives and appetites and to act in accordance with reason. This exercise of will—its willing of what judgment suggests is reasonable and good and its nilling[20] of what judgment determines to be unreasonable and bad—would not represent an exercise of freedom if will did not also have the capacity for perverse willing and nilling (that is, the capacity to will what judgment calls bad or irrational and to nill what judgment calls good or rational). The freedom to consent entails the freedom to resist.

Will includes the capacity to decline and to ignore reason itself; not just through error (which could characterize a specific act of judgment), but through intent (which is volitional). If this were not inherent in will, if—to speak the language of the Apostle Paul—"sin did not dwell within me," will would not exist. Unlike judgment, will has the incredible freedom to be irrational if it so chooses. Unlike judging, willing does not cease to be willing when it abandons rational intimation. Unlike judgment, which can exist only in a world of incomplete knowledge, will could exist meaningfully in a world where man was omniscient and therefore where judging had ceased to exist. Constrained only by what one perceives, whether accurately or not, as within the realm of the possible, will is otherwise constrained only according to its own choice. Thus, while not free to ignore deliberately all the constraints of reason, once reason has assessed the possible, will is absolutely free to leave the guidance of reason behind and to fly in the face of not only the true but also the good and the beautiful. And only because it has this option, will remains radically free in its choice even when it chooses to be more thoroughly constrained, or guided, by reason.

Thus human volition must be seen to be, through and through, a radically free act. Even in willing that which reason suggests to it, the willing-ego does so on its own volition, uncompelled in the sense that reason is compelled, in the extreme regarding even openness and objectivity as options subject to its own choice. As impressive and as awesome as is the freedom that man is given in his ability to judge, his freedom to will is much more fundamental. Even if he had only the freedom that is available to him in judging, he could not justifiably be likened to a robot, or—as is more common today—be interpreted on the model of a computer. Yet it is the freedom that characterizes his willing that gives him his greatest stature. It is perhaps this incredible freedom of the human will that provides significance to the Judeo-Christian image of man as "created in the image of God." For through his ability to will, man is—in effect—able to create, or recreate, at least in his own mind (and to a sometimes alarming extent impose that will upon his universe), the work of his Creator according to his own standards. If we assume, as is suggested in the accounts in Genesis, that God created the universe *ex nihilo* (that is, unbound by any preexisting laws or conditions), then we must suppose that God, as Hannah Arendt says, "was entirely free to create a different world in which neither our mathematical truths nor our moral precepts would be valid. From this it follows that everything that is might possibly not have been—save God Himself."[21]

The miracle of human will is that by virtue of it man can assume a similar posture of transcendence. Although lacking in divine omniscience as well as in the divine omnipotence that assures the practical effectiveness of will, man nevertheless can either will or nill the "compelling" laws that appear to govern his bodily drives and appetites, the very laws of morality, even his and his fellowman's existence. Here we are speaking of a radical capacity of the will that takes us considerably beyond its role in reflection and understanding, that is, beyond what is required in initiating and sustaining our thinking and understanding. Man's ability to will and to nill arises out of his natural inclination toward freedom, his desire to be more than a part of the necessary laws (formal or intimational) of the universe. It arises, further, as Hannah Arendt suggests, "out of a natural revulsion of free men toward being at someone's bidding." More fundamentally, man's freedom of will is an expression of his desire to participate in the issuing of the imperatives of his existence even as he obeys them, to be a coauthor of his universe and its laws. It arises, indeed, out of man's God-given freedom to accept or reject the very word and work of his Creator. In this context, we can more clearly understand what we described as the will's reflexive consciousness of itself as willing-ego. Thus, Arendt suggests that "the will always addresses itself to itself; when the command says, Thou shalt, the will replies, Thou shalt *will* as the command says—and not mindlessly execute orders. That is the moment when the internal contest begins, for the aroused counter-will has a like power of command. . . . The I-will inevitably is countered by an I-nill."[22]

Theologians speak of God as standing "outside" of time in that time itself is part of the created world. They conclude that therefore God is not contingent (that is, dependent) upon the laws of the temporal world. Although man, as a temporal being, cannot claim to transcend in similar fashion the laws of temporality, as is evident in his experience of both birth and death, and although his very categories of thought are temporal-bound, through his will man has the capacity for complete spontaneity, for unnecessitated action. The will, in its radical freedom, represents a beginning not bound or necessitated by other beginnings.

Because of the will's radical freedom, demonstrated in its unique capacity for initiative and spontaneity, will occupies a position of de facto jurisdictional supremacy (not to be confused with ontological supremacy, which—Nietzsche notwithstanding—rightly belongs to reason) over both reason and appetite. We noted earlier that even in those instances where will is guided by reason, reason rules only by will's consent. That is to say, even where reason wins out over willful whim, will itself is the final arbiter. Will can also give its consent, as well as its dissent, to rule by irrational appetite. And even in those instances when the baser passions manage to prevail through the abdication of will, this too testifies to will's supremacy. Where the appetites win out over the resistance of the will, here too the superiority of will deserves recognition, if not in terms of its power at least in terms of its jurisdictional authority—an authority that, because of will's incredible freedom, transcends rationality.[23] Whether we experience the conflict as one between desire and reason, or between will and reason, or between will and desire, it is will itself that must be the final arbiter.[24] For neither reason nor desire is able to make the kind of reflexive "I propose that . . ." choice that characterizes will. In other words, will itself must decide how it will be guided—by reason, by appetite (or by other irrational drives such as fear, etc.), or by whim—if will is to function at all. And since the contest is not, in fact, simply between desire and reason (except where will abdicates), or between will and reason, or will and desire, but is really a contest within the will itself, since it is really—as we have suggested—a contest between the will and the counterwill, a struggle between the I-will (*velle*) and the I-nill (*nolle*), it is not given to reason (or to desire) to make the final choice. Again, it is will that emerges supreme.

In this sense, it seems appropriate to understand the moral self primarily in terms of will. In our cognitive and judging activity we are totally intentional; that is, in the quest for knowledge our object and focus are entirely outside ourselves. We are totally absorbed in our intended object. Thus, in thinking of this sort I can lose my consciousness of self and experience self-abandon. Regarding myself, as subject, I become in a sense "absentminded." Indeed, I must if I am to be thoroughly open and to apply myself fully to the inquiry. Willing also has its object, its intent, its purpose. But, as we have noted in speaking of the special reflexivity of will, in the act of willing we are at least as much conscious of the self as subject (that is, as willing-ego) as we are of the objective of our willing.

The difference here between rational reflection and willing is the difference between "This is the way things are" and "This is the way I propose that it be." Even thought, in the effort to determine "the way things are," to the extent that this involves us in judging, represents a dialectical process and therefore a division within the judging-ego. Yet this division is essentially other-oriented, that is, essentially responsive to and reflective of the "heuristic field" of intimations that guide reason. On the other hand, the process involved in determining how "I propose that it be," although also represented by a divided mind, is nondialectical—each will (that is, will and counterwill) asserting itself autonomously and self-assertively. The division is not essentially reflective of an external reality, but—as we have seen—of the self's own claim to freedom. Indeed, it is only because we have this essentially self-oriented and subjectively based counterwill, which entails the possibility—even at times the inclination—to nill that which is rational and worthy (or to will perversely), that we can speak of moral worth. The waging of the intellectual contest, not characterized by the same intensity of self-assertiveness, does not, as a result, carry the same intensity of self-accrediting "worthiness." In the act of willing I am involved in making more than a decision. In willing I put myself on the line, so to speak, by way of making an endorsement; I commit myself, sometimes to the extent of suffering, of risking my status, my livelihood, even sometimes my life. In willing I cannot absent my activity from an awareness of myself as a willing person. Indeed, Professor Heidegger suggests that in willing "we encounter ourselves as who we are authentically. . . . Self examination [that is, the examination of ourselves as mere reflective, reasoning selves] never . . . shows how we are ourselves. But by willing, and also by nilling . . . we appear in a light that itself is lighted by the act of willing. To will always means: to bring oneself to one's self . . . to will one's own self . . . [to will] the self that wants to become what it is."[25]

Hannah Arendt observes that willing fashions "the same self that the thinking activity disregards . . . into an 'enduring I' that directs all particular acts of volition. It creates the self's *character*. . . ."[26] We might say that the moral self consists of the sum total of commitments one represents through his willing and nilling. To the extent that the will is rational (that is, rationally guided), through its reflexivity it is able to react to the appraisals made by judgment of the self that emerges from acts of willing.

Will is in a very real sense born of the differentiation of reality between the immanent and the transcendent and of the resulting existential tension, wherein we are called upon to identify ourselves through our commitments. It is our very moral existence that is at stake. Our willing—whether we will and what we will—is decisive. It is within the awesome capacity of our will to create whatever moral identity we have. In the radical freedom of our willing, our moral existence has been (to use Heidegger's terms) "abandoned to itself." Modern man, for the most part having lost faith, therefore often experiences much anxiety at the prospects of willing.

In these instances the abandonment of will, that is, not-willing —as we have seen—has become an increasingly recurrent phenomenon. When this occurs, however, it cannot be a matter of choice—that is, of will. We can, logically, neither will to will nor will to not-will. Not-willing, therefore, is more accurately attributed to a failure of will or to a "paralysis" of will, rather than to willful choice, especially where our confrontation with the high stakes of willing gives rise to extraordinary anxiety. Viewing not-willing as mere unwilled cessation of will seems reasonable in light of our experience of willing as an activity that—as in the case of thinking—is not sustained by an inherent momentum. Willing continues only as long as it is spontaneously rekindled, only as long as it is recurringly self-initiated. (Willing, we have said, *is* spontaneity, beginning.) Therefore will must be seen to be as susceptible to the law of entropy as anything in our physical universe. Willing must immediately lapse into not-willing as soon as willing is not actively engaged in. The burden of initiative and sustenance is upon him who would will, not upon him who abandons willing.

Experience suggests, further (as the classical philosophers amply demonstrated), that where the initiative of willing has been weakened, whether by anxiety or simply lassitude, the appetites—which do not depend, as do reason and will, upon the elusiveness of trust and hope, but thrive on the prospects of immediate gratification—often take over in providing both initiative and direction to human behavior. And the consequent sating invariably leads to further lassitude and weakening of willful resolve.

However, inasmuch as all thinking, for its initiation and sustenance, must be encompassed by willing, the condition of not-willing is one of virtual unconsciousness—or, at best, a condition of sheer mechanical cognition—"unthinking" habitual and rote response. More fundamentally, not-willing marks, through the elimination of the will, the extinction of one's self. It appears that the inordinate "anxiety of existence" (to use Professor Voegelin's term) that results from a failure to relate constructively and realistically to one's world through faith, hope, and thoughtful willing leads in the end to a destruction of the very existential tension whereby rational willing, and therefore human existence, are possible.

Yet as man is aware of the high stakes of his willing, he also is not unmindful of the extraordinary cost of not-willing. Accordingly, Heidegger observes, "A terror of the void essentially permeates all willing," for the alternative is "the extinction of the will in not-willing," that is, "nothingness." Although modern man has shown himself increasingly capable, even at the cost of self-annihilation, of abandoning willing when confronted with his self-created anxiety over willing, throughout history down to the present time man has shown an even greater propensity to cling, desperately and amidst anxiety, to willing even when the outcome has been the forfeiture of his moral character. Quoting Nietzsche, Heidegger suggests that "our will 'would rather will nothingness than not will.' . . . 'To will nothingness' here means to will . . . negation, . . . destruction, . . . laying waste."[27] Confronted with the terror of self-annihilation through the abandonment of willing, and unable to will rationally and responsibly, man—preferring ignominy to oblivion—has often willed the most unimaginably cruel and unconscionable treatment of his fellow beings.

We can hope to avoid repeating these brutalities of our past and present only if we reject that part of the classical model of man which, by suggesting that brilliance cannot be compatible with perversity, denied the radical freedom of man's will; and if, at the same time, in realizing the awesome powers of both creation and destruction entailed in that freedom, we do not lose sight of the still more radical differences that, by our created nature, distinguish us from both God and superman.

J. M. Porter · *Democracy and Autonomy in Rousseau*

The conception of the individual as autonomous has played a major role in the various theories of democracy. Carl Cohen has expressed the view that autonomy and democracy are intertwined: "Democrats are not necessarily committed to a Kantian position in moral philosophy; but anyone who respects and treasures what Kant called the 'supreme principle of morality,' the autonomy of the will, will find democracy intrinsically valuable. In it, as in no other system of government, this principle is clearly and fully embodied."[1] That autonomy has a role is generally agreed, but the interpretation, given its relationship to democracy, has dramatically changed conventional meanings of democracy.[2] Thus, it is necessary to examine the concept of autonomy: How, specifically, has the concept been used? In what ways does it affect our understanding of political reality, the nature of political activity, the goals of politics?

It is possible to categorize the uses of autonomy into two groups. There is a weak conception of autonomy utilized by those defending a pluralistic model of democracy. Those who have a unitary-consensual model of democracy use a strong conception of autonomy. In brief, the weak conception does not rely wholly on the autonomy of the individual in determining the legitimacy of a regime or the morality of a private or public act. The meaning of the term is normally shown by a simple contrast with compulsion or constraint. Autonomy by itself is not considered the source of authority. The strong conception is derived from the formal moral principle enunciated by Rousseau and Kant: autonomy of the will exists when the will is subject to its own law, or in Kant's terms, to the categorical imperative; in contrast, heteronomy exists when the will is subject to a law or end outside the rational will.

There is also a substantive dimension to both the weak and strong conceptualizations. Two of those essential substantive differences can be explained as follows: the strong conception emphasizes a self-exercising mastery and control whereas the weak conception stresses the constraining boundaries for the self within reality; the strong conception posits man's end as within human control while the weak conception presumes the possibility of direction or purpose for human action as outside human control but worthy of human pursuit. Because of the formal and substantive elements that constitute the strong conception of autonomy, it is, not surprisingly, a central category for any political philosopher who uses it.

An excellent illustration of the use of the "weak" conception of autonomy is found in John Hallowell's *The Moral Foundation of Democracy*.[3] In describing the historical and philosophical roots of democracy, he notes that the social and political philosophy of liberalism sustained democracy, and that at the core of liberalism was the "concept of the autonomous individual, or the 'masterless man.'"[4] In order to combine individuality with authority, liberalism also contained an idea of a transcendent law "discoverable by reason," which could through the individual conscience impose obligations. In short, Hallowell continues, liberalism was "based upon an uneasy compromise between two conflicting principles: the idea of the autonomy of individual will and reason and the idea of a higher law."[5] With the decline of Christian faith, the rise of positivism, and the loss of the classical understanding of reason, liberalism's two principles broke apart, and democracy lost its philosophical foundation. Hallowell suggests that we need, in part, to reconstitute the idea of autonomy by recourse to classical realism and natural law. Democracy, then, could remain a noble aspiration and a legitimate form of government, philosophically justified.

> The beliefs, for example, in the absolute moral worth of the individual, in the spiritual equality of individuals, and in the essential rationality of man were a heritage from the Middle Ages and have their roots deep in Christian and Greek thought. We can repudiate these ideas only by repudiating our humanity. It is the belief in the absolute moral worth of the individual that prevents the individual from being submerged, if not obliterated, in a conception of the race, the class, the nation, or some other collectivity that regards the individual as a means rather than as an end in himself.[6]

Autonomy here is clearly understood in the weak sense. Other concepts have far greater philosophical importance both for constructing a political theory and for justifying democracy. In Hallowell's thought, the idea of the constraining boundaries of the self within reality, which is the substantial meaning of the weak conception of autonomy, is derived from his more fundamental conceptions of human nature and of classical realism. The ramifications for understanding political reality or justifying democracy are thus decidedly different from those that follow from the strong conception of autonomy. Consequently, the use of autonomy in the strong sense merits exploration.

I

Rousseau is the first political thinker whose political philosophy, in large measure, was composed by examining political reality through the prism of autonomy. In most respects his view of the nature of autonomy has survived and can be easily detected guiding the vocabularies of later political philosophers.[7] It is not only because Rousseau is the influential originator that one must start with him in examining the relationship between autonomy and democracy but also because he exhibits with unsurpassed clarity the nature of autonomy, in the strong sense, and its ramifications for man's political existence.

Rousseau asserts that man's distinctive quality is to be a free moral agent, and this premise, as Andrew Levine explains, is central to Rousseau's thought.

> The end of man, his destiny, is to be a moral agent. To renounce one's liberty is to renounce the possibility of fulfilling this destiny. Thus, it is "to renounce one's quality as a man," to renounce one's essence.
>
> In *The Social Contract* this thesis is simply declared. It is not argued for; still less is it proved. Yet, it serves as the keystone of Rousseau's examination of authority and political obligation. It defines the parameters within which the fundamental problem of political philosophy is to be posed.[8]

In a passage in *The Social Contract* (bk. 1, chap. 8) Rousseau distinguishes three kinds of liberty. There is natural liberty such as exists in the state of nature, "which has no limit but the physical power of the individual concerned." Civil liberty refers to the liberty allowed by the laws of the state, which, in Rousseau's words, "is limited by the general will." In the civil society formed by the social contract one acquires, thirdly, moral liberty: it "alone makes man truly the master of himself; for to be governed by appetite alone is slavery while obedience to a law one prescribes to oneself is freedom." Rousseau reaches this compact definition of moral liberty or, in Kantian language, autonomy through incorporating will with law.

While remembering that apart from the other neither will nor law can be understood in Rousseau, it is necessary to unravel them a bit to see their joint meaning. One level of meaning to "liberty of the will" is procedural. This meaning can be seen in those passages where Rousseau emphasizes that man must prescribe for himself. For example, man will be dependent, i.e. lack free will, when obeying even a "good" law if he has not voluntarily prescribed it. Thus, there is a procedural meaning to the phrase: "obedience to a law one prescribes to oneself is freedom."

There is a second level of meaning to the "liberty of the will." It is of a formal and rational nature and is discernible when man enters society. For Rousseau the will, apparently, cannot be clearly seen when under the influence of particulars or appetites. It is as if the will itself has no discernible content in such a case. What can be seen, as in the primitive man found in the state of nature, is a potential. In the *Second Discourse* Rousseau describes primitive man as having the power of willing and choosing, and as being conscious of this liberty. He adds, in case this quality does not indisputably separate man from the animals, that man also has the very specific quality of perfectibility. He further claims that this quality, by the aid of circumstances, "develops successively all the others."[9] Accordingly, the will in the state of nature is a seemingly empty power but with the potential for perfectibility.

In civil society, however, the rational and formal level can develop. Here one can will what is general or universal. Man substitutes a "rule of conduct in the place of instinct," "duty takes the place of physical impulse," and man "consults his reason rather than studies his inclinations" (bk. 1, chap. 8). In the first draft of *The Social Contract* Rousseau stated succinctly this formal and rational feature of the will: "No one will dispute that the General Will is in each individual a pure act of the understanding, which reasons while the passions are silent on what a man may demand of his neighbour and on what his neighbour has a right to demand of him."[10] Thus, there is a rational and formal element to the will in that the source is reason, rather than instinct or appetites, and the object is the general or universal, rather than the particular.

Lastly, there is a substantive or experiential level of meaning to the liberty of the will, and this level of meaning is present whenever the sense of control and mastery is mentioned. In general, the experiences associated with control and mastery are the emotional evidence of the will, but also "control and mastery" are appropriate labels for the nature of the will itself. These experiences would thus be present in man's primitive state as well as in civil society. Man is born free and he is free in the state of nature. He cannot be free in nature in the sense of having moral liberty because man lacks the rational and formal element in his will. Man is dominated there by his twin instincts of self-preservation and compassion, but he is still free: "everyone is there his own master."[11] There is no other substantive experience that the free will can have than control or mastery at this stage of potentiality.

There are, however, three features to the state of nature that nourish this sense of mastery: equality, a dependence on things, and a lack of personal subjection. It is precisely these three features which become the articles of association for forming the social contract and thereby preserve in society the individual's sense of control and mastery (bk. 1, chap. 6). This explains why Rousseau believes that he has provided a solution to his central problem: to find a form of association in which "each one, uniting with all, nevertheless obeys only himself and remains as free as before" (bk. 1, chap. 6). We can be free as before only in the procedural and the substantial or experiential senses. We have also gained, through the rational and formal element, moral liberty, which we did not have before. The rational and moral element become the means for retaining the core experience of being a free actor, control and mastery.

In the compact definition of moral liberty (bk. 1, chap. 8) law must be prescribed in order for man to be autonomous. A true law, Rousseau explains, must in form be general and abstract. It must never be formed for "a man as an individual or a particular action" (bk. 2, chap. 6). Its source is the General Will, that is the will created in the formation of the civil society. Both the form and the source of the law make it objective, rational, and universal. There is an objective, general interest for the whole community, and it can be detected by reason and prescribed by each will for all.

The features of a properly formed will and of a properly formed law thus coalesce: the will is guided by reason rather than appetites and is concerned with the general rather than the particular; a law is abstract in form and directed toward an objective, general interest. There is no forfeiture of liberty or autonomy in prescribing such a law. Men remain equal in that the law is applied in general and in that the abstractness of the law prevents singling out a particular person's action for treatment; also, men remain independent in that the source of the law is the individual's own will. Finally, the generality, abstractness, and source of the law reflect the three levels of meaning contained in Rousseau's idea of a free moral agent: we are free procedurally because we individually prescribe the law; we are free rationally and formally because of the law's universality and its objective, general interest; we experience ourselves as free actors with a sense of control and mastery in that we are the source of our own law.

II

It is through the philosophical touchstone of autonomy that one can best understand Rousseau's writings on such topics as the General Will, political activity, and the goal of politics. Also, the internal coherence of these topics and of Rousseau's political philosophy as a whole is in large measure due to the centrality of his concept of autonomy. An evaluation or criticism of Rousseau, accordingly, depends upon a clear recognition of the ramifications of autonomy. However, it would be misleading to imply that the importance of autonomy for Rousseau is due simply to its centrality and its relation to other themes. Rather, autonomy provides the premises whereby Rousseau can solve fundamental political problems. While it is true, as Leo Strauss insists, that Rousseau inaugurated an attack on modernity, it is also true that Rousseau, in seeking solutions, does agree with modernity's chief spokesman, Hobbes: neither wants merely to ameliorate man's political predicament; each claims, however, to have a solution to it. Rousseau's solution, it might be added, is the more radical. Hobbes claims that he can provide, with certainty, a solution to the problem of disorder; Rousseau claims that in addition to order he can provide moral freedom, the highest state man can achieve. Rousseau's solution is obtained through the General Will, which combines individual moral freedom with social cohesion and order.

The General Will, both in its logical and psychological dimensions, grows out of the concept of autonomy. To reiterate, Rousseau's concept of autonomy was built from will and law. Free agency, for Rousseau, had three levels of meaning: the procedural, the rational and formal, and the substantive meaning of control and mastery. The generality, abstractness, and source of law (the second part of autonomy) dovetailed with these features of the will. It is Rousseau's thesis that autonomy, so understood, can be experienced in society provided that we create those conditions found in nature which enabled primitive man (before reason) to be happy and, in the procedural and substantive senses, free. These conditions were equality, a dependence only on nature, and a lack of personal subjection. The articles of association reenact for society these original conditions found in the state of nature. Equality is gained in that each gives up all to the community. Dependence only on nature is replaced by dependence only on the General Will; each puts his person and power under the direction of the General Will, which substitutes for nature and is better for man than nature. There is no personal subjection since the alienation is to no one in particular. Thus autonomy can be experienced in society, permitting the introduction of the rational and formal element which enables man to become a moral person with moral liberty.

In order to be a solution in any recognizable sense, the General Will must have internal consistency among the features Rousseau mentions, and it must be logically consistent with autonomy. Yet, even friends of Rousseau have apologized for his description of the General Will. It has, says G. D. H. Cole, "a certain amount of muddle and fluctuation."[12] W. G. Runciman and A. K. Sen, however, have conclusively demonstrated that the General Will is a logically consistent notion. Their argument, in brief, is that the two-person, non-zero-sum, noncooperative game known as the "prisoner's dilemma" illuminates the logical structure of the General Will. The dilemma is as follows:

> Two persons are thought to be jointly guilty of a serious crime, but the evidence is not adequate to convict them at a trial. The district attorney tells the prisoners that he will take them separately and ask them whether they would like to confess, though of course they need not. If both of them confess, they will be prosecuted, but he will recommend a lighter sentence than is usual for such a crime, say 6 years of imprisonment rather than 10 years. If neither confesses, the attorney will put them up only for a minor charge of illegally possessing a weapon, of which there is conclusive evidence, and they can expect to get 2 years each. If, however, one confesses and the other does not, the one who confesses receives lenient treatment for providing evidence to the state and gets only 1 year, and the one who does not receives the full punishment of 10 years.[13]

This is a dilemma because prisoners relying strictly on an egocentric interest would always find it rational to confess. Consequently, the outcome would be six years. On the other hand, if each person could forgo calculating his private interests and form a compact with his fellow whereby each would calculate the general interest or good of the other, then they would each will what would be to their general or common advantage, i.e., neither would confess. Runciman and Sen note the parallels: "The general will is general not only in its origins but its objects, and is 'applicable to all as well as operated by all.' It tends always to equality: and all citizens being equal by virtue of the contract, 'none has the right to demand that another should do what he does not do himself.'"[14]

There are other parallels illustrating the logical structure of the concept. The distinction between the will of all and the General Will is clear: the will of all is the sum of private interests alone whereas the general will refers to an objective interest, general to all. A person can be "forced to be free" through substituting the general interest for his calculating self-interest which would then free his true interest or will. The General Will, just as Rousseau insisted, is not determined by the number of citizens but by the common interest by which they are united. Rousseau's delineation of the General Will, in short, can escape the charge of being muddled. It has the logical coherence required of a purported solution.

The General Will, also, is logically consistent with the requirements for autonomy. Rousseau's explanation of the need for a social contract, creating a community "under the supreme direction of the General Will," is that men reach a point in the state of nature where the "obstacles to their preservation" threaten to destroy them unless they change their "mode of existence" (bk. 1, chap. 6). Given the general conditions in the state of nature, the private will was sufficient for the primitive mode of existence. With the evolution of man external and internal obstacles threaten to engulf him. External obstacles include, in Rousseau's view, man's dependence on others and the growth of private property; the internal obstacles are the accompanying growth of *amour-propre* (vanity) at the expense of *amour-de-soi* (self-respect). The General Will that creates the new mode of existence is "connected" with autonomy in two ways.

First, Rousseau explains that the relationship is analytic (bk. 1, chap. 7). Through the required total alienation of each, the individual escapes dependence on another person and inequality: by definition all rights and powers are given to the whole community, which is to no one. Rousseau describes this act as a tautology: "a contract, as it were, with himself." "An obligation to oneself," he adds, is not like "having an obligation to something of which one is a member." It is not the same thing because, as Rousseau reasons, the source of obligation to oneself remains the individual will, and because membership in an association cannot in itself constitute grounds of obligation without introducing heteronomy. This is a "rational entity," he concludes. Analytically, individual autonomy is preserved.

Second, the new mode of existence, provided by the community under the General Will, preserves the crucial experiential or substantive sense of freedom, control, and mastery. The total alienation "by each associate of himself and all his rights to the whole community" keeps each person independent and a master of himself: by the alienation of his private interest each person, as in the solution to the prisoner's dilemma, conceives of himself in terms of the other, i.e., in terms of the general or common interest, and this enables his private or individual will to now will the general or common good, which is to prescribe a law to himself. These are the ingredients for autonomy: a sense of individual mastery and control is retained while willing the general interest.

The analytical and experiential ties between autonomy and the

General Will are, for Rousseau, only different sides of the same bond. It is because the act of alienation can be conceived in analytic terms that the individual experiences no loss of his sense of control and mastery. The rational character of the act of alienation, an imposing of one's will on reality and oneself, accentuates psychologically the sense of control and mastery: one is a slave to passion, but by binding oneself through reason (a law prescribed to oneself) one is free, i.e., experiences a sense of control and mastery.

G. D. H. Cole has noted that the nature of free agency or autonomy makes possible the General Will: "it is because man is a free agent capable of being determined by a universal law prescribed by himself that the State is in like manner capable or realizing the General Will, that is, of prescribing to itself and its members a similar universal law."[15] While Cole's remarks are true, Rousseau actually claims more for the relationship between autonomy and General Will. The features of will and law that constitute autonomy dictate the features of the General Will. As Andrew Levine explains: "The general will (that aims at a general interest) is just the private will (that aims at a private interest) in a different form—*under the form of generality imposed by the equality of total alienation*. The general will is a private will compelled, by its own logic, to the requisite generality of form."[16] Full autonomy can exist in society only with the General Will. Rousseau thus logically warns: "The articles of this contract are so precisely determined by the nature of the act, that the slightest modification must render them null and void" (bk. 1, chap. 6). The result, he continues, will be the loss of "social freedom."

Autonomy serves as a prism for revealing the structure of the General Will, but, to change metaphor, autonomy is also an embryo of the General Will: the relationship between will and law within autonomy enables the individual to experience moral liberty; and the relationship between the individual will and the General Will enables the person to realize moral liberty in society.[17]

III

The theoretical concepts of autonomy and the General Will have enormous consequences for viewing man's political existence.

These ramifications can be easily seen in Rousseau's treatment of political activity and of freedom or moral liberty as the goal of politics.[18]

Perhaps the most striking consequence occurs with the metamorphosis of political activity. Before a community has been created under the direction of the General Will, political activity can be characterized as the overcoming of obstacles. These obstacles, as the *Second Discourse* makes clear, can be removed by man. After the General Will has been established political activity becomes a distinctive kind of participation.

It is Rousseau's claim that there is a true, objective, realizable, general interest. It cannot be defined as the sum of private interests or as a collation of opinions, any more than a solution to a mathematical problem is the result of a process of negotiation or of collecting the most opinions. Andrew Levine, agreeing with Rousseau, makes this point: "There is a general interest; the point is to discover it. There is no question, as in the liberal (and contemporary pluralist) tradition, of resolving conflicting social forces to produce a *fair* outcome. (Indeed, conflicting social forces are incompatible with the *de jure* state.) The point, instead, is to discover a matter of fact. For Rousseau, legislation serves the ideal of truth, not justice."[19] In the context of the General Will a politics of opinion with clashing but meritorious principles is not conceivable. What is possible, after the compact has been formed, is participation.

Participation is an apt word for the political activity of individuals within a community "under the supreme direction of the General Will." The initial great political act is not one of agreeing or compromising but one of becoming an "indivisible part of the whole" (bk. 2, chap. 6). Each is transformed and "acquires with civil society, moral freedom, which alone makes man the master of himself." The charge given to the Legislator further indicates the full scope and meaning of participation: the Legislator "must be ready, shall we say, to change human nature, to transform each individual who by himself is entirely complete and solitary, into a part of a much greater whole, from which that same individual will then receive, in a sense, his life and his being" (bk. 2, chap. 7). A new being is formed with a new "mode of existence." In principle, participation is the expression and confirmation of moral liberty or full autonomy.

In a faithful explication of Rousseau, Carol Pateman discerns three major features of participation when put in practice. Firstly, there is an educative aspect: "As a result of participating in decision making the individual is educated to distinguish between his own impulses and desires, he learns to be a public as well as a private citizen." And, she continues, "he comes to feel little or no conflict between the demands of the public and private spheres." Freedom, secondly, is enhanced through participation: "The individual's actual, as well as his sense of, freedom is increased through participation in decision making because it gives him a very real degree of control over the course of his life and the structure of his environment." Thirdly, participation has an integrative function: "it increases the feeling among individual citizens that they 'belong' in their community." It is, in Pateman's phrase, these "psychological qualities and attitudes" of individuals which are enhanced by activity within Rousseau's political institutions.[20]

Participation, as explained, requires a general interest which is objective, and participation concludes in a General Will that is always right. If judged by these two standards, political activity has no room for differences. Consequently, the thoughts and actions of individuals who might differ with the General Will can only be explained as the result of deception, or of being simply wrong, or of a partial interest (bk. 2, chap. 3; bk. 4, chap. 2). "Political activity" that is born from such partial, contentious interests and that concludes in the victory of one side cannot have the "psychological qualities and attitudes" engendered by participation. There can be no grounds in Rousseau for recognizing merit in political differences, just as there is no ground for recognizing merit in wrong answers in mathematics; and there are no grounds for recognizing the accompanying activity as worthwhile (bk. 2, chap. 4).

Rousseau accordingly develops practical institutions so that we will not be deceived or have a partial interest. The Legislator, laws, civil religion, educational systems, and even festivals and celebrations are all means for guaranteeing the authenticity and success of participation. Authority, proper institutions, and participation are integrated, because, as Judith Shklar notes, for Rousseau authority is a prerequisite for freedom.

> An ordered existence is needed to support us in a free condition. That also is why moderate desires, a capacity to live in the

> present and dependence only on things are the prerequisites of the very possibility of a free life. All of them, however, depend on an educative, preventive, curative and ordering authority. Authentic authority liberates. It gives liberty to those who are incapable of creating it for themselves.[21]

Thus, just as the tutor Wolmar, in Rousseau's novel *New Heloise*, provides "perpetual tutorial vigilance" over the life of the inhabitants of Clarens, so also must authority in its various guises be provided to guide participation in the new mode of existence of the legitimate state.[22]

IV

Can autonomy, the General Will, freedom, and this kind of participation serve to construct, evaluate, and justify a democratic regime? An answer cannot be attempted here, but two general theses can be suggested: Rousseau, I would argue, has not envisioned a political system; man could not develop his faculties and excellences well within this regime.

The political realm of human existence could be described as one where individuals are sometimes inescapably isolated, selfish, and in conflict; where they are limited in their knowledge and power and where fellow humans are treated instrumentally whenever unified action is required; and where man's happiness, however defined, cannot be protected by human constructs from fate, fortune, and history. The General Will would be inadequate for this realm. It could not capture the significant facets of political existence, and it cannot provide a solution since none is possible. The concomitant view of political activity, i.e., Rousseau's theory of participation, would also be inadequate both as a description and as a norm. For a purported political system to be legitimate it must be judged from the standpoint of fulfilling the functions of a political system, not a religious or social system. In this respect Reinhold Niebuhr's caution is apt: "Politics will, to the end of history, be an area where conscience and power meet, where the ethical and coercive factors of human life will interpenetrate and work out their tentative and uneasy compromises."[23]

Men seem capable of living in almost any imaginable political system. Yet the final criterion of evaluation for a regime, speculative or actual, must be whether man's faculties and excellences can be protected and nourished within it. Stuart Hampshire explains this approach:

> Those who, following Aristotle, take the notion of a good man as the starting-point of ethics will assess societies and governments as directly or indirectly producing or destroying the conditions in which the essential human excellences are attainable. What powers or habits will be fostered, if this form of government rather than that is instituted? What kind of man, exercising some of his powers at the expense of others, is likely to be found in a social order of this kind? Is there another social order, attainable under present conditions, which would encourage or permit a greater development of the essential human virtues?[24]

It could be argued, to illustrate, that reason and will have not been understood by Rousseau. As a consequence, his understanding of the excellence of moral liberty can be questioned: are control and mastery required in order to have self-dignity and to escape alienation? Moral liberty, misconceived, is the political goal for Rousseau, and it is not to be realized simply through self-help. The regime is "guaranteed by the armed forces and the supreme power" (bk. 2, chap. 4), and the Legislator, laws, civil religion, education, and other means will provide the help required to create this new mode of existence. Man would not, in Socrates' felicitous phrase, fare well.

Claes G. Ryn · *History and the Moral Order*

The last few decades have seen a widespread reaction against moral nihilism and relativism in social and political thought. There is a growing awareness that life is subject to a universal moral order which is accessible to philosophy. This new intellectual orientation has inspired and been inspired by a revival of interest in old Western traditions in ethics, principally those of ancient Greece and Christianity. However, even if the attempt is made, it is never possible simply to return to ideas of the past. A reconsideration of older traditions means their rearticulation and development in new intellectual circumstances. The question of how to understand the universal moral order is affected by philosophical challenges and opportunities brought by the last two centuries, especially those of historicism. The purpose here is to develop a thesis regarding the general direction that a modern affirmation of the ethical universal may take. The suggested direction can be described as that of a value-centered historicism. The possibility of a historicism that acknowledges the existence of a universal moral order is widely overlooked. An important problem within this general subject which has deep roots in Western theology and philosophy is whether to conceive of the ethical imperative in terms of reason or will.[1]

It has been common in older Western thought to associate the moral order with norms of conduct discovered by reason. This mode of speculation has been plagued through the centuries by the problem of mediating between the universal and particular situations. This problem receives considerable attention in one of the most widely read contemporary studies of ethics and politics, Leo Strauss's *Natural Right and History*. A careful examination of this book reveals a tension between two tendencies of thought. There are intellectual impulses and formulations which point toward an interpretation of natural right as immutable "rules" or "principles" of conduct. Strauss writes, for example, that it is granted both by opponents and proponents of natural right that "there cannot be natural right if the principles of right are not unchangeable."[2] But, as will be shown, such statements coexist with a tendency of thought seriously questioning natural right conceived as immutable rules. One may study in Strauss's reasoning difficulties engendered by an attempted but incomplete break with rule-oriented interpretations of the ethical imperative.

Strauss's own understanding of natural right can be gleaned in part from his sympathetic treatment of Aristotle's view on this subject. Strauss concentrates on the one explicit statement by Aristotle which he believes certainly expresses Aristotle's conception of natural right.[3] Strauss interprets this passage as an affirmation of the existence of natural right. Aristotle views natural right as a part of political right. He does not mean to say that there is no natural right outside or prior to the city but that it can become most fully developed only among fellow citizens. Only among them "do the relations which are the subject matter of right or justice reach their greatest density and, indeed, their full growth."[4]

But Aristotle also makes an assertion which becomes the occasion for some of Strauss's most interesting and philosophically promising efforts of interpretation: *Natural right must be mutable.* To establish the meaning of this "surprising" assertion, Strauss first considers Thomas Aquinas's interpretation of the same passage. Thomas contends that Aristotle's statement about the changeability of natural right must be understood with a qualification. What Aristotle means to say is that the fundamental principles of natural right are universally valid and immutable; only more specific rules are mutable. Strauss dismisses this Thomistic interpretation as reading into Aristotle ideas of Patristic origin. He points out that "Aristotle says explicitly that *all right—hence also all natural right—is changeable; he does not qualify that statement in any way*."[5]

Strauss then considers a rival interpretation of Aristotle in the medieval period. Standing against the Thomistic view with its preference for fixed universally valid rules is the Averroistic view of various Islamic, Jewish, and Christian Aristotelians. These thinkers take Aristotle as saying that all natural right is merely conventional: In all societies, certain general rules expressing the minimum needs of society emerge over time. But these rules are only seemingly universal. In some circumstances the preservation of society may demand that they be disregarded. It is to make them generally respected and effective that they must nevertheless be taught as though they were valid without exception. According to Strauss, this Averroistic interpretation of natural right agrees with Aristotle insofar as it recognizes the mutability of all rules of justice. But it is in conflict with Aristotle in that it implies the denial of "natural right proper."[6]

Strauss now poses the question, "How, then, can we find a safe middle road between these formidable opponents, Averroës and Thomas?" His answer is strongly suggestive of his own inclinations in the matter of natural right. He proposes an interpretation which first leads away from understanding natural right as general rules. This line of argument contains some of Strauss's most incisive observations on the ethical imperative. He writes: "One is tempted to make the following suggestion: When speaking of natural right, Aristotle does not primarily think of any general propositions but rather of concrete decisions. All action is concerned with particular situations. Hence *justice and natural right reside, as it were, in concrete decisions rather than in general rules*." Arguing the shortcomings of legalistic conceptions of the moral imperative, Strauss contends that "any general rule of natural law" may "because of its generality . . . prevent a just decision in a given case." The following statement might even be construed as compatible with conceiving of natural right as a practical, not theoretical, reality having its moral justification in itself: "In every human conflict there exists the possibility of a just decision based on full consideration of all the circumstances, *a decision demanded by the situation*. Natural right consists of such decisions. Natural right thus understood is obviously mutable."[7]

Explaining why natural right must ultimately reside in "concrete decisions rather than in general rules," Strauss draws attention to situations involving "the very existence or independence of a society." He points out that not even the most just society can survive without the use of espionage. And "espionage is impossible without a suspension of certain rules of natural right." In war against an unscrupulous enemy "there are no assignable limits to what might become just reprisals." "Natural right must be mutable in order to be able to cope with the inventiveness of wickedness. What cannot be decided in advance by universal rules . . . can be made visible as just, in retrospect, to all."[8]

Unlike Aristotle, legalistically inclined theorists of natural right do not sufficiently take into account the complexities of life to which morality must adjust itself. Strauss writes: "The Thomistic doctrine of natural right or, more generally expressed, of natural law is free from the hesitations and ambiguities which are characteristic of the teachings, not only of Plato and Cicero, but of Aristotle as well." No doubt remains in Thomism regarding "the immutable character of the fundamental propositions of natural law." According to Strauss, Thomas brought "profound changes" relative to the classics. The absence in his doctrine of natural law of "hesitations and ambiguities" and their replacement by "definiteness" Strauss attributes not to philosophical reflection but to "the influence of the belief in biblical revelation."[9]

Strauss offers a summary of the views of Plato and Aristotle which further exemplifies a movement on his own part away from moral legalism: "The variability of the demands of that justice which men can practice was recognized not only by Aristotle but by Plato as well. Both avoided the Scylla of 'absolutism' and the Charybdis of 'relativism' by holding a view which one may venture to express as follows: There is a universally valid hierarchy of ends, but *there are no universally valid rules of action.*"[10] Unfortunately, this very promising suggestion stays largely in the form of an undeveloped hypothesis. It is indicative of Strauss's hesitation in this area that his introduction of the idea of natural right as "concrete decisions" is diluted by the words "as it were." And in the very passage where he proposes the notion of natural right as "mutable" and as residing in just decisions "demanded by the situation," Strauss suddenly reverses direction by saying, "Yet one can hardly deny that *in all concrete decisions general principles are implied and presupposed.*"[11] The reader is thus invited to conceive of ethical choice as being, after all, the subsumption of new situations under preexisting "general principles." But this means that the original difficulty leading Strauss away from a rule-oriented conception of natural right has not really been overcome.[12] In the end the reader is left with Strauss's apparent endorsement of the idea that all right is mutable and the tendency of thought exemplified by his assertion that "there cannot be natural right if the principles of right are not unchangeable."

What, then, might be the solution to the problem which he is confronting? To give up in every form the idea of an unchangeable moral universal would be to deny a permanent fact of the moral life, the prohibition against arbitrariness, and to become mired in relativism or nihilism. At the same time, ethical realism requires that the fact of varied and continuously changing circumstances be fully recognized. Strauss's hypothetically expressed notion of natural right as "concrete decisions" suggests that there may be benefits to reconsidering natural right in terms of practical action, that is, in terms of will, and also in the light of some aspects of historicism, the "concrete universal" being one of its concerns.

Many thinkers gravitating in the direction of associating the moral imperative with laws or rules of reason see a conflict between stressing the ultimacy of will and accepting a universal moral order. According to Heinrich Rommen, morality rests on "the ability of human reason to recognize the nature of things and to recognize a natural order which, as a moral order, must be observed by all human will . . . . This means in the last analysis that truth makes the law and that law is reason; this . . . means there is a natural law." To assert the superiority of will over intellect, however, "means relativism in ethics. . . . It means positivism in jurisprudence, nonmorality in politics, denial of the natural rights of men, and the acceptance of absolute power of the state. It leaves no alternative but to profess that might is right."[13]

The view that emphasis on the ultimacy of will must bring with it some form of moral arbitrariness overlooks the necessity of distinguishing between different qualities of will. Since Rommen is writing as a representative of Christianity, it is appropriate to point out that in the Western world it is Christianity more than any other influence which has suggested the need for a distinction between good and evil will. One may cite, for example, the words of Paul: "The good that I would, I do not, but the evil which I would not, that I do." Contrary dispositions of will divide the human self. Strengthening the higher disposition so as to join the will of man with the will of God is a pervasive Christian concern. There is a will which is by its very nature good and which should therefore guide human action. The Greek tradition, too, has a considerable understanding of the centrality of right willing, this in spite of its tendency to make of morality a problem of knowledge, as in the Socratic teaching that virtue is knowledge. Aristotle's stress on the training of character is in part a reaction against overintellectualization of the problem of morality. Christianity brought a deepened awareness of the importance and normative role of will. It conceived of itself as offering salvation not primarily through a new theory of conduct but through a way of life. "I am the way, the truth, and the life." The good becomes known to man through an orientation of will, through incarnation in concrete action. Theoretical knowledge in moral matters follows upon right willing. It is possible to argue that *voluntas superior intellectu* is closer in spirit to the admonitions of Christ himself than are some later interpretations bearing the imprint of Greek and Roman intellectualization.

Morality may thus be ultimately dependent not on precepts of reason but on willing of a special quality. Turning to a thinker whose reasoning is not based on theology or revelation, this kind of understanding of ethics is developed by Irving Babbitt (1865–1933), the Harvard professor who has been as controversial as he has been misunderstood. Babbitt distinguishes in man two contrary orientations of will which together define his essential moral predicament. The one is toward self-indulgence of some kind. The other is a will to goodness. Both orientations are facts of immediate experience which become known by their fruits. The higher will is felt by the individual as a check on merely selfish impulse and as the potentiality of a truly meaningful existence. It is that moral imperative at the center of his awareness in terms of which everything is finally evaluated. To the extent that man acts from within that special will and thus disciplines opposing inclinations, he unifies his personality and tends to move into communion with others who are similarly motivated.

Babbitt agrees with Aristotle that through moral activity man achieves happiness (as distinguished from mere pleasure). The effect of indulging the selfish will is deepening disharmony and isolation from others. Babbitt avoids tying his doctrine to ethico-religious dogmas based in part on revelation, but the higher will is another name for the experiential reality of transcendent goodness which Christianity refers to variously as "love," "the will of God," "grace," or "the Holy Spirit." This ordering power, Babbitt argues, does not have to be taken on faith. It is an undeniable fact of general human experience becoming more and more firmly established in consciousness to the extent that man acts in its spirit. In Greek thought some corresponding terms for aspects of the same ordering moral force are *philia*, *agape*, and *eros*.

What Babbitt calls the higher will is in one sense particular and mutable; it is experienced by individual men and has an effect in the unique circumstances of their lives. But this will is also the same in all men; it is universal and immutable in that it pulls all in the same direction, toward the special quality of life which is its own reward by satisfying man's deepest yearning. The higher will draws each individual toward its own transcendent purpose by ordering his impulses. It is experienced as a negative, an "inner check," on inclinations destructive of the moral enhancement of life. In relation to impulses which are being shaped by the higher will into actions of the opposite quality, it becomes their inspiring sense of meaning and worth. In moral action, individuality and universality, immanent and transcendent, merge. The good is "incarnated."[14]

The infinite variability of circumstances cannot be captured in a net of rules, however fine that net is made by casuistry. The flow of life slips through its meshes. Babbitt's conception of the moral universal as will of a special type avoids entanglement in juridical excogitation. The higher will works, not in the abstract, but on the concrete particulars of given situations. It is the spirit of ultimate value in which man can always apply his faculties, regardless of circumstances. As an orientation of will it does not theoretically predefine the specifics of moral action. It inspires them. Their moral nature is precisely that they were solicited and structured by the intent of the higher will. It demands that our reason and imagination be marshaled in the effort of finding the particular actions which in given situations will most advance its purpose of goodness. While reason and imagination play large and indispensable roles in the preparation of the appropriate action, the standard of goodness itself is not theoretical; it lies in the affirmative or negative reaction of the ethical will to contemplated or incipient action. Even when preceded by protracted deliberation, the moral resolution, when and if it comes, is a nonintellectual practical act creating new reality out of unique circumstances. Provided this is understood, Babbitt would accept Strauss's idea of natural right as concrete decisions. Natural right is conceived as the infinitely applicable moral inspiration giving qualitative form to the "decision demanded by the situation."

According to Babbitt, the great wisdom of the Western heritage in ethics, founded by Plato and Aristotle, has been marred to some extent by a tendency to cloud the ultimate problem of morality. In the end, moral choice is not, as the Greeks were prone to think, an act of intellection but an effort of ethical will. The ethico-religious disposition of Asia has been more voluntaristic. Buddha and Confucius are representatives of the Orient who give precedence to will. So is Jesus of Nazareth. The Christian introduction of ethico-religious voluntarism into the Western world is described by Babbitt as overcoming the old intellectual problem of *methexis*, the problem of reconciling the universal with the particular.

> This problem as to how to escape from mere abstraction appears in the case of the chief idea of all—that of the good or of God which also coincides with what is most exalted in man. The word that stands for the idea of the good is the word par excellence, the logos. One can follow to some extent the process by which the Greek conception of the logos was transmitted through intermediaries like Philo Judaeus to the author of the Fourth Gospel. The specifically Asiatic element in the Christian solution of the problem of the logos is the subordination, either implicit or explicit, of the divine reason to the divine will. By an act of this will, the gap between a wisdom that is abstract and general and the individual and particular is bridged over at last; the Word is made flesh. The human craving for the concrete is satisfied at the essential point. The truth of the incarnation . . . is one that we have all experienced in a less superlative form: the final reply to all the doubts that torment the human heart is not some theory of conduct, however perfect, but the man of character.[15]

Supplementing Babbitt, a few additional comments on the role of reason are in order.[16] Reason is not itself the evaluative function. It is the *reflective awareness* of the moral reality, without which the latter would remain conceptually inarticulate. Upon the direct experience of the good in its affirmative or negative reactions to particular impulses follows immediately the discernment of these reactions in intellectual judgments. In them the precognitive concrete experience of moral value is transformed into *conceptual* awareness. What man knows, then, is not the moral universal in the abstract, but the universal in concrete manifestations, the incarnated good which has entered our experience. In the elaborate and systematic work of ethical philosophy, self-knowledge, which is always to some extent observation of our humanity in general, draws upon the broadest possible range of moral experience. According to Goethe, we should oppose to the aberrations of the hour masses of universal history. It is through such philosophical-historical observation of the manifestations of man's humanity that we grasp the permanent structures of life with their intrinsic ordering values. The "fact-value" distinction is alien to human self-knowledge, for the facts accounted for in such knowledge are value-realities, namely, actions having, or not having, a moral inspiration. (In the contexts of aesthetic or intellectual activity, the value-realities observed would be inclinations having, or not having, artistic or cognitive motivation, respectively.) Such moments of intellectual articulation of experience recur incessantly and are indispensable to continued volition.

A related activity which is rational in a sense but not really philosophical because not concerned with what is universal is the effort to formulate particular rules or principles of conduct. These rules range from the temporary and trivial to the long-lasting and highly significant. No individual or society can do without such rules. Respect for the law is a fundamental political need of civilization. To the extent that norms of various kinds are formulated with genuine sensitivity to the demands of ethics, they tend to induce in those who attempt to respect them a sense of that universal right which lies beyond all specific rules. Together with ethical philosophy proper, they help to orient the individual to the kind of life which is intrinsically good and happy. Yet no specific rules, however general they be or however elaborate is the casuistry used to apply them, can anticipate all possible circumstances. They offer at best pragmatic guidelines for action. In *this* sense, one can agree with Strauss that "in all concrete decisions general principles are implied and presupposed."[17] But the general principles are transcended in the moment of actual choice by the needs of the particular situation. No two situations are the same. This is obvious from the fact alone that every situation is affected by previous situations. The uniqueness of circumstances calls for a creative synthesis of the moral universal—the higher will—and the particular: The specific content of the moral act is the incarnation of the transcendent good through ethical ordering and development of the potentialities immanent in the situation. Awareness of possibly relevant rules or principles, and of philosophical truths, is a part of the complex challenge of circumstance out of which the ethical will finally creates the new action. Again, if natural right be the standard of action, it resides not in general rules but in concrete decisions.

Our understanding of the variety and mutability of life has been greatly advanced, even when it is not consciously recognized, by historicism. Unfortunately, interpreters of historicism who judge it only by what Germans like Ernst Troeltsch call *Historismus* have discovered in it little more than a movement ushering in a general relativization of morality and knowledge. In a different form it points toward a deeper understanding of what is permanent in man's existence. Stress on life's historicity and the uniqueness of circumstances need not, as is often arbitrarily assumed, exclude recognition of universal ordering values. In particular, it need not rule out acceptance of an ethical universal. As combined with such an acceptance, historicism becomes an appreciation of the infinite richness and adaptability of the good, of the possible merging of the universal with the particular, most especially with the uniqueness of human personalities and their circumstances. Of course, individual uniqueness refusing all discipline becomes the bearer of gross or even diabolical egotism. But as ordered by the higher will it is the source of the continuous renewal and expansion of the good life in changing circumstances.

The process of aesthetic creativity provides an analogy to the creativity of ethical decisions. An inspired artist starting a painting is in a sense trying to realize something already existing; he is trying to articulate a certain vision of life of compelling value. That vision both is and is not prior to his painting. As he applies strokes of the brush he is guided by a sense of direction, but that direction also becomes gradually revealed through the concretization that it receives on the canvas. The work of the artist is to some extent only tentative. He tries out strokes and colors to see if they correspond to what he wants to express. From time to time a sense of uneasiness comes over him. Some of his attempts are censured as somehow inadequate to the emerging vision. He must recover his sense of direction. The artistic vision slowly takes form through such efforts of aesthetic discrimination. The process of creation is one of trial and error, of struggle against artless impulses intruding on the work of art in the making. Deep pain and agony as well as exhilaration may attend the birth. Looking at the completed painting, there is a sense in which the artist has known all along what he was trying to create; he has been true to something beyond the impulse of the moment. But in another sense he has *not* known, so that only the finished work has revealed his purpose. What is created by an artist is to some extent always a surprise to him. Indeed, it may take him long, perhaps a lifetime, really to absorb what he has brought into being. The work is uniquely his in that it reflects his very own personality, but it also answers to an artistic need transcending particular personalities.

The revolt against the neoclassical attempts to capture the essence of artistic value once and for all in certain fixed formal rules to be adhered to by the artists was due in its most promising dimension to the budding discovery that art is a continuous revelation of artistic value in which the individual person is a creative mediator between universal and particular. Analogously, moral good comes into being through the creative ordering, not the abolition, of individuality.

The belief that true justice in the individual and society requires the imitation of a preexisting intellectual model of perfection tends to treat individuality as such as unimportant. This belief breeds suspicion of the view that government and society in general should try to accommodate diverse competing interests. Must not the moral approach be simply to disregard particular interests and to implement the disinterested moral blueprint? But such an approach to ethics and politics underestimates the requirement of continuous adjustment to the varying moral needs and opportunities of individuals and groups in a forever changing society. While the good philosopher, and the good statesman, know in advance something about the general form and direction that life should always assume, they cannot predefine the specific content of actions that are demanded by new and varied circumstances.

Sometimes we are able to perceive only with the benefit of considerable hindsight whether good or evil has been wrought by human action. Acts by others which first seemed to us a blatant disregard of morality may turn out to have had a profoundly liberating effect on the ethical life of society. Much simply escapes our attention. Alexis de Tocqueville saw the potential for evil in the forces of democracy, but intellectual humility stopped him from rigid opposition to a powerful historical movement which might also contain possibilities for more civilized development. One finds in Edmund Burke a similar combination of moral discrimination and humility before the yet hidden opportunities of history. What we know concretely about the transcendent good is only what has already been incarnated in history, and even here man's ability to discern the true significance of events is flawed.

If the good society cannot be predefined in concrete particulars, the standard of that society does in a sense nevertheless exist prior to specific circumstances. The common good is always that quality of society which can emerge when the higher will censures man's selfishly motivated inclinations and inspires the diverse activities of those who compose the society. Referring to the ordering principle of the good society as a "higher law," Walter Lippmann writes, "To those who ask where this higher law is to be found, the answer is that it is a progressive discovery of men striving to civilize themselves, and that its scope and implications are a gradual revelation that is by no means completed."[18] Like many who employ the terminology of law, Lippmann really has in mind a nonlegalistic conception of the moral universal. Deeply influenced by Irving Babbitt, he conceives of the higher law as the eternal spirit of genuine civilization finding expression in changing circumstances.

To thinkers who emphasize existence of the universal moral order without weighing the higher possibilities of historicism, the thought of Edmund Burke is somewhat of an enigma. He is often viewed, sympathetically, as returning political thought to some premodern themes such as natural law, or, more antipathetically, as preparing the way for historicistic relativization. Another possible interpretation is that Burke's thought does not really conform to either of these categorizations but represents a developing *synthesis* between belief in a universal good and a new awareness of the historical nature of human existence. Burke stands for a value-centered historicism: He sees the transcendent moral order as potentially inhering in history. While always mingled with and threatened by evil, the growing traditions of the civilized society reveal concretely something of the universal good.

In his interpretation of Burke, Leo Strauss notes that he rejects the view that constitutions can be "made." They must "grow." Burke thus calls into question what Strauss regards as the classical view, that "the best social order can be or ought to be the work of an individual, of a wise 'legislator' or founder."[19] Strauss sees this Burkean attitude as the result of "a depreciation of reason." It is more accurate to say that Burke is preparing the way for a revised understanding of reason. The classical philosophers were only imperfectly aware of the historical nature of human existence. Plato, and even Aristotle, underestimated the extent to which knowledge is knowledge of the historical. Indeed, in epistemological theory at least, they disputed that there could be any real knowledge of the individual, of the historical particular. They also underestimated the degree to which their own reasoning incorporated the intellectual accomplishments of previous thinkers. Insights carried in the living past of intellectual tradition they were prone to attribute to an ahistorical reason operating in the particular thinker. When Plato and Aristotle emphasized the social nature of man, this view had wider and deeper implications than they knew. The various aspects of the good society, including philosophical insights, are the joint accomplishments of many generations. In general, the Greeks were inclined to think of reason as not dependent on history, except that particular phenomena help trigger the intellectual ascent to the ahistorical sphere of universals. Although Burke does not himself concentrate on the epistemological (logical) dimension of a deepened awareness of the historical nature of man's existence, his attention to and respect for long-honored tradition anticipates a new conception of philosophical reason as being historical as well as universal and as having knowledge of the concrete universal, the transcendent incarnate in history.

Significantly, the kind of reasoning that Burke does reject and which he labels "abstract" or "metaphysical" is a reasoning which ignores the attainments and possibilities of life as it is actually experienced. His target is the kind of rationality that Coleridge distinguishes from Reason and calls "the Understanding." Viewing society as properly based on some intellectual design conceived in abstraction from historical reality reveals blindness to the complexity of human existence. It is presumptuous and potentially diabolical to ignore society's profound dependence on the achievements of earlier generations. Over the centuries diverse groups and individuals acting within a developing heritage of tradition and prescription are in a position to carry forward and enrich civilization in countless ways. This slow and complex process, continuously adjusting itself to the concrete opportunities and needs of the citizens, cannot be replaced by acts of abstract rational planning. Because of the very richness and continuing growth of the cultural heritage, the extent of society's dependence on the past is only imperfectly known by man at any particular time. A reason which believes that it can take the place of the accumulating experience of history or of the creativity of the many individual citizens is to that extent a simplistic and arrogant pseudoreason.[20]

One needs to add what Burke does not explicitly say, that the embodiment of good or evil in history is the subject of moral philosophy, so that philosophy is at the same time and indistinguishably reflection on our immediate and more distant past. Universal and particular coexist in its concepts. In spite of his strictures against "historicism" Leo Strauss is not without awareness of this fact. In his discussion of the meaning of natural right in political emergencies, he writes: "What cannot be decided in advance by universal rules . . . can be made visible as just, in retrospect, to all." Knowingly or unknowingly joining history and intellectual judgment, Strauss goes on to say that "the objective discrimination between extreme actions which were just and extreme actions which were unjust is one of the noblest duties of the historian."[21] Ethical judgment is thus historical judgment. The historian becomes philosopher, the philosopher historian.[22]

Leo Strauss portrays historicism as inimical to the idea of natural right. Historicism claims "the discovery of a dimension of reality that had escaped classical thought, namely, of the historical dimension." If this is granted, Strauss asserts, "one will be forced in the end into extreme historicism," that is, into complete relativism.[23] But such a view of historicism is clearly arbitrary. As Benedetto Croce and others have shown, individuality and universality are potentially one; the moral universal becomes concretized through an ordering of individuality. Paradoxically, the incorporation of elements of historicism into the ancient heritage lends philosophical substance to Strauss's undeveloped notion of natural right as concrete decisions. To conceive of the latter as some form of intellectual conclusions from general principles is to evade the problems of legalism raised by Strauss himself. A value-centered historicism, however, explains the possible inherence of the ethical universal in the particular action itself, thus solving the age-old problem of *methexis*. Moral actions are such, not with reference to rules, but in their intrinsic quality and inspiration. This understanding of ethics has significance for present attempts to refute the distinction between "facts" and "values." Critics of that distinction who are prone to place the moral order in an ahistorical sphere of reason beyond the world of concrete phenomena may, at bottom, be maintaining a fact-value distinction of their own not unrelated to the one they are rejecting.

Strauss's criticism of legalistic conceptions of natural right is based on an appreciation of the variability of circumstances. Yet he shies away from, or, rather, overlooks, the conclusion that in the end life—and not only life in "extreme" situations—defies all intellectually formulated rules of conduct, except they be of a formal kind. Strauss is inclined to viewing the universal as somehow existing outside of history, uninfected by the flux, and he is accustomed to conceiving of historicism as a doctrine of mere relativism. Hence he is worried that full adjustment of the moral universal to the historical flow of life would mean the compromising or even the abandonment of the universal. But to be kept safe and elevated above the indignities of life, the ethical universal does not have to be kept pure of history. It is no less noble, and actually more demanding, as a good seeking incarnation in particular actions. The view that the good is essentially and ultimately found in the successful conclusion of argument—"virtue is knowledge"—has a way of excusing the individual from the often painful exercise of will demanded by morality.

A value-centered historicism does not have to deteriorate into morally indiscriminate pantheism or Hegelian metaphysics. Burke is but one early example showing that this danger can be avoided. Value-centered historicism as here understood is perfectly compatible with this central truth: The ethical will is continuously threatened by the anarchic, merely particularistic will which is also a part of the human self; whatever progress lies within man's reach is achieved through constant struggle against life's potential for evil. And while the transcendent good enters human experience in concretized form, it is for us always a straining toward, not the perfect achievement of, the universal. The latter is immanent *and* transcendent. The goodness of the ethical will is never exhausted by its particular manifestations.

Thomas A. Spragens, Jr. · *David Hume's "Experimental" Science of Morals and the Natural Law Tradition*

The decline of a widespread belief in natural law that accompanied the surrender of classical philosophy's intellectual hegemony has seemed to leave an important vacuum in human social life; for the idea of natural law embodied an adherence to the existence of valid norms of human conduct, transcending the idiosyncrasies of particular individual preferences and the peculiarities of individual cultures. Without some such belief, the very meaningfulness of right and wrong seems questionable. Human actions and institutions cannot be designated as good or bad, better or worse. They simply are what they are, adjudged desirable or undesirable only by the arbitrary whim of individual taste. Such a complete abandonment of a belief in ethical standards that are in some sense "objective" in turn seems to lead, moreover, to some kind of moral and political anarchism.

Many thoughtful modern political theorists, as a consequence, have pondered whether there might be some acceptable modern functional equivalent of the natural law. Apart from the very unlikely reemergence of classical philosophy to the place it held in intellectual life prior to the seventeenth century, the notion of natural law that depended on that philosophy will not easily regain general acceptance. But can there not be some standard that could perform the intellectual and moral functions of the law of nature and still be meaningful to people of a modern, skeptical, and empirical disposition?

Such a standard, it is important to add, should not be held responsible for reaching some final and unimpeachable answer to the ethical problems of human life and politics. It should not be expected to end disputation over the right course of action in any given circumstances. Some adherents of the notion of a "moral science" emanating from the Enlightenment may have entertained such elevated hopes, to be sure. But the natural law tradition never claimed to accomplish quite as much. It did not aspire to eliminate all cases in which reasonable persons might differ. As Aristotle was quick to caution his readers, no one should demand more certainty in a given area of knowledge than it is capable of yielding. Practical reason could never be expected to attain the degree of demonstrability he attributed to the theoretical sciences. Instead, the notion of natural law sought simply to provide some sense of what an appropriate touchstone for decisions on questions of human conduct might be—and some guidance on how to discuss and adjudicate these questions. It would be improper and unreasonable, then, to expect more than that from a modern substitute.

In this essay I would like to argue that those who share this interest in finding an equivalent of natural law compatible with modern predispositions could find some very helpful leads in the moral philosophy of David Hume. My intent, I should quickly add, is not to defend each detail of Hume's theory, which I consider to be deficient in several significant respects. The aim, rather, is to suggest that Hume provides us with a framework for giving meaning to the notion of "norms for human conduct grounded in nature"—a meaning not contingent on the acceptance of any single school of philosophy or metaphysics. And, in addition, this framework suggests an appropriate method for ascertaining, however imperfectly, the content of these norms.

On its face, of course, this seems a highly heretical suggestion. Hume, after all, is generally depicted as the arch-skeptic in all matters epistemological. He is remembered for his forthright assertion that "moral distinctions . . . are not the offspring of reason"[1] but are instead the product of "taste" and "sentiment." He is remembered as the *fons et origo* of the "is/ought distinction." And he was the philosophical father of modern empiricism, which has in turn led to the emotivist theory of ethics. Surely, then, he would seem an unlikely resource for those seeking to reconstruct the notion of natural law in a modern idiom.

It would be a mistake, however, even if an easily understandable mistake, to see in David Hume an early votary of the positivistic dismissal of ethical questions as meaningless. To do so would be to misinterpret and misconstrue Hume retrospectively, misled by later developments. It would be to read back into Hume views his philosophy may indeed have encouraged, but which he himself never held and which he would in fact have found peculiar. For, although he insisted on the logical gap between is and ought statements, Hume by no means saw this distinction as entailing the meaninglessness of ethical claims. Indeed, he wrote that "those who have denied the reality of moral distinctions, may be ranked among the disingenuous disputants; nor is it conceivable, that any human creature could ever seriously believe, that all characters and actions were alike entitled to the affection and regard of everyone . . . let a man's insensibility be ever so great, he must often be touched with the images of Right and Wrong."[2] And although he held that moral distinctions were not the product of reason, he nonetheless believed that it was possible to ascertain valid norms for human behavior in an "objective" (or at least "transsubjective") manner. This is what his "attempt to introduce the experimental method of reasoning into moral subjects"—the subtitle of the *Treatise on Human Nature*—was all about.

A thoughtful examination of Hume's moral theory, therefore, makes a worthwhile visit to "the outworks of the enemy"—as Hobbes put it when explaining his extensive consideration of biblical texts in his *Leviathan*. It offers the opportunity to discover that one of the founding fathers of a tradition that eventuated in moral relativism and ethical emotivism would have found this outcome unacceptable and unpersuasive. Moreover, to find in Hume some of the components for a modern and secular account of "natural law" does not necessitate the kind of strained and sometimes bizarre rendering that Hobbes gave the Scriptures. One need only attend carefully to what Hume actually said, after divesting oneself of distortive preconceptions arising from a different and later time.

In the first place, it is important to understand what it is that Hume is rejecting when he denies the moral competence of reason. The problem here is that "reason" is a philosophical symbol that changes its meaning very profoundly from time to time. In Hume's philosophical vocabulary reason was no longer the noetic power of the human understanding as conceived by the classical philosophers. Reason had been stripped of its axiological dimension and turned into "ratiocination." In some ways, of course, this was an unfortunate development even if it was the result of some analytical advance. It was clearly helpful, that is, to differentiate the very different powers of understanding that intuit a geometric inference on the one hand and that perceive the moral stature of a Socrates on the other hand—instead of lumping them together in a kind of mystical mathematics, as did Plato. The danger, however, was that the more complex and subtle powers of the mind—especially those of practical reason—might be denigrated or written off altogether.

In any case, Hume did not bring all this about himself. He acquired a newly narrowed conception of reason; he didn't invent it. Thus, when he denied the moral competence of reason, he was—on the terms given him—neither saying anything terribly exceptionable nor was he necessarily denying the objective reality of moral norms. What Hume denied, quite correctly, was that moral judgments could be (1) the result of mere logical inference or the "comparing of ideas," or (2) satisfactorily incorporated into a moral algebra formally parallel to Euclidean propositions about lines in space.

Not only is this denial quite correct, but it also does not necessarily turn Hume into an antagonist of the classic tradition of moral philosophy—even though it does make him a critic of some of his contemporaries who anticipated the transformation of moral philosophy into a theoretical science. Hume himself recognized this point quite clearly, and he remarked upon it in an early section of *The Principles of Morals*:

> The ancient philosophers, though they often affirm that virtue is nothing but conformity to reason, yet, in general, seem to consider morals as deriving their existence from taste and sentiment. On the other hand, our modern enquirers, though they also talk much of the beauty of virtue, and deformity of vice, yet have commonly endeavoured to account for these distinctions by metaphysical reasonings, and by deductions from the most abstract principles of the understanding.[3]

Hume indeed seems to go beyond this quite narrowly grounded rejection of the role of reason in moral judgment where he adds that morality "consists not in any matter of fact, which can be discovered by the understanding."[4] Here Hume does seem to verge on denying altogether the role of cognition in making moral claims and to verge on denying any objective grounding to these claims. This is the side of Hume that does give rise later on to the consignment of ethics to the intellectual dustbin. Before jumping prematurely to the inaccurate conclusion that this is where Hume wished to leave the matter, however, one must immediately recall that Hume nevertheless insisted on the possibility of grounding a valid ethical system "on fact and observation."[5]

This apparent contradiction stems from a profound tension, confusion, or ambiguity in Hume's philosophy. This is a problem that is not unique to Hume, moreover, even if it is especially evident and potentially misleading here. Instead, it is a recurrent problem in the empiricist tradition. Hume is caught up in a difficult semantic problem—one that has more than semantic consequences—caused by the coexistence in his writing and thought of clashing, or at least different, conceptions of "fact" and "real" and "objective." On the one hand is his abstract and metaphysically determined conception of real and objective matters of fact as corpuscular, primary qualities. On the other hand is his commonsense conception of real and objective fact as anything that exists. The difficulty and the confusion comes about because moral qualities are for him not facts in the former sense but they are facts in the latter sense. Vice and virtue, like colors and sounds and heat and cold, fall into that ontologically troublesome netherworld of "secondary" qualities: "Modern philosophy" tells us, says Hume, that they "are not qualities in objects, but perceptions in the mind." They are not "out there," one might say, in the discrete bits and pieces of things that compose the corpuscular cosmos. But at the same time, "nothing could be more real."[6]

These competing conceptions of facticity and reality ultimately cause Hume—and most of his fellow empiricists—a great deal of trouble. Their presence should not be allowed to mislead us, however, about what Hume wants to say, even if he has difficulty saying it clearing and coherently. Moral norms, he holds, are not grounded in matters of fact in the abstract and metaphysical sense. They cannot be constructed out of primary qualities. They do, nonetheless, possess the same kind of reality as do the human passions, interests, needs, and desires that produce them. In this sense, they are very real indeed.

The moral distinction between vice and virtue, then, is not made by reason, which is "perfectly inert" in Hume's view. Ethical judgments are based on human "sentiment," instead. They are, in a sense, "emotive," then. And in one classic formulation Hume sounds very much like the contemporary emotivist I have insisted he isn't. "When you pronounce any action or character to be vicious, you mean nothing, but that from the constitution of your nature you have a feeling or sentiment of blame from the contemplation of it."[7] A. J. Ayer, one might think, couldn't have said it any better when he staked out the high ground (or low ground, some might aver) of the emotivist doctrine in *Language, Truth, and Logic*. The very significant difference between Hume and the emotivism of twentieth-century logical empiricism, however, is contained in what seems to be a very innocuous phrase in the proposition just cited: "from the constitution of your nature." For an emotivist, indeed, this phrase would be a substantively insignificant rhetorical flourish. For Hume, on the other hand, it was a significant phrase indeed—one that reflected his conception of where these moral sentiments came from and why they were not arbitrary. What lies behind this phrase, in other words, is what opened the way to his "experimental" approach to moral questions.

In the strong version of the emotivist doctrine, the "preferences" that actuate the pseudopropositions of ethical utterance are or can without objection be: (1) idiosyncratically individual and particular, (2) a function of simple self-interest, and (3) arbitrary or whimsical. For Hume, in contrast, any legitimate ethical claim was a meaningful and potentially transsubjectively verifiable proposition that: (1) was grounded in sentiments common to all humanity, (2) embodied a general good, and (3) was in a sense "necessary" and "natural" rather than capricious.

The enabling presuppositions underlying this account were two: (1) that there was such a thing as "human nature," transcending the peculiarities of different individuals and disparate cultures, and (2) that part of human nature was some degree of social feeling—i.e., "sympathy" for the welfare of others and for the commonweal. Concerning the first of these presuppositions, Hume writes:

> It is universally acknowledged that there is a great uniformity among the actions of men, in all nations and ages, and that human nature remains still the same, in its principles and operations. . . . Mankind are so much the same, in all times and places, that history informs us of nothing new or strange in this particular. Its chief use is only to discover the constant and universal principles of human nature, by showing men in all varieties of circumstances and situations, and furnishing us with materials from which we may form our observations and become ac-

quainted with the regular springs of human action and behaviour. . . . Nor are the earth, water, and other elements, examined by Aristotle, and Hippocrates, more like to those which at present lie under our observation than the men described by Polybius and Tacitus are to those who now govern the world.[8]

Concerning the sympathy that Hume sees as one of the sentiments found within this universal human nature, he writes: "'tis that principle, which takes us so far out of ourselves, as to give us the same pleasure or uneasiness in the characters of others, as if they had a tendency to our own advantage or loss."[9] And, he continues, it is only a very rare and singularly depraved human being who is not moved to some degree by this sympathetic fellow-feeling: "Let us suppose such a person ever so selfish; let private interest have ingrossed ever so much his attention; yet in instances where that is not concerned, he must unavoidably feel *some* propensity to the good of mankind, and make it an object of choice, if everything else be equal."[10]

Moral judgments, then, allegations that such and such deeds or such and such ends are good or bad, virtuous or vicious, are judgments about what conduces to the welfare of humanity. And they are motivated by the sentiment of sympathy that prompts individual concern for the general good. Ethical discourse, in consequence, is in an important sense rational, even if ethical distinctions are not themselves the product of reason narrowly defined. Furthermore, the goods that ethical discourse seeks to ascertain are in a certain sense natural. And, finally, the propositions of ethical discourse are, in a certain rough sense, subject to verification.

The rationality of ethical judgment, in Hume's account, consists first in its grounding in reality. Ethical claims are not arbitrary or capricious. They are rooted in the real needs and natural ends of human beings. Ethical claims are also rational in their generality. No legitimate ethical statement, Hume argues, can be individualistically particularistic in its reference: it must instead express a general perspective. What Kant imposes upon normative discourse by his stipulation that a rational being can act only according to what he could will to be a universal law Hume finds inherent in the logic of ethical discourse itself. Hume's point is ostensively linguistic, but it carries normative force at the same time. The parallel to the analyses of contemporary linguistic philosophy, where some utterances are ruled out as incapable of being said clearly or coherently, is rather close here. Anyone who wants to play the language game of ethical discourse cannot speak idiosyncratically. He must instead predicate his speech acts on the commonweal.

In the *Treatise* Hume expresses it this way: "'Tis only when a character is considered in general, without reference to our particular interest, that it causes such a feeling or sentiment, as denominates it morally good or evil."[11] And in the *Principles of Morals*, his account takes the linguistic turn:

> The more we converse with mankind, and the greater social intercourse we maintain, the more shall we be familiarized to *these general preferences and distinctions, without which our conversation and discourse could scarcely be rendered intelligible to each other*. Every man's interest is peculiar to himself, and the aversions and desires, which result from it, cannot be supposed to affect others in a like degree. General language, therefore, being formed for general use, must be moulded on some more general views, and must affix the epithets of praise or blame, in conformity to sentiments, which arise from the general interests of the community.[12]

Hume's insistence on this point clearly differentiates him from the twentieth-century emotivist who equates "x is good" with "yea, x!" even if he is the emotivist's philosophical progenitor. For, as Hume sees it, anyone who resolves ethical statements into individual preferences simply demonstrates that he doesn't know how to speak the English (or any other) language.

Just as ethical judgments are rational in their intrinsic generality, the ethical sentiments behind them may be said to be in a significant sense natural. At least, I would argue, the sense in which Hume recognizes moral precepts to be natural is sufficient to make his account compatible with the main tenets of the natural law tradition.

Hume's position on this question is somewhat tricky. It certainly cannot be understood by repairing to one or two brief quotations taken out of context. The problem is, as Hume tells us, that "there is none more ambiguous and equivocal" word than "nature." This semantic ambiguity leads to formulations in Hume that seem contradictory. One must always ask, then, in what sense he is using the word "natural" in any specific case, or complete confusion will result. Thus, when Hume writes that "'tis impossible that the character of natural and unnatural can ever, in any sense, mark the boundaries of vice and virtue,"[13] he seems to be denying more than he really is. What he means here is that virtue is neither identified by its statistical incidence in nature nor invariably produced by natural causes. Moreover, Hume denies that moral precepts are natural where natural is taken to mean innate or instinctual.

On the other hand, if natural means common or endemic to the species rather than rare or unusual, then "if ever there was anything, which could be called natural in this sense, the sentiments of morality certainly may. . . . These sentiments are so rooted in our constitution and temper, that without entirely confounding the human mind by disease or madness, 'tis impossible to extirpate and destroy them."[14]

Moreover, and most important, Hume allows that "in so sagacious an animal, what necessarily arises from the exertion of his intellectual faculties may justly be esteemed natural."[15] And since the rules of justice are necessary in this sense, they may justifiably be deemed to be natural. If justice is in a sense an "invention of men," Hume writes, that fact should not mislead us into seeing the rules of justice as capricious or mutable.

> Most of the inventions of men are subject to change. They depend upon humour and caprice. They have a vogue for a time, and then sink into oblivion. It may, perhaps, be apprehended, that if justice were allowed to be a human invention, it must be placed on the same footing. But the cases are widely different. The interest, on which justice is founded, is the greatest imaginable, and extends to all times and places. It cannot possibly be served by any other invention. It is obvious, and discovers itself on the very first formation of society. All these causes render the rules of justice steadfast and immutable; at least as immutable as human nature.[16]

Accordingly, it is not inappropriate to label these rules of justice as laws of nature. For

> where an invention is obvious and absolutely necessary, it may as properly be said to be natural as any thing that proceeds immediately from original principles, without the intervention of thought or reflection. Tho' the rules of justice be *artificial*, they

are not *arbitrary*. Nor is the expression improper to call them *Laws of Nature*; if by natural we understand what is common to any species, or even if we confine it to mean what is inseparable from the species.[17]

Hume's discernment of the source of virtue in the natural necessities of humanity generates some further resemblances between his ethics and the account that Plato—generally considered an adherent of natural law—provides in *The Republic*. For example, Hume argues that it is neither possible nor appropriate to mark off a precise boundary between virtues and talents—since both are cases of doing something well. Using ordinary language for confirmation once again, he observes: "I do not find that in the English, or any other modern tongue, the boundaries are exactly fixed between virtues and talents, vices and defects, or that a precise definition can be given of the one as contradistinguished from the other."[18] This conflation of virtues and natural talents, vices and natural defects, would have been scorned by Kant, who saw it as a "lax and low" account of morals. For Kant, no merely "heteronomous" quality, nothing valued by natural human desires, formed any legitimate ground for the pure rational obligations of true morality. But Plato, I think, could hardly have been scandalized, since the notion of *arete* involves a quite similar acceptance of continuity and overlap between natural and moral excellence. Thus, in chapter four of *The Republic*, Socrates builds his interpretation of the virtue of the soul on the basis of an analogy with the proper functioning of natural organs, such as eyes, and of tools, such as pruning knives. Hume is aware of the similarity here, noting in defense of his views that "the ancient moralists, the best models, made no material distinction among the different species of mental endowments and defects, but treated all alike under the appellation of virtues and vices, and made them indiscriminately the object of their moral reasonings."[19]

Also reminiscent of the Platonic account is Hume's explanation of why the virtuous life is to be recommended. Virtue, he writes, "is an end, and is desirable on its own account, without fee or reward, merely for the immediate satisfaction it conveys."[20] This satisfaction is analogous to the condition of health in the body, a condition that likewise is intrinsically desirable and self-justifying.[21] And the result is that Hume's virtuous man, like Plato's philosopher, can be deemed to lead a more enviable life than the vicious or unjust man. The reason is the same in both cases. As Plato has Socrates say in comparing the just and unjust lives, "the happiest man is he who is first in goodness and justice . . . and the most miserable is that lowest example of injustice and vice,"[22] because the just man enjoys the inward serenity of the rightly ordered soul. He is "at rest from his travel."[23] Likewise, Hume argues in the same way that the virtuous man is the truly happy man, for he possesses "inward peace of mind, consciousness of integrity, a satisfactory review of [his] own conduct;" and "these are circumstances, very requisite to our happiness."[24] Hume's good man, like Plato's philosopher, is depicted as enjoying a higher form of pleasure than do "knaves," who "will discover that they themselves are, in the end, the greatest dupes, and have sacrificed the invaluable enjoyment of a character . . . for the acquisition of worthless toys and geegaws."[25]

Thus grounded in the natural necessities of humanity, moral precepts are subject in Hume's view to "experimental" (we would today say "empirical") validation. If the good achieves its status by contributing to the welfare of human beings, then one can attain a tolerably reliable account of good and evil by finding out what people commonly consider to be good and evil. Everyone is by definition a reliable authority on this issue, since his taste is the legitimate standard. Only to the extent that anyone might be somehow deluded about his own feelings—about his own welfare—would his moral sentiments be invalidated. In Hume's hands this criterion in practice means that moral judgments will be deemed reliable "where men judge of things by their natural, unprejudiced reason, without the delusive glosses of superstition and false religion."[26]

Moral theory for Hume then consists of two parts, the first being resolutely empirical and the other being essentially analytic. The empirical part amounts to a survey of the uncorrupted moral judgments of mankind. The moral theorist is to "consider every attribute of the mind, which renders a man an object either of esteem and affection, or of hatred and contempt." Framing this catalogue, Hume believes, should not be a terribly difficult or complicated task. "The very nature of language," he asserts, "guides us almost infallibly in forming a judgment of this nature; and as every tongue possesses one set of words which are taken in a good sense, and another in the opposite, the least acquaintance with the idiom suffices, without any reasoning, to direct us in collecting and arranging the estimable or blameable qualities of men."[27] Once this collecting and arranging is accomplished, the only remaining task is to examine the lists of estimable and blamable qualities to discover the underlying common attributes. These common attributes may then be justifiably considered to be the "universal principles" of good and evil; and the goal of a satisfactory ethical theory "founded on fact and observation"[28] will be successfully achieved.

On the basis of his own survey—admittedly one that would not be considered very scientific by the standards of present-day statisticians and pollsters—Hume concludes that the universal principles of good and evil are "the *utile* and the *dulce*." Uncorrupted human taste accredits as good those things which are "useful or agreeable to the person himself or to others."[29] Virtue is revealed as a gentle mistress.

> The dismal dress falls off, with which many divines, and some philosophers, have covered her; and nothing appears but gentleness, humanity, beneficence, affability; nay, even at proper intervals, play, frolic, and gaiety. . . . She declares that her sole purpose is to make her votaries and all mankind, during every instant of their existence, if possible, cheerful and happy. . . . The sole trouble which she demands, is that of just calculation, and a steady preference of the greater happiness. And if any austere pretenders approach her, enemies to joy and pleasure, she either rejects them as hypocrites and deceivers; or, if she admits them in her train, they are ranked, however, among the lesser of her votaries.[30]

As I intimated at the outset, the point of this essay is not to recommend Hume's theory for anyone's total or uncritical embrace. His theory has, it seems to me, its very real problems. Before concluding, I would like to identify those problems that I consider most serious; for before Hume's theory could be successfully adapted for current use, these flaws in it would require attention. These problems, I would argue, fall under three general headings: methodological, substantive, and philosophical.

Methodologically, Hume appears to underestimate the problems confronted by his approach to moral theory. These inadequately addressed problems, moreover, appear at both stages of his enterprise—the empirical and the analytic.

The weaknesses of the empirical part of his procedure center around the problems of authority and false consciousness. Hume simply does not take very seriously the question of whose judgments are to be given what weight in his grand survey of moral sentiments. Prima facie, no one would seek out the views of the prepubescent to guide his sexual conduct or consult the psychopathic to guide his social relations. Judgments on matters of ethics, like judgments on matters of music or botany or baseball, require some degree of "backing" in relevant experience or knowledge to make them count. And, as both Aristotle and Rousseau insisted in their accounts of how to delineate the natural, accidentally disfigured specimens must not be averaged in on a par with normal and healthy specimens.

Hume exhibits some appreciation of this problem, but he confronts it only cursorily and tendentiously. His "exclusionary rule," if one could call it that, when it comes to counting moral sentiments seems directed only at those deemed to suffer from "the delusive glosses of superstition and false religion."[31] No serious attention is devoted to other problems of insufficient experience or of false consciousness. And, taking Hume's apparent skepticism in matters religious together with his lack of attention to identifying the scope of the "false" in "false religion," one wonders whether his survey might not include everyone other than those with religious convictions. The village idiot could receive a serious hearing and a "dismal" religious thinker like Pascal be discounted. Perhaps this interpretation caricatures Hume's account, but it seems safe to say that he fails to give this problem the attention it requires and thereby leaves his casual comments on the matter open to serious objections.

Similarly, Hume gives relatively little attention to the analytic problems of his venture. His accounts of this part of his experimental enterprise suggest that it would be a very easy and almost mechanical matter to distill the general underlying grounds of the moral sentiments from the empirically ascertained lists of "estimable and blameable qualities." However, as he does seem to realize in the thoughtful "Dialogue" that was appended to the second edition of his *Principles of Morals*, this task might not be so easy. Even a cursory review of extant systems of mores and morals reveals conflicting notions and views—not the unproblematic harmony of voices that Hume seems to suppose in his methodological passages. This fact, of course, is the "data base" for cultural relativism; and, although the matter is not by any means so easily determined as the sophomoric type of relativist often supposes, the problem is clearly a much more serious one than Hume generally recognizes or concedes. The "Dialogue" does mark a thoughtful first step in confronting this difficulty, with Hume arguing that "the principles upon which men reason in morals are always the same; though the conclusions which they draw are often very different,"[32] because of different circumstances. Nevertheless, even someone sympathetic to the basic thrust of Hume's argument here would have to concede that his account needs further attention.

Hume's substantive conclusions about what is good are also inadequate in several respects. The morally estimable qualities, as noted earlier, he determines to consist of the useful and the agreeable, the *utile* and the *dulce*. Both of these principles, I would argue, are not really adequate when presented, as Hume does, as fundamental and exhaustive principles.

First, Hume makes the counsels of virtue too "sweet"—much as one might like to acquiesce in his overly simple and sanguine views on this score. We can perhaps agree that many of the more stern-faced and rigorous moral theorists, whether Kantian or Puritan or Stoic, seem, rather like the dull hero of *The Pirates of Penzance*, to miss the point of ethics—to mistake instrumental austerities for the ultimate goal of human fulfillment. At least, however, their accounts do recognize the obligatory dimension of moral precepts; they do account for why we speak of ethical demands rather than, say, of ethical tactical advice. The truly good human being, as is commonly and legitimately recognized, exhibits at least some element of self-restraint and even self-sacrifice in his behavior. And this requirement, as Hume fails to appreciate, is not wholly reducible to the easy affability in which he clothes his "gentle mistress," virtue.

(Hume's somewhat facile dismissal of the demanding side of virtue perhaps is a consequence of his overly sanguine psychology. In Hume's psychology contention over property emerges as virtually the sole source of human conflict. Once rules concerning property are fixed and observed, he writes in a noteworthy passage, "there remains little or nothing to be done towards settling a perfect harmony and concord. All the other passions, beside this of interest, are either easily restrained, or are not of such pernicious consequence when indulged.")[33]

Next, Hume's reduction of both virtue and justice to what is useful or agreeable seems clearly to be unconvincing. Although rules of justice obviously have great utilitarian value for human society, the two (justice and utility) are not identical. It is not difficult to imagine numerous situations in which the claims of justice and the dictates of utilitarian calculation collide rather than coincide. The distinction between justice and utility, moreover, seems to be confirmed by the somewhat different "moral sentiments" they arouse—a point that Hume should have noted, given the significance his theory attached to these sentiments. The moral indignation aroused by the sense of injustice seems absent from merely utilitarian judgments. Departures from the norms of utility may be seen as unfortunate or irresponsible, but they are usually not felt to be unfair.

The same objection can also be made pertinent to Hume's reduction of virtue to utility. And here, interestingly enough, Hume did seem to be aware that his account was not confirmed by common moral sentiments. We don't respond to human virtue and to useful artifacts in the same way. Rather than reconsidering his theory, however, Hume simply writes off this anomaly as "inexplicable": "On the other hand, a convenient house, and a virtuous character, cause not the same feeling of approbation; even though the source of our approbation be the same, and flow from sympathy and an idea of their utility. There is something very inexplicable in this variation of our feelings; but 'tis what we have experience of with regard to all our passions and sentiment."[34]

Finally, Hume's theory affords too little protection against a slide into pure and simple hedonism. Hume surely does not intend to embrace the ethic of "if it feels good, do it!" But pronouncing the good to be whatever is felt as useful or agreeable can easily lead toward this conclusion. At the very least, it would be necessary to provide a qualitative dimension to Hume's utilitarianism to make clear why this hedonistic outcome is not appropriate—why, to use the formulation of a later utilitarian, it is better to be a dissatisfied Socrates than a satisfied pig. And Hume does not really provide a basis for such a qualitative distinction in his theory. At some important junctures, he very clearly seems to appeal to the presence and validity of distinct levels of pleasure. For example, such a recognition is central to his explanation of why the virtuous person is happy. However, he only manifests an awareness of this phenomenon; he does not account for it. And perhaps this weakness is not merely fortuitous. Perhaps it reflects some of Hume's deeper philosophical inadequacies: he probably could not find the basis for the necessary distinctions within his own theoretical framework.

The third fundamental weakness of Hume's moral theory, then, is precisely this inadequacy of its philosophical underpinnings. Hume's rather primitive corpuscular ontology simply does not possess the capacity to support his philosophical anthropology, which in turn is the basis of his experimental science of morality. This problem could stand considerable elaboration, but perhaps a couple of key examples can indicate the nature of the difficulty. In the first place Hume's moral theory is predicated upon the existence of a "common and universal" human nature. It is this "common humanity" that produces the fundamental consensus of the moral sentiments that gives credence to his experimental approach. But it seems difficult indeed to imagine how human beings as "heaps of impressions" could possess this kind of common essence. Similarly, Hume never can provide a very satisfactory account of the passions that are fundamental to his theory. This incapacity was observed by the nineteenth-century editor of a reprinting of the 1777 edition of Hume's *Enquiries*, with particular reference to the sentiment of "sympathy"—a passion central to Hume's ethics. "How it is possible," he wrote, "to find room for sympathy in so atomistic or individualistic a psychology as Hume's, is one of the most interesting questions which are raised by his system."[35]

Looking at the subsequent course of the empiricist tradition, one is led to the conclusion that this philosophical inadequacy proved the undoing of Hume's intent in moral theory. Rather than setting morals on a new empirical footing—i.e., in fact and observation—Hume opened the way for the dissolution of moral theory. Hume's ontology, in effect, cannibalized his moral theory. His sensationistic and corpuscular philosophy was deemed to be more persuasive than his belief in the reality of moral distinctions; so when it became recognized that the two parts of his thought could not really be made compatible, it was the moral theory that lost out.

Hume's own elaboration of his experimental moral theory, then, has some significant defects. The problems with his theory as it stands, however, are not beyond repair. Someone who sees merit in the basic project could conceivably salvage Hume's project if he were willing to: (1) address the problem of the "relevant sample"—i.e., of whose moral sentiments may be accorded what weight; (2) take more seriously the analytical and interpretive problem presented by the diversity in moral cultures; (3) provide an account of the good that is more genuinely empirical than Hume's own parochial and reductive account; and (4) develop a more adequate philosophical base for the theory than Hume's corpuscularism afforded. Clearly, these are not trivial tasks. The last of them, indeed, is more like the work for a generation than for an individual. But there are no a priori theoretical obstacles to accomplishing what needs to be done.

This reclamation of Hume's fundamental project, I want to suggest, might be a highly worthwhile undertaking for those of us who (1) are sympathetic to the essential concerns and claims embodied in the traditional notion of natural law, and (2) would like to have an account of these claims not open to dismissal on a priori philosophical grounds by those "of positivist or skeptical predispositions."[36] For better or for worse, any contemporary defense of natural law that begins with "first, let us assume the persuasiveness of classical philosophy" is going to speak to a somewhat limited audience. Simply as a tactical expedient in the contest with the modern relativism that claims its base in empiricism and that often slides toward nihilism, then, it might be extremely useful to have an account of a meaningful and transsubjective morality arrived at by a procedure that is inductive and philosophically neutral (or at least compatible with a variety of philosophies). Hume's experimental science of morality, properly refurbished, might offer such an alternative.

For those who cannot imagine any possible confluence between Hume's approach and natural law ideas, a few intimations of analogies between Hume and specific adherents of natural law might be suggestive. First, if the experimental sample in Hume's science were circumscribed in a particular way, his approach to ethics might resemble the inductive part of Aristotle's ethics. If it could be persuasively contended, that is, that the appropriate group to consult in one's survey were those of great experience and fundamental probity, then one would be approximating Aristotle's reliance on the judgment of the *spoudaios*. Second, if one interpreted the available experimental data somewhat differently than did Hume, he might find himself in fundamental accord with C. S. Lewis's attempt to provide empirical confirmation for the natural law.[37] Finally, if the focus were placed on the abstract formal content of Hume's account, its fundamental similarity with Walter Lippmann's definition of the public interest should be evident. For in Hume what is good is what answers to "the true interests of mankind"[38] as discerned from the general perspective forced upon us by the requisites of a common language. And in Lippmann the public interest is defined as "what men would choose if they saw clearly, thought rationally, acted disinterestedly and benevolently."[39]

At the very least, we should be aware that this Scottish fount of modern empiricism was no modern emotivist, despite his oft-cited remarks about the gap between is and ought and about reason's subordination to the passions. His moral theory instead was a thoughtful, if flawed, attempt to interpret the meaningfulness and validity of moral distinctions that are neither subjective (in the sense of idiosyncratically particular) nor purely conventional (in the sense of arbitrary or variable). In their appropriation of his ideas, I would argue, Hume's philosophical descendants threw away a lot of the wheat and kept a lot of the chaff. There is no reason for us not to improve on their faulty judgment.

Fred H. Willhoite, Jr. · *Biocultural Evolution and Political Ethics*

> ". . . contrary to the postulates of contemporary thought, a human nature does exist, as the Greeks believed."
>
> Albert Camus, *The Rebel*

However profound and enduring their insights may be, political thinkers are always goaded, challenged, or inspired by the major trends and events of their own times. The demoralization and disillusionment of democratic Athens after defeat in the Peloponnesian War, the short-lived coup of the Thirty, and the trial and execution of Socrates left their marks everywhere on Plato's political philosophy. Similarly, political-religious-economic conflicts in seventeenth-century England which culminated in the Civil War must have impelled Hobbes to stress above all the problematic nature of political order.

What of our own time, this century which, supremely, has verified the clearest words that Hegel ever wrote: "History [is] the slaughter-bench at which the happiness of peoples, the wisdom of states, and the virtue of individuals have been sacrificed. . . ."?[1] We do not yet have sufficient historical distance to know whether our century's terrible events have inspired enduring political thought. But these bloody nightmares have surely haunted the minds and imaginations of thinkers and writers as diverse as George Orwell, Hannah Arendt, Leo Strauss, Albert Camus, Alexander Solzhenitsyn, and John Hallowell.

Much less significantly, the once-unimaginable political horrors of the twentieth century have inspired my own efforts to understand the nature of political life—and death. I still remember my shocked incredulity upon first reading about Hitler's Holocaust and Stalin's Great Terror. These fantastic, massive slaughters of the innocent seemed so remote from my own experience of growing up in a placid, somewhat provincial area of the United States after World War II that I could not begin to comprehend them.

Three decades later, after much reading and thought, I still cannot—though I can never, never forget them. Nor can I imagine losing interest in why these kinds of political horrors occurred—and continue to occur—and particularly in what they teach us about human nature and politics.

As an undergraduate I first encountered the great political philosophers; both their ideas and their ways of trying to provide adequate interpretations and explanations of recurring patterns in politics captivated my attention. As a graduate student under John Hallowell's tutelage I began to explore their theories in much greater depth. At that time I was much attracted by Reinhold Niebuhr's "Christian Realism," and I have continued to believe that the most important requirement for political theory is to take fully into account the world as it actually is, whatever our normative judgments or desires to change it.

This concern for realistic understanding led me increasingly to believe in the necessity of testing political philosophers' ideas by the methods of empirical science. That is much more easily said than done, since, to put it charitably, the behavioral and social sciences are notoriously inchoate and inadequate. History, I have always thought, provides the most promising material for anyone trying to comprehend human nature in depth. But as we all know, historical facts do not speak for themselves, and conflicting interpretations of history are as numerous as disagreements over methodology and significance in the social sciences.

I decided therefore to start at what seemed the scientific beginning by trying to learn what the biological sciences teach about human nature. I was also intrigued by Konrad Lorenz's then-current popularization, *On Aggression*, even though its political interpretations and prescriptions struck me as extremely naive. A decade and a half later I am still learning about both biological and cultural evolution and cannot imagine thinking about human nature and politics outside an evolutionary framework.

In recent years there has emerged a new type of evolutionary theorizing which seeks to apply Darwin's central concept of natural selection to the interpretation of the behavior of all species, including humans. This approach—dubbed "sociobiology" by a leading practitioner[2]—has stirred up a hornet's nest of criticism and ideological outrage among some biologists and a number of social scientists. But whatever the shortcomings of particular works and theorists, evolutionary assumptions and approaches are spreading rapidly within anthropology and psychology, and more slowly but surely in sociology, political science, and economics.[3]

This seems to me an approach eminently worth pursuing in the quest for a truly realistic understanding of human nature in politics, though I strongly desire to avoid any pretense of having discovered a "royal road to truth." Human finitude and fallibility surely remain irremediable.

Specifically, I have been trying to develop a natural selectionist or sociobiological interpretation of the origins and biocultural evolution of politics, government, and the state.[4] Here I shall attempt to summarize this perspective, then explain what I believe are some of its major implications for political ethics. Schematically speaking, natural selection theory holds that the most fundamental behavioral tendencies involved in human evolution have been "nepotism" and "reciprocity." In basic terms, evolution functions primarily through the differential reproduction of alternative types of genes. Types which help produce organisms that most effectively propagate themselves are genes which are most likely to persist and spread within a population over a number of generations. Since genes can be replicated only through the reproductive activities of individuals, one would expect the evolution in every social species of a central tendency for individuals to discriminate in favor of their own offspring as, in most cases, the prime repositories of the reproducers' distinctive genetic material.

In many species individuals may also tend to aid discriminately other close kin, since this kind of behavior can result in their propagating some distinctive genes identical to those of the assisting individual. Among mammals, for example, full siblings share on the average the same proportion of genes which are identical by descent—one-half—as do parents and their offspring. Nepotistic behavior, favoritism toward offspring and other close kin, has been strongly selected for when it tends to promote individuals' "inclusive fitness"—the sum total of the organism's success in replicating its genes, whether directly or through assisting the reproductive efforts of close genetic relatives.[5]

Reciprocity refers to exchanges of people, goods, and services which enhance the exchangers' chances for increasing their inclusive fitness. Since natural selection operates through the differential reproduction of individuals' genetic material, sociobiological theory holds that nepotistic and reciprocating tendencies would have been overwhelmingly favored as reproductive "strategies." The latter term, one should note, implies nothing about conscious awareness but refers only to the functional outcomes of behavior.

Archeological evidence and ethnographic studies of small-scale "primitive" societies strongly suggest that nepotism and reciprocity were intricately intertwined during hundreds of millennia of human evolution. In most band and village societies there is little exchange of goods and services among nonrelatives. Except usually between parents and their dependent offspring, there is some expectation of return for gifts and aid provided one another by relatives. The adaptiveness of limiting exchanges mainly to kin presumably lies in the possibility of a genetic "return" (through enhanced inclusive fitness) for a donor who is "cheated" by a recipient of his aid.[6]

Natural selection is, inexorably, a competitive process. Each generation is dominated numerically by offspring of the more successful strivers for reproductive success in the previous generation. Nepotistic and reciprocal aid and cooperation have been selected as competitive strategies because they have generally had the genotypically selfish effect of enhancing the reproductive success of individual "strategists." But helping my kin group or my political coalition invariably means damaging the interests of competing groups and coalitions.

In short, we have evolved as ambivalent, selectively social creatures, "to have *individually separate interests*, and to strive *in relation* to one another, because each of us is genetically distinct." Furthermore, since reproductive success is always relative to competitors', "there is no automatic finiteness" to individual striving, only the limits imposed by abilities, ecology, and competitors.[7] I believe that it requires much ingenuousness or ideological blindness to deny the ubiquity and fundamental shaping influence of competition in human history and on social life at all levels, from individuals to enormous states; almost all cooperation can be most realistically interpreted as a competitive strategy.

Competitive techniques take varied forms across species, but attempts to dominate, intimidate, defeat, drive away, and even to kill competitors for reproductively valuable resources are by no means uncommon. Nearly every long-term study of primate species in the wild in recent years has produced observational evidence of intraspecific killing which can most plausibly be interpreted as a mechanism of reproductive competition.[8]

None of this implies that humans—or even monkeys and apes—are driven by genetically encoded, invariant, and irresistible aggressive and killer "instincts." Contrary to its critics' charge, sociobiology is definitely not a type of "genetic determinism." It might better be labeled "evolutionary probabilism," since it involves efforts to understand what kinds of behaviors are likely to occur under given circumstances because of their adaptiveness for individuals of a particular species. The "proximate"—ontogenetic and situational—causes of behaviors may include a high degree of learning and flexible, highly varied responses to differing ecological and social circumstances.

Within the human evolutionary process, it seems quite probable that opportunistic violent conflict between independent groups was not only an important competitive strategy but a strong selective force promoting species-wide increases in mental abilities.[9] This very definitely does not imply that humans must inevitably kill or make war on one another, much less that these practices are morally justified. But the likelihood that serious intergroup conflict has long been a potent sociopolitical fact of life has prompted evolutionary biologist Richard Alexander to advance an intriguing "Balance-of-Power Hypothesis":

> This hypothesis contends that at some early point in our history the actual function of human groups—their significance for their individual members—was protection from the predatory effects of other human groups. The premise is that the necessary and sufficient forces to explain the maintenance of every kind and size of human group above the nuclear family, extant today and throughout all but the earliest portions of human history, were (a) war, or intergroup competition and aggression, and (b) the maintenance of balances of power between such groups.[10]

This provocative formulation provides a sociobiological platform from which to launch an exploratory inquiry into the biocultural evolution of political authority. The great social contract theorists were justified in regarding the origins of political hierarchies as problematic. On natural selectionist theoretical grounds, one would not expect individuals to submit to the authority of nonkin whose fundamental reproductive "interests" would likely conflict with their own. Even more compelling is archeological and ethnographic evidence that no society-wide, extrafamilial authority—in the sense of a right to command matched by a duty to obey—existed within the small (several dozen individuals), autonomous hunting-gathering bands in which all members of our species and its ancestors lived for at least two million years.

Hunting-gathering societies are integrated solely through kin ties (nepotism) and reciprocal, cooperative exchange of goods, services, resources, and people. They are not free of conflicts and rivalry—especially men's disputes over women and interband clashes over hunting territories and wild plant and water resources. But parties to a quarrel within a band can usually leave to join relatives in another band, and in prehistory a beleaguered band could often migrate to an entirely new region. In neither case would it be possible to establish a dispute-settling authority, which would erode or terminate the autonomy valued by individuals, families, and bands.

My hypothesis is that authority systems emerged originally from the ancient processes of reproductive competition interacting with changing demographic and ecological circumstances. In prehistory, population levels in certain regions ultimately made a hunting-gathering mode of subsistence impossible. Rather than starve or risk death at the hands of their neighbors, certain peoples began to apply their extensive observational knowledge of plants to the tasks of deliberately planting, cultivating, and harvesting them as a primary food source.[11] Farming was much harder work than hunting and gathering, but it paid off in a great increase in calories per unit of land per person. More abundant concentrated food supplies became available, and men most successful at supplying it could support more wives and offspring and gain a new edge in the evolutionary game of reproductive success.

Ethnographic evidence suggests that that is precisely what occurred at the autonomous agricultural village stage of sociopolitical evolution. New types of kin-based coalitions—"lineages" and "clans"—developed, employing extended nepotism, reciprocal mate exchanges, and coercion as instruments of reproductive competition among adult males.[12]

Even though disputes multiplied, true political authority did not emerge from within agricultural villages. The anthropologist Robert Carneiro argues that history records a uniform "inability of autonomous political units to relinquish their sovereignty in the absence of overriding external constraints."[13] So long as defeated factions in a village quarrel could move away and establish their own new village, or militarily weaker and threatened villages could also migrate, they would not submit to enduring domination by their rivals.[14]

Authority systems probably developed first in geographically or socially circumscribed regions where population growth had eventually terminated the supply of vacant land. Defeated polities could then either submit to domination by their conquering overlords, paying regular taxes and tributes, or face extinction. In cases where the more adaptive choice was made, institutionalized relationships of dominance and subordination were established, and conflicts between ever-larger political units led ultimately to early historic states and empires.[15]

Political authority systems first emerged in "chiefdoms," which represented extensions of the lineage basis of social organization, a primarily nepotistic principle. But lineages now were "ranked"; some had greater dignity and privileges than others. Within the highest ranking one the chiefly position became hereditary. With authority came official ideology, a highly ritualistic religious doctrine. The chief was often head priest as well, representing the beneficent but capricious and demanding gods. Chiefs' injunctions were usually backed by magical or ceremonial sanctions rather than regularized coercive force, though the latter could often be mobilized if necessary.[16]

To keep order within their multicommunity domains, many chiefs established courts or similar mechanisms of authoritative dispute settlement. Subjects often came to feel genuine gratitude for this chiefly service because it averted many potentially dangerous quarrels and feuds.[17] But in addition to reverential deference, chiefs also received sacred tributes, superintending vast storehouses from which they redistributed goods at ritual feasts and in hard times. This norm of reciprocity could lead to actual restraints on chiefly power. If perceived as extracting far more in labor and produce from their people than was returned to them in tangible benefits, chiefs risked losing their thrones in uprisings led by ambitious men of the chiefly lineage.[18]

Chiefs and similar kinds of small-scale monarchs were typically superpolygynists, highly successful reproductive competitors: "The very first tangible benefit of political power seems to have been reproductive fitness, long before material wealth was converted into tombs, temples and palaces."[19]

Continued warfare, the threat or actuality of conquest, and inexorable population pressures within circumscribed regions led beyond chiefdoms to the development of polities organized on a territorial rather than a lineage basis—full-fledged states with centralized governments able to "collect taxes, draft men for work or war, and decree and enforce laws."[20]

Broadened nepotistic opportunities were seized upon by royal houses and their allied aristocracies. They tended to monopolize official positions, using them to build great wealth for their families, gain additional wives and concubines, and ensure hereditary transmission of their power and resources. "Pseudonepotism" accurately characterizes the legitimating ideology of such monarchies. The king would be portrayed as the supremely wise, omnipotent divine "father" of all his people, even though there were no actual kinship relations between the royal family and the mass of commoners.[21]

Reciprocal coalitions comprised of rulers and their assistants—priests, ministers, officials, generals, tax-gatherers—sharing the spoils of war and regular tributes exacted from peasant and craftsman commoners, constituted the dominant governing class of the state. Their economic relationship with the mass of the population was primarily "a form of redistributive explotitation."[22] But in supplying institutionalized means for peaceful dispute settlement and military protection against predatory neighboring polities or nomadic raiders, rulers did provide a vital and highly valued service for commoners. The experience or threat of a Hobbesian state of "Warre" can strongly encourage acceptance even of an exploitative exchange relationship.

But commoners' obedience to rulers also secured protection against their coercive power. Early states—and all subsequent ones—feature a huge difference between government and governed in the ability to mobilize violence. I agree with Weber that an effective ability to enforce commands by the use or threat of violence is the defining characteristic of the state, a necessary though not sufficient condition for its existence. Early states, in fact, most states, have featured cruel and extensive punishments for lawbreakers, and unspeakable tortures and grisly executions for suspected or actual opponents. In numerous early states the institution of ritual human sacrifice both reinforced the ideology of divine right and intimidated the populace by demonstrating rulers' control over life and death.

To this point I have proposed a biocultural explanation of how and why stratified power in the form of political authority first emerged in human societies. The ultimate "why" was the natural selective process of reproductive competition. Because of the particular abilities and ecological adaptations of our ancestors, this process took the form of an accelerating positive-feedback system strongly favoring individual and coalitional success in directing or controlling the lives of others. Changing ecological, demographic, and social circumstances made possible the creation of greater and greater imbalances of power within and between polities.

I am suggesting that human power-seeking evolved originally as a proximate means to the ultimate (evolutionary) end of enhancing individuals' chances for reproductive success. Even though rapid cultural evolution has produced a considerable loosening of the bonds between power-seeking and reproductive striving, power continues to be intrinsically rewarding but not intrinsically limited. It is additionally reinforced by extrinsic rewards of prestige and material gain, which also originally functioned in human evolution as proximate means to reproductive success. Not everyone's desire for effective power—"the capacity of some persons to produce intended and foreseen effects on others"[23]—flows into political channels, but there has never been a shortage of ambitious competitors for political eminence.

For populous, complex societies political power can be usefully compared to water: in predictable, appropriate amounts and in the proper places it is absolutely essential to life, but when superabundantly concentrated and uncontrolled it rages, crushes, and kills. The most appropriate and indispensable form of political power is wielded by authoritative governments, those accepted by the governed as truly legitimate, while regimes which feature enormously concentrated and monopolized power may flood the world with their people's blood.

Political legitimacy has become increasingly problematic in the modern age, since the ancient doctrines of divine-right, pseudonepotistic patriarchy became discredited by religious, political, and intellectual revolutions. No acceptable ideological basis for authority remains, from Locke to Lenin, except reciprocity: governments are legitimate only if they exercise power in the interests of the people.

It is tragically ironic, then, that the twentieth century, the temporal apex of enlightened modernity, has produced political leaders and elites who have slaughtered their own subjects on a scale unimaginable to the most arrogant and heartless despots of the premodern world. My deep conviction, given the actuality of Hitler, Stalin, Pol Pot, and their lesser imitators, is that the primary and overriding ethical problem of politics today is to prevent the worst—regimes which claim the right to kill anyone whom their rulers consider obstacles to the fulfillment of their movement's ideological destiny.

What does a biocultural evolutionary perspective imply about understanding and responding to this supreme challenge? It shouldn't, in my judgment, imply stunningly novel ideas but rather strong support for prudential observations in which theorists of diverse philosophical and religious persuasions already concur. Some critics will no doubt view this outcome as simply an effort to claim scientific authority in support of preexisting ideological bias. Obviously I disagree, but there is little to be gained by endless recriminatory exchanges about ideological distortion and blindness—though I would be among the last to deny their significance in most thinking and writing about politics.

At any rate, I shall focus on what I see as the two major implications for political ethics of my evolutionary understanding of politics. First, political utopianism is a delusion and a fraud and should never be endorsed as a legitimate rationale for wielding governmental power. Marxist-Leninist ideology has been the most audacious and influential modern representative of a utopian version of reciprocity: "from each according to his ability, to each according to his needs," in a system where harmonious cooperation and individual "goodness" render coercive government so superfluous that it "withers away." On the way to this social paradise the "revolutionary vanguard of the proletariat" must rule dictatorially to crush counterrevolutionaries at home and abroad. Only the Party represents the truly progressive, historic interests of the working class, who gratefully acknowledge its legitimacy in exchange for its leading the inexorable march of mankind toward communism.

The practical fraudulence of this rationale for irresponsible power has become so apparent—especially considering the actions of the Polish proletariat since August 1980—that a diminishing number even of professionally leftist Western intellectuals seem able to take it seriously. The Gulag Archipelago, the emergence of a new power-monopolizing class which arrogates to itself both material and nepotistic privileges,[24] and an enormous increase in the coercive and intrusive powers of government combine to produce a formidable absolutist system within which "might" clearly defines "right," whatever the official legitimating ideology.

In my judgment a natural selectionist view of human nature should at the very least inspire extreme skepticism about the possibility of sociopolitical utopia, and knowledge of enthnography and history should finish the job of relegating it forever to fantasy-land.

Since humans have evolved "to have individually separate interests, and to strive in relation to one another,"[25] egoistic and nepotistic biases are almost certain to influence our ideals and desires, and the interests and purposes of diverse individuals and their coalitional groups can never be completely harmonious and friction-free within any realistically conceivable social order. Both theoretical and practical wisdom combine in the irrefutable conclusion that "politics is the art of the possible; it is not a science of perfection."[26] Marxist-Leninist totalitarianism has demonstrated that a fraudulently promised "best" is enemy not simply of the good but of the humanly tolerable.

Second, political power is not self-limiting, and when not restrained in any practical way, it poses inherent dangers to a sizable proportion of its subjects: "The widespread diffusion of power is essential if that power is not to be abused."[27] Roughly speaking, the Lockean version of political reciprocity has been institutionalized in modern constitutional democracies. In these systems the constitution is supposed to embody a mutual agreement among the people (ideally, all adults) to be governed by institutions and processes which are kept responsive to popular opinion through freedom of expression and competitive elections. Laws and policies made in accord with constitutional requirements are to be accepted as legitimate, even by those who disagree with them. Particular individuals are given official power to make governmental decisions so long as they obey the law and do not displease enough voters to result in their dismissal from office.

Like all other kinds of political authority systems, constitutional democracies are subject to centrifugal pressures; if severe enough these can lead to destruction of the regime (Germany and Spain in the 1930s, Chile and Uruguay in the 1970s). Firm and widespread belief in its fundamental legitimacy may be essential to prevent inevitable conflicts and disagreements from escalating to a point where mutual distrust, hatred, and violent tactics put an end to constitutional processes and the rule of law.

Also, like all other systems, constitutional democracies are imperfect. Whatever they do will be considered unsatisfactory, unfair, even oppressive by some. But it would be wise to understand that that has been true of all human societies, even small stateless communities. From an evolutionary perspective, "While individuals try to choose behaviors which are optimal for their inclusive fitness, the overall group pattern of behavior is unlikely to be ideal for any one individual. Rather, it can be expected to represent the outcome of conflict and compromise among individuals with differing interests."[28]

To cultivate a political ethic of prudential moderation, of mature understanding and acceptance of the realities of irreducible human variety and conflicts of interests, and of a determination to cope with them indefinitely and interminably through the frustrating processes of mutual deliberation, compromise, and accommodation seems an appropriate outcome of viewing human political nature in evolutionary-historical depth. Compared to all other attempted ways of organizing political power in large-scale societies, constitutional democracies incorporate realistic means of limiting its exercise by institutionalizing the principle of "power checking power." If one evaluates regimes not by unattainable standards of perfection but by achievable criteria of political reciprocity, essential for protecting the most vital interests of the great majority of people, constitutional democracies possess enormous ethical value and therefore legitimacy.

Michael Oakeshott has wisely observed: "If it is boring to have to listen to dreams of others being recounted, it is insufferable to be forced to re-enact them . . . the conjunction of dreaming and ruling generates tyranny."[29] Political dreams, however seemingly benign and beautiful, can only generate nightmares of oppression, mass murder, and spiritual death when, instead of inspiring a humane prudence, they rationalize total power. A deep awareness of this truth must energize us to an unapologetic defense of constitutional democracy, with its many flaws and frustrations, against the champions of all utopian "final solutions."

Barry Cooper · *Ideology, Technology, and Truth*

"There is more bother," wrote Montaigne, "about interpreting the interpretations than about interpreting the things, and there are more books about books than about anything else. We do nothing but write glosses upon each other." In this essay I shall offer an interpretation of the things indicated in the title, but of necessity I must also say something about books. This is because the things have been modified by books, by words, speeches, or discourse. In addition, the things are also semiotic. They are interpretations or textual analogues. Accordingly, they require deciphering and representation in a way one hopes is persuasive. Having said that, however, I must add that the title, "Technology, Ideology, and Truth," is intended to indicate that the main topic is discourse, not hardware, pollution, or the social consequences of microchips.

I should say as well that this attempt to do honor to Professor Hallowell is in the form of an essay rather than a piece of research scholarship. An essay, as I understand it, tries to push an argument to its limit, with a minimum of qualification or second thoughts, and in a mood of considerable speculative confidence. An essay presents a perspective rather than new information. Much of the argument is, therefore, allusive. Where I have elaborated a contention elsewhere, I have been immodest enough to refer to my own work. Some years ago I had occasion to thank John Hallowell for turning me away from the more futile and sterile areas of political science. I still feel enormously grateful, though there is perhaps scarcely a trace of his prudence and common sense in this contribution.

The three terms of my title, and the context of their interplay, namely modern politics, are padded by assumptions that express but do not always clarify our everyday experiences of these realities. I would like to be clear about what I mean and so would offer a brief description of the two most obvious things, modern politics and technology. Next I will discuss ideology, its relationship to technology and modern politics, and a criticism of this complex technology-ideology-politics that is based on an ancient notion of truth. Finally I will consider a modern notion of truth that ties it to power. This final topic raises a new family of issues, I believe, but it does not point to their resolution.

Modern Politics

I begin with politics because, by a long tradition, politics provides the context for other practices. It will soon be clear, however, that I do not really believe that politics is a context for technology and ideology. Originally the political referred to the public doings of the polis, a community that included other communities such as the family or tribe or business alliance but was not included by any higher community such as an empire or community of religious believers, that is, a church. Today, one could just as easily say that technology provides the context of politics and ideology, or that ideology provides the context of technology and politics. But one must begin someplace. Like Plato's butchers we should aim to carve at the joints.

Our commonsense understanding of politics is bound up with activities of government or of the state. These activities may conveniently be divided into administrative matters and nonadministrative ones. Included in the first category are things such as the conventions regarding the regulation of traffic: green means go, etc. On the other hand, there are some Canadians, living in the administrative units of Quebec and Alberta, who believe that certain political acts are needed to preserve their particular and good way of being human against others whom they find menacing. These others are willing to sacrifice the particular qualities cherished by some residents of Quebec and Alberta in the name of higher goods, called "national unity," or "national energy policy," for example. It is perhaps foolishness to debate the justice or goodness of administrative conventions such as traffic lights, but it is essential to dispute questions of particular good. Perhaps it would be more accurate to say that questions of particular good are essentially disputable.

In any event it is clear to me at least that modern politics is heavily weighted to the side of administrative matters. Certainly in Canada our elections have become increasingly plebiscitarian with the real choices being confined to one or another set of administrators and with the actual experience of politics coming to resemble major sports events like the Stanley Cup. The cause of what several years ago Bernard Crick called the decline of politics[1] is, I would say, the relative absence of conflict concerning the highest political good or, in an ancient language, what constitutes the best regime. For nearly all of our fellow citizens and, indeed, for most of the politically visible population of the planet, the highest political good is the creation of the technological society. The most fundamental premise of that society is that the overcoming of fortune or chance, which in the past had taken on the appearance of capricious gods and a wild nature, is the highest human good. This activity, the overcoming of chance, is carried on by the application of the natural and human sciences to external things.

The most accurate and comprehensive name for the regime that is presently being actualized by technical activities is the universal and homogeneous state. In my opinion this regime was exhaustively described,and its genesis accounted for, in Hegel's political science. Hegel, I believe, following Alexandre Kojève,[2] identified the germ of that state with the Napoleonic Empire whose consolidation he witnessed at the battle of Jena in 1806, the day after he finished the *Phenomenology*, a book he identified as the introduction and first volume of *the* System of Science. In the *Phenomenology* Hegel described a state where, in principle citizenship is held by free and equal men and women, where everyone but a few idiots or criminally insane persons would be open to the wisdom presented in natural and social or human science. There are additional interesting features of the universal and homogeneous state—its citizens are necessarily atheists, for example—but the aspect I wish to emphasize now is that this necessary openness to the wisdom of natural and human science promises that men will be ruled by a common, indeed universal, standard of reason and not the passions, loves, or particular quirks of other men. Because all men would be reasonable (apart, as I said, from idiots and the criminally insane) they would agree about what is good and dispute only the means of quicker or more perfect actualization. Consequently our common life would be—and I would say, has become—increasingly ordered and organized by administration or by administrative techniques.

Technology

Secondly, there is the thing indicated by the term technology.[3] It is a modern neologism coined from the two Greek words *techne* and *logos*. A techne was a kind of production, that is, literally, a leading forth, but of a special kind, one that is mediated by human or other agency. For the Greeks techne was also a kind of knowledge, the knowledge of leading things forth: tables can be led forth or produced from lumps of wood by persons who know carpentry, and so on. It was in principle concerned with things that might or might not be: lumps of wood could be burned to keep warm, for example, instead of being used to make tables.

In contrast to technical knowledge was theoretical or scientific knowledge, what the Greeks called *episteme*. Episteme was concerned not with what might be but with what must be. What must be, they said, was timeless, without beginning or end. I must confess I have a great deal of difficulty understanding what that might have meant after I have read books that claim persuasively to describe the first three minutes of the universe. The Greeks, however, concluded that there was a proper distinction between theory and technique or between science and art, to use the Latinate equivalents. This distinction was sustained by the real difference between the eternal and the temporal, between what must be and what might be.

Our modern understanding of scientific or theoretical knowledge, in contrast, includes an element of making. For example, scientific knowledge of disease depends upon instruments such as stethoscopes and microscopes and body-scanners, all of which are fabricated. And in turn the fabrication of these machines depends upon the scientific knowledge of optics, acoustics, physics, and so on. This copenetration of scientific knowledge and making is a historical novelty. Or, to put it the other way around, the old distinction of theory and technique is no longer made. Consider what we mean by technology in contrast to what the Greeks might have meant.

A logos, for the Greeks, was a coherent or systematic discourse: it hung together and made sense. Now obviously there are coherent discourses about the arts, but that is not what we mean by technology. On the contrary, the copenetration of art or technique and science or logos has changed the very nature of the arts by means of the speeches. To take the same example, the art of medicine has been utterly altered by the speeches of chemists and biologists and physicists and all their amalgams. And the reverse is also true: new inventions—think of a linear accelerator—make possible new speeches, by particle physicists for example.

Moreover, the new arts and the new speeches call forth thoughts about them. Mostly these thoughts are in the form of questions, which is understandable since we are seeing novelties and are curious about them. But we are more than curious. The invention of magnificent powers of making and unmaking has occurred at the same time as the makers have seemingly become ignorant of what is worth making or unmaking. Power and ignorance also apparently copenetrate. For example, supposing it were possible to make a race of human slaves who were content to be slaves and found all meaning in life through service to their masters. They could be identified easily, say, by having a certain color of skin. Most of us would call such people, if we called them people, monsters. Monster is a term that derives from the Latin word for warning; if we saw these slaves as monsters, or if we called the making of them monstrous, we would know already that it must not be done. It is not at all clear to me that we have that knowledge. In fact, I would say that the imperatives of technology make such knowledge impossible or meaningless. Robert Oppenheimer sought some solace, or perhaps justification, after the explosion of the atomic bomb by quoting the Vedas. Beforehand he remarked: "If the experiment is sweet one must proceed with it." He was expressing a new imperative that had nothing to do with the old Greek knowledge of what must or must not be. One might say that, knowing only what might be, we must make it so.

The Greeks, with their puzzling notion of eternity, never had to face this problem because they knew clear limits to what must be made and unmade. Some things must not be made and so were termed unnatural. Nature, then, was somehow connected to what was timeless, and good was connected to appropriateness or, you might say, naturalness. With the copenetration of arts and science, that is, with the advent of technology, the authority of the scientific account of nature has dissolved the sense that used to be included in the ancient knowledge. One knows the objects of nature, in part because one has made them. To put it another way, because modern men experience no restraints in nature, we have learned to do what we will. All limits are therefore temporary or historical, not eternal. They are problems crying out for solution, challenges to the will, not mysteries to be respected or feared or reverenced.[4]

Ideology

The third topic to be described is, of course, ideology. The term, as everybody knows, was coined by Destutt de Tracy to describe what he called the science of ideas.[5] To his enlightened mind, an "idea" was something that eventually could be traced to sensation. He thought Descartes had made a serious error. In place of *cogito ergo sum* he set a new tag: *sentio ergo sum*. Ideology was intended to be a science that overcame what were seen to be the abstractions of metaphysics and the unreliability of opinion.

Seldom, however, are the circumstances under which the new science was conceived given proper emphasis, namely the Terror of 1793–94. De Tracy was incarcerated in the town hall at Auteuil and then in a former church at Carmes. Each Monday for several months one or more of his fellow prisoners, some of them his friends, left jail to be sliced apart by the guillotine. He appealed his doom, protesting quite rightly his loyalty to the Revolution. He was, however, also an aristocrat and something of a snob. (Before the Revolution he had commissioned a genealogy that traced his origin to 1419 when four Scottish brothers named Stutt crossed the Channel to serve as archers in the army of the Dauphin against the English during the Hundred Years War.) When in jail he read Condillac and Locke and formulated in the spring of 1794 a discourse that would apply to society the science of Lavoisier, who had been guillotined on May 8th, and the equations of Condorcet, who had died in jail on March 27th. He himself was scheduled to take his last walk on the eleventh of Thermidor, July 29th. But on the ninth of Thermidor Robespierre was overthrown and citizen Tracy was saved.

The circumstances attending the birth of ideology remind one of another celebrated jailing, that of Socrates. Socrates, moreover, once called philosophy the practice of dying. There are, of course, several differences that ought to be borne in mind. De Tracy was not executed and Socrates was. De Tracy lacked a Plato and took upon himself the role of explicating the experience of being in jail awaiting death. Socrates appeared to be far more at peace than some of his friends who visited him before he died. De Tracy was so upset by what had happened to him that when he finally emerged from jail early in October his hair had turned completely white.

Ideology, then, was not only linguistically modern, but owed its genesis in part at least to a thoroughly modern institution, terror. Taken alone, the Terror of the Jacobins seemed to be meaningless: the *ancien régime* had fallen and with it had gone tradition, religion, and stability. There was no conformity since there was nothing, neither community nor state, to conform to. Wordsworth's sentiment,

> Bliss was it in that dawn to be alive
> But to be young was very heaven

suggests the experience of open potentiality that unrestricted terror inspires in those who, generally for a short while, make use of it. At the same time, sheer potentiality amounts to complete emptiness, what Hegel called the absolute freedom of the void, the negative action that accomplishes only the fury of destruction. He compared it to slicing up heads of cabbage or slurping a draught of water.[6] From this I would conclude that ideology is a symbol that both expressed the experience of meaningless death and was designed to render the approach of nothingness meaningful.

The Terror and the appearance of meaningless negation was superseded by the Napoleonic state. As mentioned earlier, I believe the genesis and nature of this state were described by Hegel's political science. In developing his own discourse, Hegel said many extravagant things about Napoleon and his work. Napoleon, however, said nothing about Hegel and some very nasty things about de Tracy, his anti-clericalism, and his proposals to reform French education.[7] Perhaps that was to be expected. It should not, however, obscure the fact that ideology was, from the start, a practical business. In his address to the Class of Moral and Political Sciences on April 21, 1796, de Tracy stressed that the aim of all science, and especially the master science of ideology, was "the knowledge of effects and their practical consequences." The connotations of the term ideology have changed since de Tracy's day but the essential feature, its practicality, has not.

Before proceeding further, I would like to gather up a few threads of the argument. In general I am concerned with discourses about things. Discourses, I believe, are part of the world rather than reflections of or on it, because the world has its nervous system constituted by what is said in it. The horizon of practical activity, following Hegel, is the universal and homogeneous state, a political order that gives primacy to rules and administrative technique. Technology, of which administrative technique is a part, has resulted from the copenetration of knowledge and making and is deployed against what used to be called human and nonhuman nature. It does so in a manner that is autonomous and self-augmenting, and consequently is unlimited. There exists, however, a limitation to the individual, namely death. It was from the experience of that limitation, during the Jacobin terror, that ideology came into being.

In a general way that indicates the things. Now one must consider the discourses that provide interpretations of this combination of unrestricted and unrestrictable technology and meaningless death within the universal and homogeneous state.

Pagan Philosophy and Biblical Religion

I shall outline three interpretative strategies that attempt to come to grips with the problem. I should say as well that I am not so fascinated by Hegel that I am fixated on the number three. There may be other options than those I am about to discuss.

The first amounts to something like a rearticulation of Greek philosophy, say that of Plato. Our lives would then be ordered according to experiences historically antecedent to ideology and would be centered in institutions such as the polis, which would be understood to be natural and for which we are inherently fitted. We would, moreover, stand in awe before an eternal and divine nature. Pollution would be a spiritual reality requiring ritual purgation, not a material one requiring more technology. A variation on this theme involves what Nietzsche called Platonism for the many.

Consider the argument and plea of George Grant. Ideology, he said, is a particular characteristic of modern progressive empires, which here is used as a synonym for the universal and homogeneous state.[8] It has arisen because of certain presuppositions concerning that state. Before the modern era, before the highest good was conceived as the overcoming of chance and the actualization of that state, the most thoughtful Western human beings were of the opinion that the practice of Biblical religion and Greek philosophy were necessary in order for tolerably decent communities to exist. Moreover, philosophy and religion were distinguished. Sometimes they were radically separated and sometimes they were harmonized, but always the relation between them was considered complex and difficult to understand. It was a matter for deep reflection and very prudent speech.

One of the marks of modern thought, according to Grant, is the belief that philosophy should absorb religious revelation. Here again I would emphasize the importance of Hegel's science of wisdom as a synthesis of what used to be called philosophy and religion. However, to revert to Grant's terms, the imperialism of philosophy was both a success and a failure. There was, he would say, something unnatural in the attempt. All the clever philosophers could do was criticize and ridicule the old religion. They could not obliterate what religion expressed and fulfilled, which Grant called a need for reverencing. The need for reverencing, he implied, is inherent in human nature. And when the traditional reverences were destroyed by philosophy, ideology filled the void and answered this need. Ideologies, he concluded, are surrogate religions pretending to be philosophies or surrogate philosophies trying to replace a dissolved or eclipsed reverence. Either way they are ersatz.

Accordingly, they do great harm to our public life by masking the proper or true or even natural positions of philosophy and religion. They deny that reverence is central to human life but at the same time they slip reverence in the side door in the form of race, class, nation, progress, or the state. But these things are not worthy of reverence, according to Grant. They are idolatrous. They claim to give a reasonable account, a knowledge, of what is going on in the world but do not give it. They destroy both common sense and moderation, which according to the now displaced classical pagan philosophy were the great preservers of public decency. Ideologies are not just religious idolatry, they are what Plato would have called lies in the psyche.

What, then, is to be done? The future, Grant said, stretches before us as trackless, and the chief compasses of the Western past (Biblical revelation and classical pagan philosophy) have ceased to be readable by most of us. It is, therefore, foolish to anticipate that future in any detail. Nevertheless, if the question of how to live well is a permanent one, as Grant maintains it is, a certain pattern of events can be anticipated, of which a prelude was found in the late 1960s.[9] The politics of administration attempts to foreclose any discussion by its understanding of reasonableness as technique. If, nevertheless, the reality of administrative politics is experienced by people—Grant calls them those of noble minds and open hearts—as not living well, and if reason in its full, Greek philosophic sense is not available because, as he said, it is a compass we cannot read, then we may expect ideological responses. As the universal and homogeneous state is ever more completely actualized, those who find in it no comfort and no meaning other than as a threat and a menace, will embrace ever more urgent and illicit ideologies, and eventually will find meaning only in the practice of violence. Here one should ponder the meaning of the monstrous novels of Anthony Burgess.[10]

Grant was not pleased with what he anticipated. He feared both sides, and was at a loss to know how to respond. On the one hand, he said, one must respect the necessities of public order even if that order appears as an administrative tyranny backed by the boundless potential of physiological and psychological technique. On the other hand, one must respect the rebellions against that order, for spontaneity is a manifestation of human good. Yet those rebellions are expressed in the form of illicit, unnatural, and, he anticipated, even mad ideologies.

So one asks again: what is to be done? This time I will quote from the concluding essay, called "A Platitude," to *Technology and Empire*. In fact they are the concluding words. "In such a situation of uncertainty," Grant said, "it would be lacking in courage to turn one's face to the wall, even if one can find no fulfillment in working for or celebrating the dynamo. Equally it would be immoderate and uncourageous and perhaps unwise to live in the midst of our present drive, merely working in it and celebrating it, and not also listening or watching or simply waiting for intimations of deprival which might lead us to see the beautiful as the image, in the world, of the good."[11]

One recalls that those who listen may hear the word and that the original watchers were the theorists of ancient Greece. And if the compasses are truly unreadable, and revelation and philosophy are irretrievably lost, then we must wait to see or hear again, by learning of our deprivals. If we find them monstrous we should also recall that only a benevolent nature or god would warn us. Grant's powers of analysis, his open-hearted honesty and his courage are admirable, but one is not necessarily persuaded by his remarks. His allusions to the events of the late 1960s, for example, are far too sombre. The gaiety is missing. As Dr. Leavis would say, the proper response to such discourse is "yes, but."[12] I will try to voice that "but" in a few minutes.

Values Chatter

A second interpretative strategy is probably more familiar than Grant's, since its language is that of modernity and social science. The centerfold of modern social science is the celebrated distinction between judgments about facts and judgments about values, and the doctrine that the scientist deals with the former only, translating the latter into psychological facts. Reason, they say, cannot judge what is valuable and, likewise, what is valuable is necessarily unreasonable. When this hermeneutic was given its present form by Max Weber, the purpose was to transcend the intense ideological conflicts of his German homeland. When his younger contemporaries introduced the procedure to the new world it served a specific ideology, liberal-democratic pluralism. In this way, the universities became servants to the private and public corporations that constitute the apparatus of power in liberal pluralist democracy. These corporations are the means by which the great task of overcoming chance and building the universal and homogeneous state is organized, at least in the West. The rhetoric of pluralism and the irrationality of values has permitted a privatized but persistent individualism. From within this understanding of reasonable discourse the second interpretative strategy has been developed.

The argument is simplicity itself. The values that are actualized in the world by our technological society are in conflict with what are usually referred to as human values. If we are to maintain the quality of life, it is said, we must pursue certain ideals that ensure the creation of a fuller humanity. We need new goals and objectives by which to guide our collective lives. People who talk this way are quite possibly high-minded and sincere. One must, however, pierce the veil of good feelings and insist upon the unpleasant reality that he who talks of values and ideals, of building a humane society or achieving the goal of a fuller humanity uses a rhetoric indistinguishable from the expressions of technological will. Indeed, the reluctance to challenge directly the iron circle of technology amounts to a kind of moralizing sadism cloaked by the hypocritical language of liberation and the never-redeemed promise of actualized freedom.

The advantage of immediate intelligibility, of being in touch with the language and experience of technology, which was apparently absent from Grant's reliance on philosophy and revelation, this advantage is wiped away by the complicity of the critic in sustaining what he pretends to wish to change. Grant himself has made a splendid analysis of the statement "the computer does not impose on us the ways it should be used."[13] There he showed that this statement was full of an absence of thought. It is not news to learn that computers in fact can be used only in one way, to store and process information. The essence of information is its homogeneity: rules of classification, of identity and difference, can operate only within the n-dimensional flatness of a conceptually homogeneous space. It cannot, therefore, be used neutrally with respect to heterogeneity, with respect, for example, to autochthony. Accordingly, the statement hides the fact that the computer's capabilities limit its use to homogenizing ways, so that the meaning of homogenization is forgotten. The reason for this forgetfulness is that the very terms that suggest that the computer is a machine that we can bend to our will stem from the reasoning that builds computers in the first place. That reasoning is incapable of understanding properly its own apparent object because it is a part of the form of reasoning embodied in the object.

The problem with the modern ideological criticism of ideology and technology is exactly the contrary to the problem of interpreting madness. Madness has been deprived of its language by psychiatry so that while one can speak of madness, madness itself has no speech of its own. With the dialectically concentrated complex of technology, ideology, and politics it seems as impossible to speak in a nonideological and nontechnical language as to entertain seriously that the universal and homogeneous state is not the best, and so, necessary, regime. Accordingly it may seem that one is reduced to encountering various voices of silence, like Grant's, or the incoherence of humane ideologies.

Truth and Power

I come, then, to the third interpretative strategy. If it is successful it will be intelligible to our modern understanding, unlike the evocation of eternity, and it will be coherent and insightful, unlike the chatter about values. This is more easily said than done, so what I have to say is highly tentative.

Let us return to the Ideologues of the Directorate and empire. In the same speech to the Institute that I quoted earlier, de Tracy said that ideology was the basis of grammar, which was the science of communicating ideas, of logic, which was the science of combining them and reaching new truths, of education, which was the science of forming men, of morality, which was the science of regulating desires, and finally it was the basis "for the greatest of arts, that of regulating society in such a way that man finds there the most help and the least possible annoyance from his own kind."[14] De Tracy's colleague Servan stated more explicitly that ideology was a technique of control. The mind provided the surface upon which power could be inscribed: bodies could be made to submit because they were controlled by minds, and minds were directed by ideas. "A stupid despot," he said, "may constrain his slaves with iron chains; but a true politician binds them even more strongly by the chain of their own ideas; it is at the stable point of reason that he secures the end of the chain; this link is all the stronger in that we do not know of what it is made and we believe it to be our own work; despair and time eat away the bonds of iron and steel, but they are powerless against the habitual union of ideas. They can only tighten it still more; and on the soft fibres of the brain is founded the unshakeable base of the soundest of Empires."[15] The anchor at the end of the binding chain of ideas and embedded, so to speak, in those soft tissues, was reason.

One can always say: "No; that is not reason. That is ideology. Reason is disinterested; it provides access to truth not power." But such a reason belongs precisely to classical pagan philosophy, to theory, to that now unreadable compass that is said somehow once upon a time to have charted the ways of eternity. The burden of its glorious past is what seems to make it unconnected with modern technology except, perhaps, as a means of proving that technology is unnatural, impossible, and must not be. Instead of pursuing the implications of classical pagan reason into regions increasingly remote from modernity, let us follow the implication of de Tracy and Servan: power and knowledge form an ensemble.

The interconnectedness and copenetration of power and knowledge or of power and truth has recently been studied by Michel Foucault and it is upon some of his formulations that I am relying.[16] If knowledge is immanent to relations of power, it neither reflects nor distorts them. It is just as impossible for power to be exercised in the absence of knowledge as it is that knowledge not engender power. They directly imply one another. Accordingly, knowledge can never be pure but is inherently political, not because it may have political consequences or uses, but because its condition of possibility is a specific configuration of power. No scientific discourse, no knowledge, or if you like, no theory, can create its own conditions of possibility because these are found in power-relations. Knowledge is not neutral or objective or true: it is legitimate or illegitimate according to a particular set of power-relations.

Knowledge and truth are produced by discourse, but the production of discourse is controlled, selected, organized, and redistributed within society according to procedures whose purpose has nothing to do with knowledge or truth, and everything to do with averting danger and managing unpredictabilities.[17] There are overt procedures of exclusion such as censorship and prohibition, but there are also extremely subtle forms of exclusion that come from the division of true and false. In this instance, it is not a question *within* any particular discourse, of an arbitrary division between true and false. On the contrary, then, there is nothing arbitrary. But if you ask why do we wish to know, where does this will to know come from, then a kind of exclusion appears inasmuch as the operations of knowing are an imposition of will. Historically speaking, true discourse, truth-saying, meant meting out justice and giving each his rightful share. Greek poetic prophecy announced what would happen and thereby contributed to the fabric of fate. Between Hesiod and Plato truth ceased to be what discourse *was* and turned into a property of what was *said*. It seemed no longer to be linked to the exercise of power. And yet even Platonic truth-tellers rely on institutions of exclusion—libraries, pedagogy, books, academies, laboratories, and the value set by our, or any other, social system upon knowledges, some of which, like carpentry or computer programming may be seen to be outside the constraints of truth.

There are also controls internal to the production of discourse. These include received commentaries, which say again what has already been said, and by that activity refine and regulate its meaning; there is the notion of an author, which acts as a principle by which writings may be unified and deprived of their heterogeneity; and there are disciplines, quasi-anonymous bodies of propositions that are held to constitute a theory or a set of rules or methods for the production of truth. A third group of controls determine the conditions under which discourse is employed. There are ritual qualifications that must be met before someone can appear as a speaker; there are fellowships of discourse, learned societies that are not open to just anyone, where speeches are exchanged in a specialized tongue; there is, finally, the appropriation of discourse through educational institutions, which serve as the political mechanism by which legitimate speeches are maintained and modified.

With all these procedures in operation, a general law or norm of discourse is produced that is equipped with an internally defined rationality. This rationality is the principle of their expression and therefore constitutes a denial of their particular, restricted, and refined character. One is therefore directed away from an inner core of meaning that is mysteriously invested with the value of eternal truth to the conditions of possibility of a discourse, to the practice that speech imposes on things, to its violation of their being. Truth and knowledge, which are the products of discursive practice, are not the offspring of protracted solitude nor the reward of free spirits soaring in the empyrean. Truth and knowledge are produced by constraint and induce power. They are weapons by which society manages itself.

Every society has its own regime of truth comprised of four typical elements: specific kinds of discourse that are acceptable and legitimate and that function as true mechanisms, methods by which true and false statements are distinguished, techniques that are considered valuable and useful in acquiring truth, and lastly statuses and positions of people who are tasked with saying what is to count as true.[18] In short, truth is the ensemble of rules according to which the true and the false are separated and specific effects of power are attached to the true. It is a system of ordered procedures for the regulation, production, distribution, circulation, and operation of statements. Accordingly, it is linked directly to systems of power that produce and sustain it and to effects of power that it induces and by which it is extended.

The existence of a regime of truth alters the meaning of ideology and of what it is to do philosophy. The contemporary usage of the term ideology, which owes a great deal to Marx, misses the point. The problem is not one of distinguishing ideology from science or truth or knowledge but of seeing how the effects of truth are produced in discursive practices. Likewise the philosophers or "intellectuals" cannot be the disinterested conscience of society, and their claims to universality are necessarily fraudulent.[19] Like everybody else they can speak only of what they experience and know. It is for this reason that Foucault has spoken of his work as archeology or genealogy. Like his dead friend Nietzsche his genealogy is grey, a great contrast with the blue skies of the great ideas.[20] But at the same time, that greyness liberates one from the crushing power of the great truths, the great systems, the great syntheses, by turning hypothetical, playful, and *frölisch*.

These remarks have some bearing on the matter of technology or ideology. To begin with, the contemporary, modern regime of truth is centred on scientific discourses and the institutions that produce them. These discourses are the object of constant political and economic demand. They are diffused and consumed by means of educational and informational apparatuses under the control of a few political and economic organizations, the universities, the private and crown corporations, the media, and the government. More importantly, this regime is animated with a will to knowledge whose cruelty, viciousness and general malice was brought to our attention a century ago by Nietzsche. In *The Dawn* (1881, para. 429), he wrote: "The desire for knowledge has been transformed among us to a passion that fears no sacrifice, that fears nothing but its own extinction. It may be that mankind will eventually perish from this passion for knowledge." The will to truth had no limit, so it practiced violence upon those who were happy in their ignorance and destroyed the illusions by which humanity had protected itself. It did so in the name of reason, the sole and imperious sovereign of the mind. It did so by declaring unreason to be madness and locking it up. That is, the same act of violence constituted at the same time scientific discourse and the lunatic asylum. It covers itself with the name of progress.

I would conclude, as did George Grant, with a platitude. We know all too well the benefits of technology and the bountiful life lived within the horizon of the universal and homogeneous state. The mechanisms of knowledge and power do not cease to inform us. It is more difficult and subversive to see how we are deprived, because the triumph of reason has silenced, disciplined, or normalized unreason. No one can be willfully modern and live according to the systems of meaning provided by myth, Biblical revelation, or philosophy. No longer does it make sense to subscribe to the old philosophical tradition wherein one is supposed to be "on the side" of truth or "in favor" of truth. That dream has been all dreamed out. With the end of history and the end of that picture gallery of representations and powers that Hegel chronicled and accounted for, with the advent, that is, of the present world that was inherited long before we were born, the purpose of thought has come to be the discovery of the status of truth and the political and economic role it plays. One thinks today by undertaking that discursive practice that accounts for the way that truth is geared to the restraints of scarcity, but also to the exuberance of public recognition, which accounts for the way truth is able to justify the invisibility of those it eclipses but also the glory of those it exalts. In a large measure this means no more than expressing what is our common experience. But one must do so by unblocking what a subtle system of power and truth, power and reason, has invalidated by rendering too familiar what we pretentiously call knowledge.

The special problem for a genuine historian of the present, for one whom, even more pretentiously, we call a thinker, is the temptation of authority, the temptation to become the issuer of sober words and dispenser of deep judgments. It matters not a whit whether those words are those of an apologist or of a "conscience to power" since either way they will be ground into the reinforcements of reason. Style is therefore important because it can function as a rejection of the language of reason whose standardized, measured monotony strives to impart a tone of objectivity and truth. What one actually says about one's experiences will vary according to one's opportunity, disposition, talent, courage, intelligence, and so on. Some sort of limit, however, is set, it seems to me by the following analogy of circumstance. In the early Christian centuries people wondered about the return of Christ and what to do in the meantime. Nowadays the second coming seems to be that of revolution. And yet, so many revolutions have been betrayed. The messages of the modern synoptic gospellers have been seared into our being even as we await the transfigurative discourse of a contemporary St. John, who we shrewdly suspect cannot possibly exist.

Gerhart Niemeyer · *Communism and the Notion of the Good*

The question, "Communism: is it or isn't it a threat?" continues to disturb us. It has been phrased in this manner: "Do they behave like human beings? Certainly. Do they behave like Russians? Indeed. Do they behave like Communists?" If the last question is answered affirmatively, it brings up further questions: "Often?" "always?" "occasionally?" "typically?" and, above all: "What does 'behaving like a Communist' mean?" This last question should be narrowed down, for our present purposes, to: "In what way is Communist politics moved by goodness?" This formula already structures the answer, since it removes the problem from the ground of psychology. To the extent to which the practices of Communists differs significantly from that of other human beings we must look for an explanation not in conditions but in ideas, the ideas shaped into an ideological system by Marx and Lenin. Both insisted that ideas and practice should be united, that the point of ideas is not to explain the world but to change it, and that the appropriate type of practice must be revolutionary.

There is no denying that a strong moral element is present in the Communist call for action. The call draws its power from both moral indignation and a moral vision. The initial appeal of communism to outsiders is always moral. On the other hand, the fear of communism is also primarily moral. It is not primarily a concern of rich men for their wealth. Quite the contrary: rich men have tended either to observe an attitude of indifference toward communism or else have sympathized with it, from a distance or, on occasion, even actively. Nor is it an aversion to rapid change as such. Among those who fear communism have been many socialists who themselves have initiated systemic changes of society. What is feared is, first, Communist terror, Communist unscrupulousness, Communist untrustworthiness. Deeper down we find the fear of Communist godlessness and of the "public falsehood." If, then, the initial Communist impulse has been moral, the Communists have encountered a resistance no less moral. This induces us to take a closer look at the moral element in Communist theory and practice.

A modern movement appeals from the later Marx to "the early Marx," supposedly the "humanist Marx." As we pick up Marx's early writings what strikes us is the negative form of his morality. His emphatic concern is with "critique," a watchword of all left-Hegelians. "Critique" was exalted as the process of negation which, as the "negation of the negation," would open the way to higher realities. Among the left-Hegelians Marx alone pushed on, from "Critical Critique" to "radical critique" and "practical critique," i.e., revolution. In other words, he moved from an epistemic negation to practical-subversive negation. The present system, he wrote, "dehumanizes" men, the "feeling of man's dignity [has] vanished from the world," and thus the world is in "a dream" from which it must be "awakened." "Social truth" cannot be found in men's consciousness but can be "developed everywhere out of this conflict of the political state with itself."[1]

Marx's critique of "the political state" became, almost immediately, a total critique of society, as he rejected a "*merely* political revolution" on the grounds that it "would leave the pillars of the house standing."[2] Moreover, he praised the French "critical and utopian socialists and Communists," whose ideas he in general rejected, for "the critical element" in their writings: "They attack every principle of existing society. Hence they are full of the most valuable materials for the enlightenment of the working class."[3] This emphasis leads Marx to his concept of a "negative representative of society" as the carrier of the revolution. It must be "a class with radical chains, a class in civil society that is not of civil society, a class that is the dissolution of all classes, a sphere of society having a universal character because of its universal suffering and claiming no *particular* right because *no particular wrong* but *wrong in general* is perpetrated on it."[4] The burden of the accusation could not be graver. It amounts to deriving evil as such from the institutional structure of society. The tone of the indictment reminds one of the prophets of Israel, and thus a moral standpoint is strongly implied.

It is implied but never explicitly set forth. In the case of Israel's prophets, their starting point is the covenant between Yahweh and his people. Yahweh is the God whose concern is righteousness, and his commandments are no mere implication but a clearly defined way of life. Marx, who had embraced Feuerbach's "critique of religion," would not draw his indignation from a divine source. But when speaking of "dehumanization" he certainly invokes something akin to "human nature" in Aristotle's sense. He quotes Aristotle in the context. His total critique of society, however, has the side-effect that it negates not merely the present but all of the past, and thereby eliminates any experience of human nature. If no humanity has ever been actual, Marx might dream of a human nature but could not claim any knowledge of it. He did say explicitly that he hoped to discover "the social truth" in the course of revolutionary practice. In terms of the historical record, however, Communists must profess agnosticism with regard to human nature.

The "implied moral standpoint," then, has no basis other than that of radical negation, the total critique of society. The good is chiefly seen as the opposite of that which now exists. Present society is bourgeois and capitalistic, so the good must be proletarian and socialistic. Hence, as Bakunin put it, destruction is to be held a "creative force." Goodness is not now, nor has it been, but will be, after radical revolution, in the future. On the other hand, not much is known about the future, but, since it will be utterly different from the inhuman present, it must by definition be good. The resulting moral justification chiefly supports the historical struggle as "absolute" (Lenin's term). The struggle as such carries hope, since by virtue of the total critique of present society it is necessarily a struggle against what is seen as wholly inhuman, unjust, and alienated: an apocalyptic war against wickedness as such, to the end of its final elimination.

Fourteen hundred years before Marx, Augustine had criticized the "present society" of Rome in terms as radical as those of Marx, but without losing the foundation of his positive morality. A total critique of society, then, does not always have the undesirable side-effects that showed up in Marx's case. One is led to inquire into Hegel's system as the likely cause of this devouring negativity. Hegel made history into the ultimate reality of everything. In all the great cultures of the world, however, morality seems to have been experienced as an aspect of some ultimate "givenness." One thinks of the Hindu concepts of *ṛta* and *dharma*, of the Chinese *tao*, of Plato's *Ideas* and Aristotle's *Nature*, of the Stoics' *Cosmos* and the Hebrews' *Creation*. Buddhism, it is true, does look for a *Nirvana* that can be seen as the annihilation of everything given, but still the Boddhisattva's *compassion* is positive goodness.

Nor is this "givenness" denied by the obvious fact that good character requires a process of formation. For learning, not only of good moral habits but of other kinds of habits as well, seems to be attended by an intuition of rightness. A child is taught words, and of a sudden begins to speak entire sentences never heard before. An athlete is shown the various motions of hurling a ball but then, all at once, intuits how the parts combine into a single motion. A musician faces many notes, but the wholeness of the music comes to him beyond these particulars. A detective sees the unity of a multitude of facts, in a flash which has no explanation. Such experiences are at the back of the manifold symbols of givenness, e.g., the idea that knowledge is above all memory. Morality, then, is conceived as attached to such constants as gods, essences, nature, being. More important, though, "the good" itself, i.e., its content, is experienced as something given rather than something consciously invented or subjectively preferred, so that Plato refused to define it. In the common law tradition we still say that the judge is supposed to find the right measure rather than to make it up. Nor is this experience of givenness incompatible with the philosophy of process. If Aristotle had no trouble in conceiving a nature as the development of an entelechy, the perception of a chain of events is likewise not incompatible with structure.

All givenness vanishes, however, when such concepts as being, nature, creation are replaced by history. History differs from "process" in kind, process being eminently analyzable in relations and successions, while history is characterized by the play of countless singularities whose ensemble defies any kind of universal concept. In no ways can history serve as a substitute for such a concept as, e.g., nature. In its Hegelian meaning, which underlies most of contemporary thinking, it stands not for "process" but rather for "coming to be," a coming to be not of existing things, but rather a coming to be culminating in some perfected future kind of being. Thus it both requires and entails a claim to "knowledge" of the future. This is not the kind of knowledge that enables one to predict the outcome of an ongoing project, but rather knowledge of a future condition that contains all of history's meaning.

All the same this humanly foreknown future sheds no light. It does appear bright, but its brightness casts deep shadows over past and present human existence. As for the past, it tends to disappear in the abyss of "not at all"; as for the present, it lingers in the twilight of "not yet" (cf. Ernest Bloch, *The Principle of Hope*). Thus Camus wrote: "Nothing is pure: that is the cry which convulses our period. Impurity, the equivalent of history, is going to become the rule, and the abandoned earth will be delivered to naked force, which will decide whether or not man is divine."[5] At this point defenders of Hegel and Marx like to point to the Christian faith which believes in a Kingdom of God yet to come. The comparison, however, is misplaced. The Kingdom of God is also "at hand," and the faithful endeavor to live now in a manner worthy of it. The Kingdom of God was "opened to all believers" by Christ's death on the cross, so that it is also indissolubly linked to the past. The Kingdom of God is both given and coming. It bears no likeness to a reality which is supposed to have no being at all until some future generation will be able to say that it has "become."

In that perspective nothing can be said to be real except becoming, the coming to be of being which is not yet. That becoming was given by Hegel the character of negation, and by Marx that of revolutionary struggle. Now a struggle that carries the becoming of reality is of such transcending importance that it must divide all humanity into two opposing groups. On one side is the very small group of those who, possessing the key knowledge of the ideology, have anchored their consciousness in mankind's future, who are therefore conscious of their own "historical mission" and, by virtue of this consciousness, detached from all "spontaneity." Aware of that which is to come they form "the vanguard," not merely of the proletariat or even of mankind, but of history itself. On them lies the burden of bringing about mankind's destiny. The others, bulking in numbers, are all counted as the vanguard's opponents, not necessarily by intention, rather by situational definition. Social origin makes them into opponents, spontaneity makes them into opponents, so does attachment to the present, or even a merely passive trust in history's self-movement; for the vanguard, having apprehended what is yet to come, must actively lead. The struggle being defined in such terms, nothing remains that these two groups could have in common. A Manichaean gulf divides them, as the forces of light from the forces of darkness. Again, this terminology bears no comparison with "children of light" and "children of darkness," which says something about subjective orientations that may yield to conversion, while the Communist concept of embattled class forces postulates a situation that can change only in the moment of the vanguard's total victory.

Now one of the basic assumptions of morality is an acknowledgement of sameness, or equality, between humans. Martin Buber has insisted that the well-known Biblical commandment should be translated: "and (love) thy neighbor as *one like* thyself." A realization that we share an ontic or transcendent equality—whether we call it "the human condition," "human nature," a "divine image," or a common "fatherhood of God"—lies at the root of what Bergson has called "absolute morality." This is the attitude of the "open soul," which experiences obligation beyond what is relatively owed to a particular society.

> Suppose we say that it embraces all humanity: we should not be going too far, we should hardly be going far enough, since its love may extend to animals, to plants, to all nature. And yet no one of these things which would thus fill it would suffice to define the attitude taken by the soul, for it could, strictly speaking, do without all of them . . . it has not aimed at this object; it has shot beyond and reached humanity only by passing through humanity.[6]

Nothing of this attitude has a place in the Communist mind which, rather than opening the soul, closes it in on a small part of humanity and its "historical mission." All the same, their "narrowing of the soul" has, paradoxically, a moral character for it is motivated by the vision of "human emancipation." Some call it a peculiar "love of mankind." It would seem more correct to speak of a "love for Communism's 'sublime vision' of the future." As far as mankind short of that future is concerned, Communists see in it nothing but a basic and unremediable inequality between the two opposed groups. There can be no rights for the enemies of history, but the Communist party has the historical right to make sure that all others support it unconditionally, for the future's sake.

Thus we are thoroughly mistaken if we attribute to communism an advocacy of equality and justice. Marx rejected both principles in his scathing criticism of Proudhon, *The Poverty of Philosophy* (1847), and, later, in *The Critique of the Gotha Programme* (1875). There is no need to appeal to authority, though, for the concept of Communist inequality follows logically from a morality centering on history's coming to be and on revolution as the mode of that becoming. In Communist eyes their commitment to two standards has the same moral character as the initial impulse of the revolution. Still, Communists are quite aware that they do not share a common conscience with the rest of humanity, so they feel the need to keep the principle of Communist inequality hidden, and to play publicly on the conscience of "the others." Thus hist'ry does make liars of us all.

On the same grounds the struggle itself, seen in terms of light against darkness, enjoys exemption from all moral restrictions. The "sublimity" of the goal justifies any method required to reach it. Lenin explicitly enjoined on the comrades both violence and trickery, dissimulation and brutal force, concessions and deception. He also succeeded in giving to foreign affairs the color of the class struggle, in which the class enemy has no right to exist. One may say that Communist operations are characterized by moral immorality, immoral practice that is moral in its ultimate justification. The immorality is real, though, while the moral justification is merely implied. After all, the future is not yet. Communist "moral immorality," then, is composed of a moral element amounting to a begged question and an immoral aspect that is consummated practice. If one should wonder why the moral *petitio principii* is still socially effective and appealing to outsiders, one should remember that our age tends to deify humanity and to exalt politics to the rank of a redemptive enterprise. The Communist vision therefore touches the deepest hopes of many who, though not sharing the Communist ideology, look for cultural perfection in this world.

It may not be superfluous at this point to look briefly at the merits of the Communist vision of the good, as if it were conceived as a utopian blueprint—which, in fact, it is not. The only feature of the future order that Communists profess to know is its socialism, i.e., social ownership of the means of production. The concept looks for the overcoming of human egotism through collective economic production, secured by appropriate institutional arrangements. A book by the Yugoslav philosopher Svetozar Stojanovic, *Between Ideals and Reality*,[7] criticizes the Communist ideology by pointing to the way in which things have gone wrong in practice. The condition now prevailing in the Soviet Union he calls "statism" rather than socialism, arguing that socialism would have required self-management and self-determination by the workers. The main thrust of his critique is that a wrong kind of institutional arrangement was chosen for the new society. One asks, why? To which question a possible answer is that institutional arrangements were not, and can never be, entirely under the control of social planners, since all institutions have a momentum of their own that is never fully predictable. Likewise, the relation between institutions and their effect on personal morality are not known and possibly not knowable. This answer is underscored by the fact that Stojanovic's criticism comes late, long after the fact. That implies that at the time of the choice no prediction of the moral effect of new institutions was possible, so that the experiment amounted to nothing more than a wager.

Another way in which things have gone wrong bears the Communist name of "opportunism," the persistence of petty self-seeking and self-advancement even in the framework of socialist collectivism. Complaints about opportunism in the ranks of the party itself continue to be voiced, implying the acknowledgement that, in spite of the "correct" institutional change, no transformation of personal morality has occurred. This entails basic doubts whether any moral regeneration can be expected from a reshuffling of institutions. Moreover, Marxist-Leninist analysis of extant immorality rests on the premise that avarice is the root of all human evil. The ineradicability of selfishness, even in a socialist economy, strongly suggests that there are other roots of evil in the human soul.

Finally, one doubts the entire notion of the merging of human individuals with the social whole. That notion, we remember, was in modern times first set forth by Rousseau, who asserted that a "collective moral being" would result if every person "alienated" his individuality to the community. Now we are all aware that self-centeredness is something to be overcome and that, to be saved, we must give ourselves to the service of a higher and better reality. The question whether a collectivity is better than the individual, however, is begged. A social whole is still a whole of human beings. Even on the level of collectivity, humanity is still imperfect. Rousseau and Marx were wrong. Collectivism is no salvation.

After this brief excursion into the realm of socialism as a utopia, we return to the ideological edifice that Marx and Lenin erected. Both in their analysis of the present society and in their prefiguring of the future, their thought concentrates wholly on the economic order. It is political order, however, which is measured by the concept of the good. Communist ideology has failed to produce, and probably will not be able to produce norms, principles, and concepts regarding the good political order of existence. One reason for this failure is Marx's insistence that power consists in ownership of the means of production, an apolitical concept that he himself found not applicable to the "Asiatic Society" which drew his attention in the middle 1850s. The other reason is the ideology's emphasis on history's coming to be. Marx and Lenin, with Engels and Stalin thrown in for good measure, produced principles of political action only in the form of principles of revolutionary strategy and the "dictatorship of the proletariat," the latter being political order in "the period of transition." Lenin added to this a strategy of "the socialist camp" in the setting of politics among nations. Strategy, by definition, aims at the preconceived goal of victory, which means that it also aims at the peace of victory. The Communist concept of peace, however, is futuristic, vague, and speculative. Most definitely it is not peace in the present setting, i.e., peace between socialists and the forces and units of the present-day society.

Strategy is the Communist manipulation of these forces to the end of ultimate and total victory, but peace will come by eventual social evolution, and that evolution is speculatively asserted. Peace is something for which Communists typically are waiting, even while continuing the prime duty of the struggle. That same waiting also applies to Communist domestic policies. "Building" there is, but always in the expectation of effects which no man can fully predict, e.g., the coming of "the new Soviet man." Since the building is done in the period of transition, one does not build primarily in order to live in the present. All Communist building is strategic. Therefore no state concept is presently possible, and, as for the future, the state is said to wither away. At any rate, all good, for Communists, still lies in the future, except "the good" of the struggle itself. Some point to the welfare aspects of the Soviet system as a modicum of common good, but then one also remembers that state-administered welfare was in fact introduced by Bismarck as early as the 1880s, when there was not even a parliamentary government in Germany.

Soviet rule, then, labors under the absence of a concept of political order. It does have a concept of the party's rule, the supremacy and highest authority of the party over the state, the people, and the entire Russian tradition. But one bears in mind that the party regards itself as a "movement," implying the very opposite of the word "state." Human law, as Boethius rightly perceived, imitates eternity, as laws are designed not strategically but normatively. Since the Soviets have no political theory, in spite of repeated efforts in that direction by Marx, Engels, Lenin, Stalin, and Khrushchev, they have found it impossible to conceive of abiding principles setting limits to state action. Whatever limitations are occasionally conceded must appear, in the words of Zhores Medvedev, as "humane forms of arbitrariness." As long as Communist ideology continues to motivate Russia's rulers, the idea of government as a servant of present human good, common good, will remain a dream. For the same reason, an effective and realistic notion of peace will elude the Soviet leaders. One may say that they are doomed to continue, until the day of the great conversion, in the peaceless and restless prison of their dogma of history's movement.

James W. Skillen · *Societal Pluralism: Blessing or Curse for the Public Good?*

The chief concern of politics should be the public good—the health, welfare, peace, and justice of the public order. We know, however, that this "public thing" is a highly complex social order, so it is difficult to understand its exact identity. One of the longest standing political questions presses upon us today with greater demand for an answer than ever before: "How can the good of the entire public be achieved in face of so much complexity and diversity in society?" Or to put it another way: "Is public justice compatible with highly differentiated societal pluralism?"[1]

Contemporary events demonstrate the urgency and difficulty of the question. Polish workers have recently struggled against a restrictive conformity imposed by the Communist party. They have succeeded, at least at the time that this is written, in establishing an independent trade union that further enlarges the scope of structural pluralism in Poland—a pluralism undergirded by the independence of the Catholic church. But what has made this differentiating process possible? In part it has been due to the willingness of workers to maintain solidarity in a single movement. In part it has arisen from the high degree of Catholic unity among the Polish people who know little of the ecclesiastical diversity that Americans experience. And, of course, the contemporary events in Poland bear witness to a nationalism among the Poles that allows the church, the workers, and even many in the Communist party to work for a common (Polish) good that is quite distinguishable from the international communist unity sought by leaders in the Soviet Union and elsewhere. Certainly, then, we can ask the question: "Are we really witnessing the emergence of greater pluralism in Poland, or is it the unfolding of a newer form of public unity? Or, could it be that both differentiation and integration are taking place at the same time?"

Nicaragua recently threw out the dictator Somoza who had defined the public good so narrowly that most of the people knew it did not include them. But how to achieve the common good for all people?—that is a more difficult matter. The new government wants greater freedom for more people—education, economic opportunity, popular politics. It wants to achieve greater independence for Nicaragua among the American states, especially over against the United States. But such independence and societal pluralism seem impossible to achieve without national unity and solidarity. Much of what we perceive from the outside in Nicaragua appears to be strongly directed public conformity, with some forms of pluralism being delayed or repressed altogether.

The problem of societal pluralism and public unity is as contemporary as Poland and Nicaragua today. It is also as old as the contentions between prophets and kings in ancient Israel, or Aristotle's criticism of Plato's attempt to reduce the family to a mere function of the polis. A problem or question that is both so old and so contemporary must be addressed by every political scientist and government official. A general pragmatic or functionalist approach to solving problems is insufficient.

How should we understand the public good? Is genuine societal pluralism a curse or a blessing for public solidarity? What does justice demand? Toward what end is history moving—unity or diversity? Surely it is not possible simply to aim for the avoidance of anarchy and totalitarianism without having a healthy conception of what we do want to achieve. The mean between extremes can hardly be defined merely as a negation of extremes.

We face a moral question of utmost seriousness: "What are the norms for a healthy public order?" And the question is pushing us ever more rapidly beyond the confines of particular domestic situations. The differentiation of states and of societal institutions around the world, especially since World War II, has coincided with growing evidence of global interconnectedness. Our question is truly international in character: "Does the public good of the entire world demand principled support of societal pluralism, or does it require the overcoming of that cursed hindrance to global unity?"[2]

In his book, *Main Currents in Modern Political Thought*, written in the years immediately following World War II, John Hallowell begins the final chapter this way:

> It has been suggested throughout these pages that the basic insights of the Christian faith provide the best insights we have into the nature of man and of the crisis in which we find our-

> selves. That crisis is the culmination of modern man's progressive attempt to deny the existence of a transcendent or spiritual reality and of his progressive failure to find meaning and salvation in some wholly immanent conception of reality. Modern man's worship of the Class, the Race, or the State has only further alienated him from reality, plunged him deeper into despair and impelled him further along the road to destruction and annihilation. Only through a return to faith in God, as God revealed Himself to man in Jesus Christ, can modern man and his society find redemption from the tyranny of evil.[3]

This profound confession, I am convinced, has everything to do with the question of pluralism and the public good. One might ask, of course, whether the reviving influence of Christianity in Poland and in some parts of Africa and Latin America, as well as the revival of Islam and Judaism in various parts of the world, are cause for encouragement and hopefulness today. Whatever the evidences of spiritual liveliness, it is not clear that public justice always flows as a consequence from such revivals. Those of us who, with John Hallowell, are convinced of the truth of God's revelation in Jesus Christ, must nonetheless continue to ask about the political meaning of that faith.

Biblical revelation offers a testimony that is not only ancient in its wisdom but also powerful as a light on our contemporary path. Without doubt that revelation has been and still is abused by imperialists, nationalists, racists, and other crusaders who have attempted to manipulate biblical doctrine for their own ends.[4] But the biblical testimony is thorough and consistent about two characteristics of reality that bear directly on our question.

The first characteristic to which I refer displays itself in the relationship between God's transcendence and the locus of power and authority on earth. From the biblical perspective the only ultimate point of integrating focus for earthly life is in God's own monarchical authority and purpose for the creation. Every creature, including every nation, is "at His disposal" as servant and steward—to be blessed or cursed according to its deeds. Israel's "good" is dependent on God's covenant. The life of the nations, both Jewish and gentile, according to the New Testament, is dependent on the universal kingship of Jesus Christ—a kingship that is not simply "of this world." In other words, the public good of any particular (or even universal) political community on earth cannot find its ultimate point of integration in any human authority or idolatrous "ism." The highest central purpose toward which all societal institutions and functions should be directed is God's glory and kingdom, not "the nation," or "our race," or "our form of government," or "military supremacy," or "economic growth." The public good, as defined and served by political authorities, may not lay claim to total or even reductionistic power through which human persons or institutions attempt to place themselves on the throne of God.[5] Rendering to Caesar the things that are Caesar's and to God the things that are God's is clearly interpreted throughout the biblical texts to mean that everything (even Caesar) belongs to God, while only a few things belong to Caesar under God's dominion.

The second characteristic of reality that biblical revelation illuminates is the pluriform shape of the creation—including the world of human relationships. God's covenant with Israel is a normative recognition and definition of many types of human responsibility and community, each with its own sphere of authority and accountability before God and among the people. The New Testament epistles, in all their compactness, display the same perspective: parents, employers, farmers, priests, kings, judges, teachers, and others all have a calling from God, an office of creaturely responsibility to fulfill. Business and agriculture are not merely functions of a national or international economy. Homes are not simply civic or economic training centers. The authority for most human responsibilities does not originate with either civic or ecclesiastical law. Rather, the plural character of a diversifying human world comes from the identity of the creation itself, and thus from the hand of God.[6]

To speak of God's sovereignty and the order of creation is not to speak in terms of static rationalism or in terms of natural and organic models. The biblical testimony is historically dynamic, directing human beings to act creatively in response to divine norms. The Bible does not speak of conformity to ideal forms, but of obedient responses to divine commandments in the course of history.

God gives his creatures genuine responsibilities—stewardly jobs of shaping life on earth. As human beings have unfolded the creation through agriculture and art, science and technology, trade and education, so the complexity of social life has grown. But the

Bible nowhere unveils an ideal political form that will take care of this complexity once and for all. In each new generation citizens are called to do justice to every neighbor even as they continue to find new ways of caring for their families, raising crops, pursuing technological development, and doing countless other nonpublic things.

The shape of public justice will vary from time to time and place to place. But the implications of these two simple truths—God's sovereign transcendence and the world's complex creatureliness—are not ambiguous. To our original question they suggest the following answer. Societal pluralism is not only a blessing for the public good; it is constitutive of an authentic public order. A truly just public order can be constituted as a whole only by recognizing the independent pluralistic diversity of society from the outset. The unity of any public order—whether a small town or the whole globe—can only be healthy and just if it is built as a complex whole. In other words, its very character as a public order must arise through definite constitutional (and other legal) means that do justice to the unique identity of families, schools, businesses, churches, voluntary associations, animals, natural resources, and all other things that exist by virtue of their creaturely identity and capabilities and not by virtue of governmental fiat.[7]

Analogies, if used carefully and not pressed too hard, abound. The sculptor's statue can come into existence only if he does justice to the medium of stone or wood with which he begins. The orchestra conductor can bring forth a harmonious symphony only if each player has room, time, and will to give his own talent to the whole.

In practical political terms this means that a just state or political community will recognize its own limits both as something less than God and as a respecter of the other creatures and human associations to which God has given authority and responsibility. Binding a territory together under one public law will be just and good to the extent that its unity is sought not by obliterating diversity and not by concentrating all authority in the public order itself. To "sculpt" or to "orchestrate" such a public order will require great insight into the particular office of responsibility that government has in a state or in an international public order. It will require the willingness and determination to respect (in public legal ways) both its own limited office and the God-given rights of all that the Creator has made.

While one might appreciate the reaction of an Ayatollah Khomeini to the Western materialistic subversion of Islam, or the reaction of a so-called "moral majority" in the United States to certain secularizing tendencies that seem to be undermining traditional moral values, it is not possible to sympathize with movements that seek to reconstitute public moral wholeness in ways that do not recognize the necessary diversity of a complex public whole.

This was the chief error of Jean Jacques Rousseau, and of countless subsequent reformers or revolutionaries who have sought to build or to regain public moral communities. While one can appreciate Rousseau's (and later, Marx's) reaction to the dominating control of the public order by one or more private interests, Rousseau's theoretical effort to create a community governed by the general will did not make room for a genuinely complex whole. As he said in the *Social Contract*, "It is therefore of the utmost importance for obtaining the expression of the general will, that no partial society should be formed in the State, and that every citizen should speak his opinion entirely from himself. . . ."[8] The Dutch Calvinistic pluralist, Herman Dooyeweerd, expresses appreciation for Rousseau's struggle to overcome "the undifferentiated feudal notions of governmental authority" and to reach for a new conception of the res publica.[9] But Dooyeweerd is critical of Rousseau's failure to grasp the complex reality of a genuine public thing. For Rousseau,

> a state which is an authentic expression of the humanistic idea of freedom cannot possibly recognize the *private* freedom of the individual *over against* itself. Such a state must completely absorb the natural freedom of man into the higher form of political freedom. . . . In a truly free state the individual cannot possess rights and liberties over against the *res publica* because in such a state the total freedom of the individual must come to expression.[10]

The difficulty here, according to Dooyeweerd, is that Rousseau's effort to overcome unjust grants of public privilege to private groups and persons leads him to concentrate all authority in an undifferentiated public totality. "Like Hobbes's Leviathan, Rousseau's radical democracy is totalitarian in every respect. It expresses the humanistic motive of freedom in a radically political way, in absolute antithesis to the biblical creation motive underlying the principle of sphere sovereignty. The notion of radical democracy contains the paradoxical conclusion that the highest freedom of man lies in the utter absolutism of the state."[11]

Clearly the paradox of Rousseau's effort to create the means for achieving ultimate human freedom is rooted in presuppositions which deny both God's transcendent authority and the genuine diversity of creaturely responsibilities before God. As Hallowell explains, here in Rousseau "is born a conception of law which is radically modern and absolutely contrary to the Judaeo-Christian tradition. It is not God who is the ultimate author of law but 'the people' and this is true whether the form of government be democratic, aristocratic, or monarchical."[12]

Without doubt we live in a day when public justice is threatened from all sides—from private business interests and from anarchic terrorists, from nationalists who have little regard for global justice and from some internationalists who have little regard for the proper place of societal and national diversity. Adequate responses to these threats cannot come from libertarian reaction to totalitarianism or from nationalist and collectivist reactions to anarchy. A healthy response can come only by efforts rooted deeply in principle to build communities of public justice—public legal bonds that integrate a diversity into a complex unity. But the unity must have a very special and limited character, displaying a recognition that God has also given place, identity, and purpose to nonpublic associations, institutions, and individuals, each of which must be allowed to fulfill its calling in the creation. God alone rules the whole creation as Creator, Judge, and Redeemer. His revelation gives a light to our path which we cannot afford to ignore. In the midst of distress and darkness it points the way with steady brilliance to the opportunity for genuine human political responsibility today.

Mulford Q. Sibley · *The Problem of Coercion*

Coercion was defined long ago by a religious leader as "any compulsory force put upon a man or group to compel assent or action against the will of the man or group."[1] This definition is as good as any. It suggests that coercion can take many forms, including not merely the employment of physical force but also the use of social pressure. It also assumes the possibility of voluntary action with which coerced conduct is in sharp contrast.

However much religious institutions may have been involved (as they have) in some of the most horribly coercive acts, there has always been a kind of tension between higher religious consciousness and coercive methods. The religious mystic seeking truth opens himself to the upper reaches of consciousness in which the constraints of time, material resources, and space are forgotten in absorption by that which lies beyond time, material limitations, and competition.

In politics, of course, we have a meeting of the material and the spiritual as human beings seek to go beyond the ordering of human groups by mere wont or custom and to develop that ordering deliberately and rationally. As the individual person seeking to direct his own life encounters the problems of ethics, so do those attempting to order the collectivity discover the dilemmas of both ethics and politics.

But the very word "order" suggests the possibility of disorder, and disorder, that of coercion to restore the order. To many religionists, the existence of disorder both reflects and accentuates one of the most ubiquitous factors in the religious consciousness—alienation from God and alienation from other human beings. At the same time, the suggestion that coercion be used to promote order is viewed by some as itself a species of disorder and therefore of evil.

The highly sensitive religious consciousness is, moreover, aware that the problem of coercion is above all reflected in humanity's relations with the scarcities of Nature. We exploit and mine Nature, as it were; yet Nature, even with human help through technology, still gives but grudgingly, compelling us to ration material resources either directly or through the pricing system. We are admonished by our faith to love one another, yet our economies and their accompanying social and political structures seem inevitably to deny love in the restrictions they impose on unwilling human beings, and in grossly inequitable distributions of economic power. The issue touches theological heights; for the God of love seems to many to contradict the God of power. Or can the two attributes of divinity be reconciled?

These are the kinds of questions at stake in the Western religious debate about coercion and politics. To make the terms of that debate more explicit, we first remind ourselves of the main lines of the historical discussion and then evaluate the issues raised by the debate.

Coercion in Western Religious Thought

The Hebrew prophets dealt in many contexts with the problem of coercion. Their constant warnings against idolatry seemed to suggest that the human tendency to idolize natural objects and human creations would inevitably lead to the enslavement of human beings: thus the creature would coerce the creator. Then again the prophets often warned against the tendency to trust in the latest war technology of their day—the Egyptian chariot. For, they contended, the only one to be trusted was the Lord.[2] To Jeremiah, it was better to meet the threat of Babylonia without arms than with them, although we do not know precisely the basis for what may have been a policy of nonresistance or nonviolent resistance.[3] "Not by might, nor by power, but by my spirit," said another prophet.[4]

Interestingly enough, the views of Socrates (at least on one of his many sides) seem to be similar. In the *Republic*, for example, we even have an anticipation of Jesus. When it is suggested that a rough-and-ready definition of justice is "to do good to your friends and harm to your enemies," Socrates replies that it can never be just to do anything to a human being which would impair his humanity: we should never so treat an enemy that he would deteriorate.[5]

Although Jesus did not speak of coercion as such, his teaching is a good example of the dubiety with which it has been viewed by so many, particularly when it becomes violent. Jesus makes the ancient Hebrew saying, "You shall love the Lord your God with all your soul, all your strength, and all your mind and your neighbor as yourself," an epitomization of all the commandments. We are admonished to love even our enemies.[6] We are not to condemn harshly. One of the most striking Temptation stories is that in which the devil offers all the kingdoms of this world if Jesus will only bow down and worship him—a worship which implies utilization of the means traditionally employed to conquer power (war, revolutionary violence, assassination). But Jesus resists the beguilements of the devil in this one of the most obviously political temptations.[7] And when a disciple uses a sword to strike off the ear of the high priest's servant, Jesus tells him, "Put up your sword, for they that take the sword shall perish with the sword."[8] Biblical scholars have debated the exact meaning of these and similar texts, but surely in a cumulative sense they point to a position which distrusts coercion, and particularly violent coercion, and which might agree with Socrates' well-known proposition: "It is better to suffer injustice than to commit it."

This interpretation was, by and large, sustained by the early Christian community, as modern studies like those of Harnack and Cadoux have confirmed.[9] Until fairly late in the ancient period, most Christians apparently refused to hold office, enter the army, or remain in the army after conversion, at least in large part because of their attitudes to coercion and particularly violent coercion. While writers like St. Paul advocated submission to the "powers that be,"[10] Paul never sanctioned serving in the magistracy (where one often had to condemn criminals) or in the army.

Down into the fourth century, moveover, even after many had begun to depart from these earlier uncompromising positions, the great church fathers maintained the original views. Thus Origen admitted that Christians had scruples against entering the army but said that if all persons would adopt their attitude, the barbarians would no longer menace the empire.[11] And both Tertullian and Lactantius took a similar position. The martyrdom of Maximilianus in 295 was the result of his refusal to join the army on grounds that military service was incompatible with Christianity.[12] And in the fourth century Martin of Tours, a recent convert, left the army because of conscientious scruples.

But long before the period of Martin, the great majority of Christians had given up their opposition to military service and to the coercive magistracy. Compromise with "the world" became the keynote of most thought after the reign of Constantine. Rationalizations even of violent coercion began to supplant such uncompromising positions as those of Origen and Lactantius.

The more relativistic position was aided and abetted by the development of the notion of original sin, according to which Adam's and Eve's primitive alienation from God tainted all their descendants. St. Augustine was greatly troubled by the problem of coercion in general and, in particular, by the issue of whether the state could legitimately coerce heretics and schismatics. He eventually came to accept coercion but with great reluctance, since he had always held that religious conversion must be the act of a free human soul. He eventually began to believe that sometimes a preliminary dose of force was essential to awaken the consciousness of those in error.

Political and coercive institutions such as property, war, and the state, the Augustinian view held, arose out of the Fall of Man but, in divine providence (for God knew that man would use his freedom to fall), were at the same time a coercive corrective for sin. Although tainted by their origin in sin and apparently harsh in nature, they also mitigated in some measure the worst effects of alienation from God.

Thus despite early religious dubiety, coercion and its institutions came to be given a religious sanction. The repudiation of all war gave way to the doctrine of the just war, in which an effort was made to legitimize some types of violent coercion. Private property, certainly no institution in Eden, where a kind of free communism reigned, came to be justified relative to man's fallen state.

Yet the religious conscience was never easy about what Troeltsch has aptly called "relative natural law," or principles applicable to human beings in their fallen state. Thus it is said that many executioners during the Middle Ages used to apologize to their victims for what they were about to do. The clergy, in theory at least, were forbidden by canon law to shed blood. The practice of monasticism sought to hold up the idea of a freely embraced life of communism and personal poverty as one most nearly perfect.

In many sectarian movements, of course, the dubiety about violence was emphatic. Thus the Waldenses took a frankly pacifist position, as did a number of other groups. And the medieval religious radical often appealed from the property institutions of the day to the life of communism in Eden.

In early modern times there was often an emphasis on the Thrasymachan view that "justice is the interest of the stronger"—a position exemplified in Thomas Hobbes, where the ethic of love became a counsel of expediency and a part of the so-called laws of nature which themselves were rooted in mutual fears rather than in a natural sociality. A great religious figure like Luther, in his doctrine of the two kingdoms (one of power and the other of grace) seems to allot a very wide scope to the coercive element in the economy and polity. He appears to set a private ethic of love over against a public ethic which can justify extreme harshness and near-vindictiveness. Human beings have to learn to live in a schizophrenic condition: called upon to be hangmen by public authorities in one situation, they may then in the next moment be asked, in their private relations, to live out the ethic of love of enemies.[13]

To be sure, a few Reformation sects, like some of the Anabaptists, endeavored to retain a pacifist position by means of an ethic of withdrawal from a world in which coercive factors seemed to be inevitable. And groups like the Quakers sought, while living in "the world," to be carefully discriminating in the types of coercion they permitted: thus in Pennsylvania they allowed what might be called the coercion of law, while rejecting the violent coercion they saw implied in the maintenance of an army or in any war against the Indians or others. They thought that the implementation of a just social order—including fair treatment of the Indians—would, in words which they constantly repeated, "take away the occasion for war."

The traditional Augustinian position assumes that the state is designed primarily to repress sin and to coerce wicked men. Before the Fall there could have been no state. Suppose, however, that one conceives the state to be more than an organ of repression: it is also seen as one of positive coordination and a framework for affirmatively discovering and implementing the good common to all persons. If one accepts this view—often associated with the position of St. Thomas Aquinas—then the state in its role as coordinator existed even in Eden: it is not simply the consequence of the Fall, although its coercive features may be. Even if all were sinless, the state would exist to reflect the social and political nature of humanity. A position of this kind should be sharply distinguished from both Augustinian and Hobbesian views.[14]

Turning to modern perspectives, the issues which stand out in the twentieth-century world are the increasingly destructive nature of war, the problem of distributive justice, and the treatment of the offender. "Tender" religious consciences will differ from one another on precisely how these questions are to be approached.

One response would be that of a religiously grounded anarchism. Leo Tolstoy is perhaps the greatest exponent of this position in the twentieth century. He sees both state and civilization as repressive and as violative of the central ethic which pervades the Gospel, that of the Sermon on the Mount.[15] We are not to judge our neighbors, which implies a rejection of the criminal law. We are to share material goods with one another, which suggests the elimination of property institutions. We are to love our enemies, which commands the dissolution of armies. We are to live simple, unostentatious lives, which entails a return of closeness to Nature and an erosion of civilization, with its protectors the state and the law. How eliminate the state? When enough religiously dedicated persons refuse to enter the army, serve on juries, administer criminal law, live ostentatious lives, and obey law, state institutions—which are identified by Tolstoy as essentially coercive—will collapse. Spontaneity and harmony would then characterize human life. Tolstoy pleads his case with great earnestness and carefully distinguishes his position from that espoused by liberals, Marxists, and socialists—all of whom, he maintains, are willing to violate the Gospel in various ways.

There is about the whole Marxian paradigm a religious flavor which cannot be mistaken: one might, indeed, term it a theodicy. It builds on very ancient religious interpretations of history when it suggests that human experience develops from primitive communism to the class conflicts that characterize human history, to a new communism in which both class and coercion will wither away. All this reminds one of the medieval Joachimites who saw history moving from the Age of the Father, or harsh coercion to maintain order, to the Age of the Son, or the relatively mild coercions of the church, to the Age of the Holy Ghost, in which all external institutional controls and coercions will disappear.

Both Tolstoyan and Marxian views assume that as political institutions wither, a sense of individual responsibility expands, which raises the question of whether one can coerce oneself. If we assume a sharp dichotomy between inner and outer, and the latter form of coercion is abolished, is inner coercion any less onerous? This is the kind of question raised by Ursula LeGuin in one of her novels.[16]

Other twentieth-century religious principles would carry on many features of the traditional debates. Thus Niebuhrian outlooks remind one of characteristically Augustinian positions on coercion. Many conservatives who build on religious foundations would echo traditional Burkean positions, stressing the dangers of rapid social change, with its often arbitrary uprooting of human beings, its harsh coercions, and its frequent denigration of human personality. While religiously grounded conservatives would not be unaware of problems of distributive justice, they would tend to say that often the perils of change, in terms of an expansion of coercion, might outweigh any gains that might be attained. The problem of religious conservatism, as of conservatism generally, is how a truly conservative position can be held once one accepts the imperatives of an ever more complex technology—demands which seem to make impossible any building up of the kind of social order envisioned by conservative outlooks. "Throne and altar," the slogan of much conservatism in the past, can hardly be reconciled with the almost frenetic social change—and its accompanying coercions—engendered by acceptance of ever more complex new technology.

Cutting across all modern attitudes to coercion is, of course, the issue of pacifism. Anarchists can be either pacifist—rejecting all war and violence—or nonpacifist, accepting some version of relativism or a just-war theory (thus Peter Kropotkin supported the Allies in World War I). Nonpacifists, too, find the issue a vexing one. Essentially, the historic debate about the legitimacy of violence is repeated, although many just-war theorists have in effect become pacifists by the just-war route; for they argue that no modern war can possibly fulfill the traditional canons governing the definition of a "just war."[17]

And thus the debate has continued.

Evaluation and Judgment

How should we come to terms with the debate? At the outset, we may suggest that no answer is completely satisfactory. Every response will be a ragged one, in the sense that there will continue to be a tension between life in the existential community and the call of religion. Yet to say that no answer will be immune to criticism does not imply that some responses are not, relatively, better than others.

Political life, as Father Gilby has suggested in his work interpreting Thomism, may be said to exist "between community and society,"[18] in the sense that it emerges out of a social mass in which individual personality is at a low level but implicitly looks forward to a state of things that may be described as "association without organization." Man is a social and political animal: his place in the scheme of things historically is bounded by the pole of submerged personality, on the one hand, and, on the other, by a state of things in which individual personality, with all its complexities and eccentricities, can fully flower while at the same time belong to the group. In the existential world both poles will be represented, the first by factors which make for depersonalization, the second by the call to freedom and to free and uncoerced association. Political institutions reflect these two pulls: they arise in part to provide a framework for the development of freedom; but the very institutions and organizations which, through their coordinating and restraining functions, may enlarge freedom and promote development of personality, can also repress them.

In any complex civilization, law, bureaucracy, and planning would seem to be essential if personality is to be both free and social; yet the inertia of institutions, the inequities involved in legal classifications, and the difficulties of anticipating consequences in planning often counter any liberating potentialities.

Optimistic views of the historical process foresee a day in which all individuals will be truly self-governing, in the sense that neither the threat of physical force nor that of social pressure will constrain human beings who will act spontaneously and yet always in ways conducive to the social good. More pessimistic interpretations suggest that this ideal can be fully attained only in heaven and that in the meantime we must live with the ambiguities, paradoxes, and limitations of political life. While progress in the direction of a free and unconstrained life may be possible, the pessimists might continue, its full attainment on earth is unlikely.

If we accept something like a moderately pessimistic perspective, how might the religious consciousness view coercion? We attempt to answer this question by noting the varieties of coercion and the distinction between violent and nonviolent types; examining the problem of individual responses to the seemingly inevitable coercions of life; and, finally, touching on the issue of coercion in collectives.

1. Coercion is expressed in a bewildering variety of ways, and the development of a religious conscience will depend on an awareness of this multiplicity. Differentiations between varieties of coercion are vital if we are to make well-grounded ethical distinctions. We are coerced by Nature, insofar as we perceive its scarce resources limiting us in what we should like to do or have. There are the coercions of law, in which we are prevented from doing what we might like to do. Majorities coerce us in political life. The "third degree" is a form of coercion, as is the forcible seizure of an inebriated man to "dry him out." I impose limits on my child in the house, thus inevitably repressing at least one side of him or her to some degree. The so-called laws of supply and demand coerce us in economic activities: even human beings will have their value fixed by these impersonal factors of the marketplace—in effect, they are auctioned off, reminding one of slavery. A boycott of dime stores, such as occurred during the Civil Rights struggle, is in some measure an effort to coerce dime-store owners into hiring blacks. Gandhi's boycott of British cloth had the effect of putting British mill workers in the ranks of the unemployed. Some coercion entails physical force, while other types consist of social pressures of various kinds.

It would seem that our ethical judgments of coercion should turn on the type and context of the coercion involved. Thus forcibly rescuing a child from an onrushing automobile is coercive; so is the torture of a prisoner in a Chilean or Soviet or Irish or American prison. Yet most of us—and rightly—would not put the rescue and the torture in the same ethical category. Why? Because the act of rescue is one dominated by the interest of the child and is performed in an atmosphere of love and by means which are not inevitably deadly (although accidentally the child may be injured in the process). The torture is inevitably seriously injurious to the person and is hardly carried out in an atmosphere of love and concern. Even the police make a distinction between the coercion which involves what they call "deadly force" and that which does not.

In these last illustrations, we have been endeavoring to draw a distinction between what might be called violent and nonviolent coercion. Although the line may at points and in practice be difficult to draw (and it is surely not to be equated with one between physical and nonphysical force), the attempt to draw it is highly important if we are to come to grips with the ethics and politics of coercion within a context of religious presuppositions.

Long ago C. M. Case, a sociologist and Quaker, analyzed the characteristics of nonviolent coercion,[19] in the process distinguishing it from violence. Thus he examined such phenomena as street demonstrations, the context of Quaker nonviolence in colonial Pennsylvania, rent strikes in Ireland, and so on. And in a volume I published a number of years ago, I tried to bring together a good many cases of what some have called nonviolent resistance.[20]

Case and others would argue—and it is difficult not to agree—that the difference between nonviolent and violent coercion is substantial and not imaginary. While we are never to break cooperation with others in a social conflict without first attempting conciliation, still there are times when such action is justifiable. The strike, civil disobedience, and other such methods may receive our sanction when used with care and in an atmosphere characterized by the search for justice. At the same time we must recognize that what Gregg calls "the power of nonviolence,"[21] while often highly efficacious in the quest for justice, is, after all, a form of power, with the danger of turning into violent coercion and thus becoming self-defeating.

Another way of suggesting the distinction between violent and nonviolent coercion is to say that while the former tends to run away from any self-imposed limits on action, the latter is associated with a sharply defined sense of limits. The utilization of nonviolent coercion in conflicts often has the effect of bringing the parties together, whereas violent coercion prevents long-run and permanent solutions.

The point we have been stressing, in other words, in this typology of violence and nonviolence, is that whether or not coercion can be approved ethically may depend on the kind and context of the coercion involved. Obviously, the religious ideal of free and voluntary action is to be preferred in all instances. But short of that, we search for forms of struggle which are discriminating, not inevitably seriously injurious in a physical or nonphysical sense, and compatible with the goals we seek. If the goal is a warlike society, then war is an admirable means; but if the end is a peaceful world, then the violent coercion of war would have to be ruled out under all circumstances. As someone once put it:

> Show me not the end without the way,
> For ends and means on earth are so entangled,
> That choosing one, you choose the other too—
> Each different path brings different ends in view.

God, perhaps, can use even war to praise himself. But human beings, not being gods, are strictly limited in what they can do by the organic relation between means and ends.

2. How should the individual respond to the coercions of life? In the first place, he or she will try to change the conditions which make for coercion and particularly violent coercion, keeping in mind the means-ends entanglement.

But what about individual responses to many of the coercions which seem to be beyond control? It is an old observation of Cynics, Stoics, monks, and Zen Buddhists that if one really seeks freedom and with it a life the least subject to coercion, one must reduce one's desires. The fewer the desire for, and ardent attachment to, wealth, power, status, honor, glory, the greater the freedom. The person of few desires will not regard the deprivations associated with the word coercion as impingements on his freedom, for he will never have been attached to the things of which he is deprived and will therefore not feel coerced. St. John of the Cross expresses this admirably in a religious context: "That thou mayest have pleasure in everything, seek pleasure in nothing. That thou mayest know everything, seek to know nothing. . . . In detachment the spirit finds quiet and repose, for coveting nothing, nothing wearies it by elation, and nothing oppresses it by dejection, because it stands in the center of its own humility. For as soon as it covets anything, it is immediately fatigued thereby."[22]

If we will and do the good, St. Paul and many others teach, then legitimate law and legitimate rulers will not be coercing us, for we shall voluntarily have done what the law requires. We anticipate the demands of the law, so to speak, and thus escape its coercive effects.[23]

Even the tyrant, who is lawless or acting under unjust law, cannot coerce us, for if we follow such thinkers as Epictetus, St. Paul, and St. John of the Cross, we wil not be attached unduly to physical life. By being detached from it, the tyrant can threaten it, even unjustly, without our feeling in any way coerced.

All this suggests that with these attitudes, the individual may be free in the profoundest sense of that word, even in the shadow of death.

3. But personal attitudes and reactions to threatened coercion, while vital and fundamental, are not in themselves enough. Every person lives in a community and the central political virtue is justice. What are we to say about coerion and the achievement of justice? Coercion and desirable social change?

If we assume that the central commandment of religious ethics is love of God and love of neighbor, these issues turn on the question of how we can translate love into the collective life of human beings. We have noted some of the permutations of this question historically, particularly against the background of the myth of original sin.

Without necessarily subscribing to that myth, we accept the fact of sin, or alienation from God and fellowmen, and see the task as one of abating or restricting its worst effects—narrowing the alienation, so to speak. On the one hand, humanity has a tendency to sin or to become alienated from the good; on the other, it has enormous resources of love, which have the capacity to engulf sin and remove alienation. It is along these lines that we must think of the tasks of social justice.

But, it may be asked, what role does power play in all this? Some seem to think of love and power as opposed, and Tolstoy appears to believe that we must "abolish" power. But to oppose love to either power or justice is to create false dichotomies. Nothing can be more powerful than love. Paul Tillich correctly argues that there is no basic conflict between and among love, power, and justice.[24] Justice becomes the concrete embodiment of love in human communities, while power, in the spirit of love, enables us to attain and sustain justice.

It is at this point that the personal responses of which we have spoken earlier become most important. Those who are most detached from finite and material things are the most likely to be crucial in attainment of social justice. Their nonattachment to limited things and to power will make them fearless, and fearlessness is central if we are to resist tyranny or transform the social order. As Wincenty Lutoslawski, the Polish Platonist, suggests, injustice could not long flourish if the world were populated by millions of persons who really believed that their souls would survive bodily death: with such beliefs and with actions corresponding to them, millions might simply refuse to obey the tyrant and thus render him helpless.[25]

But if our distinction between violent and nonviolent coercion has validity, those fearless in the face of death would themselves refuse to kill. There is an important distinction between willingness to kill for a cause and readiness to die for it. In the former we perpetuate the violence and injustice of the world by engaging in violent coercion; for violence and injustice go hand in hand, and violence in means, as we noted earlier, implies violence in ends. But willingness to die rather than kill suggests that in absorbing the violence of others and refusing to retaliate in kind, we can turn the situation around and set in motion the forces of nonviolent power. All this is implicitly if not explicitly suggested by thinkers like Tolstoy and Gandhi and, earlier, by William Godwin, Percy Shelley, and many leaders of Quakerism.

An outlook of this kind—which draws its inspiration from several types of historic religious pacifism—would not be anarchist. It would agree with thinkers like St. Thomas Aquinas that restraint of evil is only one side of the functions of political authority, the other dimensions being reflection of the good common to all and the coordination of labor that has been divided. Nor would this outlook require the rejection of all physical force; but where physical force was permitted, it would have to be subordinate to the general principles of nonviolent coercion which we suggested earlier. The outlook would, of course, rule out the violent coercion of war and of violent revolution. Instead, defense of legitimate rights would depend on organized nonviolent resistance, whether against domestic or foreign tyranny. This perspective would also obviously reject what we euphemistically call capital punishment, that is, the deliberate taking of a human life by the state.

Although this view rejects violent coercion on both moral and practical grounds and stresses the idea of limits in human actions of all types, its major emphasis is positive: its rejection of violent coercion is a necessary but not a sufficient condition for its affirmative faith in the possibilities of good overcoming or rather engulfing evil. Intrinsically evil acts such as killing and denigration of human personality can only perpetuate evil and not overcome it. We are stressing, with Tillich, the interweaving of love, power, and justice. We are rejecting the notion, so common today, that a realistic politics must be prepared to spurn the constraints imposed by a religious ethic of love. We are maintaining that this ethic is relevant for the relations of groups as well as for those of individuals; that it is, indeed, far more relevant for the welfare of humanity than an ethic which tends to place its confidence in armies, missiles, and threats to obliterate whole cities.

We are emphatically agreeing with the late military historian Walter Millis, who, speaking of the "uselessness of military power," argued that the United States could defend itself far more effectively under a policy of "unilateral divestment" of military weapons than it could with arms.[26] This would be particularly true if unilateral disarmament were accompanied by a genuine commitment to economic justice and redistribution of power on a world scale.

An outlook of this kind would also invite us to rethink the problem of revolution. Both the French and Russian revolutions began with relatively nonviolent strategies and tactics—in the Russian case, protests, strikes, refusals of soldiers to shoot, and so on. In later stages, however, both upheavals became corrupted as their leaders turned increasingly to violence. More recently, we have seen in Iran a remarkable movement which used the largely nonviolent strike very effectively, toppling a tyrannical regime that had pinned its faith on a large army. But, like the French and Russian revolutions before it, the Iranian affair also became distorted and counterrevolutionary as it increasingly employed harsh police repression and violence. Thus far, at the time this is written, the Polish trade union Solidarity has been a model of nonviolent self-discipline and, by most standards, has been amazingly effective. But if it should ever employ the weapons of violence, we could expect many of its gains to be lost.

Early in the sixteenth century, before the civil wars in France had devastated that unhappy land, an eighteen-year-old French lad, Etienne de La Boétie, an ardent and prescient Catholic, wrote a book called *Discourse on Voluntary Servitude*. In it he argued, on the basis of his study of ancient tyranny, that violence was unnecessary to overthrow even the most onerous despotism. Instead, he maintained, all one needed was a large group of men and women willing to disobey the despot, or, in other words, to renounce their "voluntary servitude." Without firing a shot, they could, by acts of nonviolent power, undermine even the most cruel dictator.

De La Boétie was right. The hope for genuine change in the direction of justice depends not at all on violence but rather on those willing to absorb the violent coercion of others in nonviolent acts, while refusing to utilize violent coercion themselves. The ancient slave Epictetus expressed the spirit of this in describing a "true Cynic": "See what this means. The kings and tyrants of this world have their armed bodyguard which enables them to rebuke certain persons and to punish those who do wrong even though they are wicked themselves, but the Cynic's conscience takes the place of arms and bodyguard and furnishes this authority."[27] This reflects the kind of consciousness we have been endeavoring to describe. It suggests a personal attitude to coercion and at the same time an approach that can be and has been compatible with a profoundly religious perspective in politics.

Clarke E. Cochran · *The Radical Gospel and Christian Prudence*

In the last twenty years Jesus has been rediscovered as a political figure. The radical implications of the good news he preached have been translated into contemporary terms as support for revolution against oppressive regimes, for a drastic restructuring of capitalist economies toward egalitarian distribution of goods, and for active opposition to nuclear armaments. More abstractly, this rediscovery has stimulated theological inquiry into the historicity of divine revelation, the meaning of eschatology, the concept of liberation, the prophetic in Scripture, and the insights of Marxism. It is all too easy to accept this idea of the radical gospel uncritically, but it is also too simple to reject it out of hand.[1] I believe that the radical political implications clearly present in the gospel must be taken seriously. At the same time the scriptural recommendations of prudence and discretion must be regarded earnestly. Yet the claims of prudence are not easily reconciled with the radical demands of Jesus' message.

In this essay I shall work out a preliminary description of the tension between the radical gospel and Christian prudence and a preliminary statement of the direction a reconciliation between them might take. First, I shall consider the gospel's fundamental challenge to political life and the dangers of this challenge. Second, I shall take up the contribution prudence makes to moderating the dangers of radicalism and the corresponding dangers of prudence. Finally, I shall suggest two types of prudence and how the concept of stewardship might integrate them with the radical gospel.

The good news of the kingdom proclaimed by Jesus is radical in two ways. First, to hear and receive the gospel demands a fundamental change of heart. Loyalty is to be given to God alone; all other loyalties and commitments become provisional, subject to judgment in terms of trust in and loyalty to the Father. Because their loyalties are provisional, followers of Jesus are pilgrims, sojourners on the earth, citizens of another city. Such citizenship breaks down all the racial, sexual, cultural, and class differences on which human beings conventionally rely for a sense of security and self-esteem (Gal. 3:28). Moreover, the change of heart, the new loyalty, and the universality of the gospel must be manifest in action (Jas. 1:22–25; Mt. 7:21–24). The conflict between new and old loyalties is thus social as well as psychic.

This first radicalism of the gospel is familiar enough to need little elaboration; yet it is at the same time so familiar and so radical that its demands for love, forgiveness, generosity, patience, and compassion are too readily assimilated to the conventional ways in which these virtues are institutionalized. Generosity means giving to the United Way; patience means not yelling at the children; forgiveness means not hitting back; and so on. Such easy reductions of the demands of faith may be why the gospel includes a second kind of radicalism: very specific and very fundamental behavioral demands. "You cannot serve God and Mammon" (Mt. 6:24). "Judge not, that you be not judged" (Mt. 7:1). "But love your enemies, and do good, and lend, expecting nothing in return" (Lk. 6:35). And, astonishingly:

> When you give a dinner or a banquet, do not invite your friends or your brothers or your kinsmen or rich neighbors, lest they also invite you in return, and you be repaid. But when you give a feast, invite the poor, the maimed, the lame, the blind, and you will be blessed, because they cannot repay you. You will be repaid at the resurrection of the just. (Lk. 14:12–14)[2]

Prudence, common sense, and decorum rebel at taking such a directive literally, or even seriously, and few do. Yet these particular demands are only specifications of the radical demand of faith.

Politically, the gospel is radical in the same two ways. First, the Old Testament prophetic theme that God has a special care for the poor is continued in the New. Jesus identifies himself with the poor, the outcast, and the oppressed. His first description of his mission (Mt. 5:3; Lk. 4:16–21) makes this identification, and he continues it throughout his public career. The apostolic church also stressed this mission (Eph. 4:28; Js. 2:1–13; 5:1–6) and institutionalized it in the practices of communal sharing, in the appointment of deacons, and in Paul's collection for the Jerusalem church.

Second, the gospel is politically radical because Jesus seems totally unconcerned about how his message affects political stability or about how those with power over him react to him. Neither Herod ("that fox") nor Pilate nor the politically powerful priests and scribes determine his course of action. On the contrary, he condemns the way political rulers act (Lk. 22:24–27) and recognizes that he and his followers will be perceived and persecuted as a challenge to political order (Lk. 21:12–15). "I have not come to bring peace, but a sword" (Mt. 10:34).

This perspective is familiar enough. The problem is, How are the radical sayings and the radical identification of Jesus with the poor and outcast to be taken? What does his subversive disinterest in political stability imply? How are the more outrageous counsels to be taken? Christian thought and practice have displayed an astonishing variety of responses, most of them designed in one way or another to evade the most radical demands.[3] They are often taken as outlining an ethic of intention; that is, they make radical demands on the inner dispositions, but not necessarily on behavior. Thus the demands are "spiritualized," and the harsh sayings are taken as Semitic hyperbole. Clearly this interpretation holds for some sayings ("If your right eye causes you to sin, pluck it out and throw it away"), but not for others ("Love your enemies"). Moreover, Jesus' prophetic identification with the *anawim* (the poor and lowly of the Lord) and his disregard of political order are too characteristic of his fundamental orientation to the world to dismiss as hyperbole. A second response softens the hard sayings by placing them in the context of Jesus' and the early church's seeming expectation of an imminent eschaton. Thus Jesus' demands constitute an ethic only for the brief interim before the end; they are not meant to found an enduring order. Another interpretation moves to the opposite extreme and regards them as a rule of life only for the coming heavenly kingdom. Others have regarded the radical demands as serious and possible, but only in a simple, rural socioeconomic climate.

Perhaps the most widespread avoidance mechanism, however, is to regard the radical gospel as a counsel of perfection intended only for an elite few in its full measure. After all, Jesus tells the rich young man to go and sell all he has and give to the poor only after the young man has reported to Jesus that he has kept all the commandments. Jesus also prefaces his answer with, "If you would be perfect. . ." (Mt. 19:16–22). Perfection cannot be expected of those who must scratch out a living and raise a family day by day. Thus, the radical gospel is for monks and hermits and, perhaps, priests, nuns, and ministers, but it does not demand fundamental social, economic, or political transformation.

The trouble with this interpretation is that it receives support in only a few isolated passages; for example, "He who is able to receive this, let him receive it" (Mt. 19:12) or Paul's strict view of marriage coupled with prudent advice (1 Cor. 7). But the "more excellent way" of love is clearly meant for all Christians (1 Cor. 12:31–13:13), and most of Jesus' preaching is addressed to all who hear, not just a select few. After all, the most radical teaching, the Sermon on the Mount (or Plain), is given to "the crowds" as well as to the disciples (Mt. 5:1; Lk. 6:17).

Many Christians have, of course, taken the radical gospel to heart. St. Anthony, the founder of monasticism, gave away all his wealth and went to the desert when he heard the gospel of the rich young man proclaimed. St. Francis of Assisi's inspiration was similar. These may be an elite, but if the elite are defined as those who follow the radical demands of the gospel, the question is begged. Most sectarian movements take inspiration from the radical gospel. The "peace churches" are formed by Jesus' clear condemnation of violence, even in self-defense. Other groups of Christians, such as the Catholic Worker Movement, are oriented to communal living and sacrificial care for the poorest of the poor. Christian revolutionaries in Latin America take as their model the Christ who condemned oppression in the harshest language and placed himself totally on the side of the poor. Others who work for the nonviolent transformation of unjust social, economic, and political structures have the same model. Throughout church history, to use H. Richard Niebuhr's typology, both "Christ Against Culture" sectarian movements and the "Christ Transforming Culture" tradition have been inspired by the radical gospel.[4]

Yet whatever contributions these two traditions have made, their limitations are also clear. The same Father who sent Jesus to show a new way also created the world and human beings with a need for order, culture, and stability. Those who would transform the world forget that Jesus recommended no specific plan of political change, no form of a regime, and no social-economic theory. The radical gospel sits side by side with the prudent advice of Romans 13, Jesus' evasive answer to the tribute question, and the compromise over the application of the law to gentile Christians (Acts 15:1–29).

The political danger of the radical gospel is ideology, for ideology supplies the specific political program which the radical gospel lacks. Why ideology fills the vacuum is readily seen. If what is genuinely radical about the gospel is that it claims all areas of life for Christ; if, therefore, Christians must be disciples in all they do; and if Scripture gives no fixed rules of behavior in politics and economics, then the Christian faces a dilemma. He must rely on the difficult discipline of prayer, study, and reflection to determine a course of political action, even then living with uncertainty, or he must find a table of rules and a program of principles to read into Scripture. Since a life of radical calling laden with uncertainty over how to live the call is a life in tension, the Christian is strongly tempted to relieve the tension by finding an ideological solution. Thus, even with the best of intentions, a radical political theology degenerates into a radical political ideology in which human devices and human frailties provide the heart of a program for which divine sanction is claimed. Such an ideology may be found either on the left or on the right, depending more on ideological fashion than on theological insight.[5]

This is not to say that all proponents of the radical gospel are unaware of its dangers.[6] The problem, however, is to create a Christian political theology inspired by the radical gospel but not captured by ideology. Perhaps the virtue of Christian prudence can direct such a faithful, rather than ideological, approach to political life.

Prudence and the qualities associated with it, such as discretion, shrewdness, craftiness, and wisdom, are far more prominent in the Old Testament than the New.[7] The careful, clever way is less at home in the radical atmosphere of the new covenant than in the more practical atmosphere of the old. Where prudence, wisdom, or shrewdness do appear in the New Testament, they are often treated ironically (e.g., Lk. 16:8–9 and 1 Cor. 1:19). Yet the difference is not simply between the new and old covenants, for prudence is also not prominent in the prophetic literature. Where the thirst for justice is intense, cautious efforts at reform will not slake it.

Yet Scripture at times does recommend prudence's watchful appreciation of circumstances. "Behold, I send you out as sheep in the midst of wolves; so be wise as serpents and innocent as doves" (Mt. 10:16). "For he has made known to us in all wisdom and insight the mystery of his will . . ." (Eph. 1:9). The parable of the wise and foolish virgins recommends foresight (Mt. 25:1–13). The follower of Christ must understand the signs of the times and discern in them the will of God. Thus prudence is more than mere cleverness or shrewdness. Knowledge and love of God and neighbor manifest in forgiveness, generosity, justice for the poor, and trust in the Father's love are the heart of the gospel. But the gospel also requires insight into the particular circumstances in which the Christian must act, as well as appreciation of the probable consequences of various courses of action. The evils of this world must not be condemned and attacked improvidently, lest the attack create worse evils and miss real but limited opportunities for good.

Contemporary conservatives criticize liberal Christians and liberation theology for lacking such prudence, though they tend not to use that term. Edward Norman, for example, criticizes Christian attacks on the South African regime because "very little consideration is given to the possible political consequences of bringing about the collapse of the existing structure."[8] A prudent consideration of the nature of politics dictates that power should not be radically condemned or ignored; rather, power and coercion are irremovable features of human life and may be used to promote the good where possible and to restrain greater evil where necessary. Both Niebuhr's "Christ Above Culture" and "Christ and Culture in Paradox" traditions implicitly recognize the value of prudence. The Catholic tradition enshrines it as one of the four cardinal virtues. St. Thomas transforms Aristotelian prudence into the central virtue of Christian moral and political life. Self-giving love is the supreme Christian virtue, but prudence regulates the specific means toward the end of love and makes it effective in action.[9]

Politically, the Christian recognizes in order and stability the return of grace upon fallen nature. Politics is necessarily infected with sin, but God has provided in the human propensity for association, in fear of injustice, and in love of order the materials for restraining the worst effects of sin. Tradition and authority, moreover, have not completely lost their natural goodness; they can contribute creatively to the development of human character, to the building of community, and to justice, freedom, and the common good.[10]

John Hallowell showed in *The Moral Foundation of Democracy* that politics is more than the instrument by which some bend others to their will. It can be an instrument for pursuit of the common good through deliberation in terms of common interest and commitment. Democracy in particular recognizes the sinfulness of human beings and their need for coercion, but it also recognizes their capacity for good. "It is this capacity of men to respect the common right, the public good, and the universal law, though they often need the compulsion of law to implement that respect, that makes democracy possible."[11] Democracy understands that man is passionate and self-interested, but also that he is a moral, rational, and spiritual creature. Because human beings have such capacities, persuasion through debate and deliberation is possible, and "political prudence" can direct the way toward decisions which best promote the common good in the particular circumstances in which a political regime is situated.[12]

It follows from this perspective that the prudent Christian owes a certain amount of respect to a democratic political order and that political order in general is not necessarily opposed to gospel principles. Such a favorable view, however, carries with it a danger as real as the danger of the radical gospel. When the claims of political order are taken too seriously and when the gospel becomes comfortable rather than discomfiting, Christian prudence may shade into civil religion. The church loses the distance from politics necessary to criticize it in the name of the gospel.

This is not the place to review the lengthy debate over the nature of civil religion. My use of the term is very close to Niebuhr's category of "The Christ of Culture," in which the tension between Christ and the world is lost. Those who occupy this position "interpret culture through Christ, regarding those elements in it as most important which are most accordant with his work and person; on the other hand they understand Christ through culture, selecting from his teaching and action as well as from the Christian doctrine about him such points as seem to agree with what is best in civilization."[13] Civil religion is as prone to ideology as the radical gospel, but its ideologies are of the tame and safe middle ground. Civil religion in America is either liberal or conservative. Its most prominent representative today is the new "Christian Right."

From the perspective of the radical gospel civil religion is idolatrous because it worships the values of society rather than the one God. Loyalty to God ceases to be exclusive, because it exists alongside and is interpreted through loyalty to power, nation, economic system, and class. Conservative civil religion spiritualizes Christ into irrelevance, objecting to the state only when it directly interferes with worship, but serving it loyally when it pursues its properly "secular" goals. At the extreme, such a position can paralyze Christian resistance to a clearly demonic regime, as it did in Germany during the 1930s and 1940s.[14] Liberal civil religion forgets the transcendence of God and the necessity of personal commitment to Jesus Christ because personal freedom and programmatic reform have become the true faith.

Christian prudence need not succumb to the disease of civil religion, for a more precise understanding of prudence builds up resistance. There are, I contend, two different kinds of prudence, which I shall refer to as "lower" and "higher" prudence. Each is a legitimate form of Christian prudence, and each form is recognized in ordinary language. Lower prudence is cautious and discreet. It is defensive, focused on survival and respect. These are important values, and concern with personal safety and with one's appearance to others is proper. Such prudence requires and exhibits many of the "gifts of the Spirit." It cultivates peace, patience, kindness, gentleness, and self-control, and it knows how to avoid anger, dissension, envy, licentiousness, and the other "works of the flesh" (Gal. 5:16–25).

Politically, lower prudence is conservative and realistic. It values political stability because it understands the fragility of order and the evils spawned by social chaos. It attempts to identify and distinguish changeable conditions from those which, even though unjust, cannot be changed in the short run. It resists radical attacks on the latter, because they inevitably fail and generally produce greater injustices. Lower Christian prudence is skeptical of all-embracing ideologies and plans for society. It recognizes the place of sin and self-interest in politics. Knowing that these cannot be erased, it devises and defends institutions such as capitalism and representative government which minimize their effects and channel them in beneficial directions. Lower prudence appreciates the limits of political possibility and is open to compromise.

Higher prudence, on the other hand, is active, caring more for justice than survival and for love than respect. It takes risks in the interest of realizing higher values. While it appreciates lower prudence, it demands that the lower be governed by the higher, for it is less concerned with stability than with the realization of love in concrete circumstances. More precisely, it follows the prophets in contending that the only genuine peace and stability are those founded on God's law; that is, on justice and mercy. Therefore, injustice and oppression are essentially unstable. They must be challenged for what they are and their ugliness exposed, even though such an attack runs the risk of promoting a violent backlash. The existence of higher prudence allows the New Testament to take an ironic stance toward lower prudence.

Higher Christian prudence shares the lower's suspicion of ideology, because ideology claims ready-made solutions applicable to any society. The sabbath, however, is made for man; the fabric of justice must be fitted to the circumstances of each society. Jesus' higher prudence is anti-ideological. He condemns injustice and oppression; he articulates the principles of a new order; but he leaves it to his disciples constantly to work out the particular institutions of that order in accord with the materials at hand.

Higher prudence, while not rejecting the importance of lower prudence, comes closest to the authentic understanding of prudence in Aristotle and Aquinas, for whom prudence is not a cautious virtue but a virtue in which the highest things come alive in human action. For St. Thomas, prudence operates with a "robustness and an abandon to God." "It is a virtue infused with grace; its measure exceeds that of living merely according to reason—its measure is the mind of Christ; its purpose is not to be respectable but to be a fellow citizen of the saints and a familiar of God. . . . It springs from and lives only in charity, without which one may be shrewd but cannot be prudent."[15] The lawgiver must be prudent, but his prudence is directed by a radical goal. "The entire purpose of the lawgiver is that man may love God."[16]

Jesus and Paul exhibit both lower and higher prudence. They do not directly challenge the political regime or attempt to overthrow through direct action an unjust order. They implicitly recognize, Paul more clearly than Jesus, the value of political order. But the message they bring attacks the very foundation of the Roman regime in its demand for a love which is unconditional and which is first poured out upon the poor and the exploited. When this message brings them into confrontation with the powers that be, they do not compromise it for the sake of life or reputation. Indeed, Jesus clearly recognizes that he will be killed by an unjust order for the demands he is making. Thus, the radical gospel joins Christian prudence at the point where higher prudence demands that the actions necessary to fulfill loyalty to the Father and unconditional faith, hope, and love are actions which undermine the existing order and which provoke that order to defend itself through persecution. Jesus does not recommend love of enemies or justice to the poor for reasons of prudence, that is, because they bring recognition or admiration; quite the contrary, they bring disgrace and resentment. The recurring Old Testament theme of wealth and prosperity as a return for obedience to the law largely disappears from the New. Lower prudence might practice love for its rewards; higher prudence will not.

Yet within the context of the higher, more radical prudence Jesus frequently maneuvers with a lower prudence. He does not accept the futile Zealot option of revolt against the oppressors. He simply leaves when the crowds try to make him king (Jn. 6:15). He deftly avoids the traps laid in the tribute question (Mt. 22:15–22) and the question of his authority (Mt. 21:23–27). Lower prudence has its place.

Paul frequently practices the lower form of prudence. He seems to assume that the political order is just, or at least to act as if it were just. He freely claims the rights of his Roman citizenship and defends himself against illegal and improper arrests and judicial proceedings.[17] Political order clearly has a value for Paul, as Romans 13 amply demonstrates.

But it is also amply clear that Paul considers the powers of this world ultimately to be demonic and that the Christian's loyalty is to Christ, not to the political regime. Romans 13 is not a defense of unconditional obedience to the state, nor is it a declaration of the autonomy of secular institutions. Romans 13 is situated in the context of Paul's teaching of the same radical demands made by Jesus: do not be conformed to the world, be patient in tribulation, do not repay evil for evil, but do good to the enemy (Rom. 12), and love your neighbor as yourself (Rom. 13:8–10). In short, for both Paul and Jesus the radical demands of higher prudence always control the caution of lower prudence.

A concept which captures very well the sense of higher prudence is stewardship. Though stewardship today is often limited to the context of financial support for the church, its actual range of application is the whole of life. The follower of Christ is accountable as a steward for the use of time, possessions, and talents. The steward must wisely administer all the gifts given by God, especially the grace of the gospel (1 Cor. 4:1–2; 9:16–17; Eph. 3:2; Col. 1:25; 1 Tim. 1:4; Tit. 1:7; 1 Pet. 4:10). The highest virutes—love, faith, hope, forgiveness, patience, compassion, mercy, the good news to the poor—are gifts entrusted to his followers by Jesus, and his followers must be stewards of these mysteries. A steward must administer what he receives, using it for the master's benefit. Stewardship thus requires lower prudence, so that the gifts entrusted are not squandered or invested in foolish and unproductive enterprises. But stewardship also demands risk-taking; that is, radical action or higher prudence. It is not enough for the steward cautiously to protect the gifts of God; he must administer them so that they increase, and attempting to increase a thing of value is always risky. The person who invests money in new ventures takes greater risks than the person who hides it. This truth recalls the saying that the follower of Christ must be a light shining in the darkness, not a lamp hidden under a basket. A light in the darkness is not only a guide for travelers; it is also an easy target.

Jesus, of course, tells a number of parables of stewardship, recommending the lower prudence of the "unjust" steward (Lk. 16:1–9), but especially commending the risk-taking of the good steward (Lk. 19:11–26; Mt. 25:14–30). A scrupulous weighing of costs and benefits does not fit stewardship. In creative and risk-taking care to spread the gospel entrusted to him, the steward's left hand must not know what his right is doing. The lender must not expect repayment. After all, Jesus did not worry about the ingratitude of the nine cleansed lepers who did not return; the faith of the one who did was worth the cure.

Thus the prudent steward of the radical gospel might urge his nation to take the risk of cutting arms spending before its adversary does. Such a steward might not worry overmuch about abuse of income support programs or about whether such programs are as efficient as possible. He will be more concerned about whether they are as compassionate as possible. Such a steward will preach and live the gospel in season and out, honoring and encouraging the political regime insofar as it is authoritative and promotes human character and community through pursuit of freedom, justice, and the common good. Insofar as the regime fails in these tasks, it is to be criticized and prodded by a steward church.

The lower prudence which forms a part of this understanding of stewardship must be exercised primarily defensively. That is, it must use common sense and political acumen to avoid the dangers of ideology and to guard against foolish squandering of the grace of the gospel. The steward who turns his charge over to a radical ideology or to a conventional ideology is an unfaithful steward and can be steward no longer, for he has nothing left to administer. The gospel has slipped through his fingers. The unique challenge of the gospel may be lost through the caution of lower prudence or the zeal of radicalism. Stewardship, the higher prudence, cherishes the gospel and so preserves it from loss; at the same time, the radical gospel goads the steward until he is free enough to risk himself in its service.

Ellis Sandoz · *Power and Spirit in the Founding: Thoughts on the Genesis of Americanism*

Despite the misgivings of the American founders themselves, the patriotic consciousness of the country from the very first insisted that the founding was an activity of men more than merely mortal done in close cooperation with the Deity himself. It is my purpose here to sketch the founders' "divine science of politics" as the noetic ground of popular consciousness and of the symbolisms articulating the order of our constitutional democracy in Americanism. I propose to do this by considering the authority of the founders, the character of the consensus that emerged in the formative period, and the science of politics with its penumbra of foundation myth and civil theology. The "divine science of politics" is John Adams's symbol. The equation of "the dictates of reason and pure Americanism" originates with Thomas Jefferson.[1]

I

It is evident that the authority of the founders or Founding Fathers (habitually capitalized, as befits heroic and celestial beings), has been and remains great in the American consciousness. A French visitor to the country understated the case when he reported in 1939 that "America is the only country in the world which pretends to listen to the teaching of its founders as if they were still alive."[2] We listen to them much better than if they were still alive. The founders themselves would have been amused by the twentieth-century report but scarcely surprised by it. The "canonization" of the founders began with the Revolution and Constitution themselves and culminated in the "emotional outburst" that swept the country on the fiftieth anniversary of the Declaration of Independence when the news broke that John Adams and Thomas Jefferson both had died on that day, "the point at which the American people came to remember the Revolutionary fathers for what they had agreed upon rather than for their disputes with one another."[3] But the founding generation was fully aware at the time that epochal events were unfolding, that history had taken a new turn, and that the *novus ordo seclorum* was being imprinted upon America and the world itself by the heroic mind of remarkable men in its midst. Contemporaries also were aware that this is the stuff myths are made of and themselves entered into the fabulous articulation of the tenor and significance of events never regarded as merely secular and pragmatic by leading participants. Jefferson called the Federal Convention "an assembly of demigods," and not to be outdone, Adams soon afterward and with customary irony magnified the framers as "heroes, sages, and demigods" for whom he hoped to become one of the "underworkmen." Yet at the very end of their lives Jefferson gently uttered the final encomium when he wistfully wrote of "the Heroic age" of the founding and of himself and his dear old friend Adams as among its "Argonauts."[4]

Perhaps the leading participant who was, at once, most sensitive to the momentous, portentous, and comic dimensions of the founding was John Adams. "It has been the will of Heaven," he wrote in January 1776, "that we should be thrown into existence at a period when the greatest philosophers and lawgivers of antiquity would have wished to live. A period when [we have] an opportunity of beginning government anew from the foundation. . . . How few of the human race have ever had any opportunity of choosing a system of government for themselves and their children!"[5] Less than a month before Independence, Adams wrote from Philadelphia where the Continental Congress was in session: "Objects of the most stupendous magnitude, and measures in which the lives and liberties of millions yet unborn are intimately interested, are now before us. We are in the very midst of a revolution, the most complete, unexpected, and remarkable, of any in the history of nations. . . . When these things are once completed, I shall think that I have answered the end of my creation, and sing my *nunc dimittis* . . . ." Myth taking shape before one's eyes is a disconcerting experience, however, as we see from Adams's comments of 1777 when, in the face of Washington's ascension, adulation veered toward idolatry: "Now we can allow a certain citizen to be wise, virtuous, and good, without thinking him a deity or saviour," he wrote Abigail. And some months earlier he had said to Benjamin Rush: "I have been distressed to see some of our members disposed to idolize an image which their own hands have molten. I speak of the superstitious veneration which is paid to General Washington."[6] In the following year Washington was, for the first time, indeed proclaimed "Father of his Country" in Francis Bailey Lancaster's 1778 *Almanac.*[7] Adams's irritation and misgivings were patent. They grew from his historical awareness of the danger to liberty and republican institutions posed by charismatic military leaders and the opinion that, as worthy as Washington truly was, "in this house [i.e., Congress], I feel myself his superior"—views which very nearly implicated him in the popular mind in an unsavory intrigue against the emergent legendary Father of his Country.[8]

It is with some further irony, then, that in Adams's preface to the first volume of *A Defence of the Constitutions of the United States of America Against the Attack of M. Turgot . . .* (1787) he points out that, while it "was the general opinion of ancient nations, that Divinity alone was adequate to the important office of giving laws to men," in the United States of America "it will never be pretended that any persons employed in that service had interviews with the gods, or were in any degree under the inspiration of Heaven," since "men are now sufficiently enlightened to disabuse themselves of artifice, imposture, hypocrisy, and superstition. . . ."[9] This was partly, no doubt, a swipe at the burgeoning Washington cult born of envy, perhaps, but also of the distasteful recollection that King James I and Oliver Cromwell each had been lauded as Father of his Country (*parens patriae; pater patriae*). It was also a counter to Turgot, meant to assure the enlightened *philosophe* that American lawgivers were as rational as he and relied upon "the simple principles of nature . . . reason and the senses" in contriving their new governments.[10] Still, it was the "divine science of politics" that Adams celebrated, as we shall shortly see.[11]

By 1790 Adams's irritation with the Washington myth at large in the country hatched a fleeting Swiftian satire as he sketched a "fable plot": "The essence of the whole will be that Dr. Franklin's electrical rod smote the earth and out sprung General Washington. That Franklin electrified him with his rod—and thence forward these two concluded the policy, negotiations, and war." The myth took its scientistic turn in the inevitable direction of Newtonian physics, in this parody of the country's "Saviour, Deliverer, and Founder."[12] Two decades later, long after Washington's death, Adams still ridiculed the "hypocritical cult" that idolized "*divus*

Washington, *sancte* Washington, *ora pro nobis*!" And he implored another correspondent, Dr. Waterhouse: "Do not however, I pray you, call me 'the godlike Adams,' 'the sainted Adams,' 'Our Saviour Adams,' 'Our Redeemer Adams'. . . ."[13] Recoil as he might from the rhetoric of myth, Adams jocularly stated in private correspondence what he had really long since soberly concluded. If, come what may, there is to be a Father of the Country, then his own credentials were as good as anybody's. Thus he wrote to William Cunningham: "They called me venerable Father of New England. I resented that, because if there was any pretence for calling me Father of New England, there was equal pretence for calling me Father of Kentucky and Tennessee. I was therefore willing to be thought the Father of the Nation."[14]

In truth, the matter was settled long before July 4, 1826, and earlier than when Adams staked his own claim in the letter of 1809 to Cunningham. To be sure, John Adams would have to settle for the merely collective immortality of the Founding Fathers, as befitted an underworkman. But this already had been achieved. One example must suffice. In *The United States Elevated to Glory and Honor*, the election sermon preached in 1783 by President Ezra Stiles of Yale College, Washington, Jefferson, Adams, and others of the national pantheon were mustered in a mighty "discourse upon the political welfare of God's American Israel . . . allusively prophetick of the future prosperity and splendour of the United States." Stiles exclaimed: "Already does the new constellation of the United States begin to realize this glory. . . . And we have reason to hope, and I believe to expect, that God has still greater blessings in store for this vine which his own right hand hath planted, and to make us 'high among the nations in praise, and in name, and in honour,'" quoting Deuteronomy 26:19, his text for the occasion.[15] God's wrath abated, and the Revolution ended in victory and secure independence for the American Israel, so "does it not become us to reflect how wonderful, how gracious, how glorious has been the good hand of our God upon us in carrying us through so tremendous a warfare!" Washington, true to Adams's grumblings, is lauded above all others as the leader

> Congress put at the head of [its] spirited army [as] the only man on whom the eyes of all Israel were placed. Posterity . . . inconsiderate and incredulous as they may be of the dominion of

> heaven, will yet do so much justice to the divine moral government as to acknowledge that this American Joshua was raised up by God and divinely formed by a peculiar influence of the Sovereign of the Universe for the great work of leading the armies of this American Joseph (now separated from his brethren) and conducting this people through the severe, the arduous conflict, to Liberty and Independence.[16]

Stiles, in common with other preachers of the period and even with Tom Paine (see his *Crisis Papers*), characterizes the Revolution as a Just War, retold as a heroic tale in the rhetoric of an Old Testament parable. Washington is greater than Cyrus or Caesar, and others even compared him to Jesus Christ! Jefferson "poured the soul of the continent into the monumental act of Independence," and Franklin, Adams, Jay and others "resolutely and nobly dared to sign the glorious act," thereby meriting the immortality of fame. Adams is eulogized as "that great civilian" and quoted as expressing his faith that the Revolution served the purposes of divine Providence, accelerating by centuries the progress of society toward the millennium. The language becomes apocalyptical as America's messianic destiny is meditated, to the point where the "collective body of the United States" is evoked in close analogy to the mystical body of Christ ordained to "illume the world with TRUTH and LIBERTY." And unique to the new dispensation is that it "will embosom all the religious sects or denominations in Christendom. Here they may all enjoy their whole respective systems of worship and church government complete. . . ." Thereby America's true republicanism and steadfast faithfulness may providentially conspire to attain "a singular superiority—with the ultimate subserviency to the glory of God, in converting the world" to Christianity.[17]

It can readily be seen from Stiles's sermon how the mythopoeic imagination of Americans of the formative period translated for general consumption the great events of the time into the genre of a sacred history augmenting that provided in the Bible. For all of the theoretical acuity and up-to-date rationalism of the intellectual leadership of America—not excluding Ezra Stiles himself—, the controlling self-interpretation of the founding lay in the mode of articulation just illustrated. And it remained substantially controlling as the basis of Americanism, the common sense of the nation. In Perry Miller's summary, the preachers of the time were not selling a Revolution to a people sluggish to buy in providing a religious interpretation of events, but explaining matters as they truly believed them to be. "[N]or were they distracted by worries about the probability that Jefferson held all their constructions to be nonsense. A pure rationalism such as his might have declared the independence of these folk, but it could never have inspired them to fight for it." Further:

> The American situation . . . was not what Paine presented in *Common Sense*—a community of hard-working, rational creatures being put upon by an irrational tyrant—but more like the recurrent predicament of the chosen people in the Bible. . . . The Jews originally were a free republic founded on a covenant over which God "in peculiar favor to that people, was pleased to preside." When they offended Him, He punished them by destroying their republic, subjecting them to a king. . . . Hence when we angered our God, a king was also inflicted upon us; happily, Americans have succeeded, where the Jews did not, in recovering something of pristine virtue, whereupon Heaven redressed America's earthly grievances.[18]

Because of secularization during the past two centuries, pains must be taken to supply the experiential context that makes the foundation myth plausible and intelligible. To be sure, the mythic quality of the Declaration and Constitution is apparent to some degree. The atmosphere in which Founding Fathers of heroic dimension proclaim self-evident truths respecting the creation and creatures therein, and contrive out of more than merely mortal wisdom a matchless instrument for the ordering of the lives of all future generations of Americans (a model for mankind itself), is plainly a world of mythopoeic contrivance. Yet there is missing the verdant foliage of the people's myth told in the parlance of popular consciousness. While complete on principle and aimed toward magistrates and the enlightened urbane of America and the world, the official, secular version is deficient in the pathos of which it is an intellectualized expression. The myth that arises from the experience of America as New Israel, a land apart, and of Americans as a Chosen People whose destiny lies among the stars of the heavenly firmament, of a providentially ordained history tending inexorably toward the kingdom of God is only hinted in our state papers. The decisive context must be sought elsewhere in the contemporary sources. The sense of divine election and messianic purpose that crowns Ezra Stiles's political faith, as we glimpse it in his 1783 sermon, composes a vital dimension of Americanism that need not be left to supposition and must not be ignored if we wish to understand the founding as it was originally portrayed.

The outlook of the founders is well suggested and permanently symbolized by inclusion on the reverse of the Great Seal of the United States (conceived and designed between 1776 and 1782) of the "Eye of Providence in a radiant Triangle" placed above a "pyramid unfinished" on the base of which appears the "Annuit Coeptis MDCCLXXVI" and "underneath the following motto, '*Novus Ordo Seclorum*.'"[19] As the symbols indicate, divine Providence presides over the establishment of the New Order of the Ages by its anointed people, America. Adams, Jefferson, and Franklin composed the 1776 committee to design the seal and Charles Thompson explained it to Congress in these words in 1782: "The pyramid signifies Strength and Duration: The Eye over it and the Motto allude to the many signal interpositions of Providence in favour of the American cause. The date underneath is that of the Declaration of Independence and the words under it signify the beginning of the new American Aera, which commences from that date."[20]

When Washington was inaugurated first president of the United States in New York City on April 30, 1789, the Bible was opened to the forty-ninth chapter of Genesis for the administration of the oath of office. And he laid his hand upon verses 13 to 33 which recount Jacob's blessing of Joseph as the Prince of his brethren.[21]

II

The authority of the founders (attested by the spontaneous emergence of the public cult around them which viewed them as heroic figures) rested on the conviction of the American community that their words and deeds served liberty, truth, justice, and reason. The vindication of this conviction through both the success of the Revolution militarily and of the transition from colonial to sovereign nationhood politically—marked by the framing of the Constitution, its ratification, inauguration of the president, convening of the Congress, and adoption of the Bill of Rights during a decade and a half—profoundly secured the concord of the people and durably institutionalized their vision of public order. These achievements are no less remarkable politically because of their familiarity to us two centuries later, or because we so easily concede the wisdom and good luck of the generation of '76 of whom we are beneficiaries.

The creation of a society organized for action in history is no merely pragmatic achievement, important as the practicalities indeed are. Mere utility does not evoke the passion for liberty and justice commonplace in the utterances of the period. The small politics of mutual accommodation and self-aggrandizement (always present) cannot account fully for great political achievement. And however much the high achiever may be driven to attain fame and glory, and rightly claim them when they are his due, persons as well educated as Adams, Jefferson, Madison, and the other leaders of the founding, knew (whatever Machiavelli and Bacon had said) that the timocratic men were not the true *aristoi*, noble though they might be.[22] Rather, at the pinnacle of worthy achievement of the order encountered in the American founding, one must look to vision and virtue for primary explanation. And as he looks, he should not forget that humble Socrates himself laid just claim to the highest honor Athens could bestow (*Apology* 36A–37A).

If it is true that the order of a society not only has a pragmatic dimension but a theoretical one as well, and that it represents not only a self-contained parochial truth of a conventional sort, but also existential and transcendental truth that relates the society and its citizenry to nature and the ground of being to assert the claim of universal validity, then ultimate theoretical moorings of the American mind must be sought. They can be found, I have suggested, in philosophy and Christianity.[23] What this ultimate horizon of reality comes to in certain central aspects is concisely stated by Professor Hallowell:

> The Hebraic-Greek-Christian tradition teaches us . . . that the ultimate reality behind nature and history is a creative, rational, moral, loving Will and that man, since he is created in the image and likeness of God, achieves the perfection of his being in willing submission to the Reason and Will of Him that governs the universe. Men may resist that will or submit to it, but they can-

> not change it. The ultimate reality cannot be made over to conform to our desires—it is not something we can make or manipulate but something to which ultimately we must conform. Ultimately, all our actions will be judged by a standard which is not our own but God's.[24]

Since we have come so far with John Adams, the deepest thinker among the founders, it will serve to go yet a little farther with him to ascertain the character of American concord (or *homonoia*) that made it a community bound together by affection and mutual conviction. He is a fit spokesman: "I have hitherto had the happiness to find that my pulse beat in exact union with those of my Countrymen," he wrote in 1778.[25] In Adams's view the substance of the community consisted of Christianity, moral and intellectual virtue, and love of liberty: "Governments . . . founded on the natural authority of the people . . . authority in magistrates and obedience of citizens . . . grounded on reason, morality, and the Christian religion. . . ."[26] The "divine science of politics" of the founders presupposed a virtuous citizenry, true religion, honest and able leaders. That some such community actually existed is acknowledged by John Jay in *Federalist No. 2*, and James Madison reported that the people were "knit together . . . by . . . many chords of affection." Thomas Jefferson, writing toward the end of his life, believed that he and Adams and the other authors of the Declaration of Independence had spoken nearly fifty years earlier for a unified community merely stating "the common sense of the subject . . . [as] an expression of the American mind. . . . All its authority rests then on the harmonizing sentiments of the day. . . ." "[T]here was but one opinion on this side of the water. All American Whigs thought alike on these subjects."[27]

This political science embraces a "true map of man" that delineates "the dignity of his nature, and the noble rank he holds among the works of God," that lays it down "that consenting to slavery is a sacrilegious breach of trust, as offensive in the sight of God as it is derogatory from our own honor or interest in happiness," and acknowledges "that God Almighty has promulgated from heaven, liberty, peace, and good-will to man!"[28] With customary power Adams reaffirmed his views long years after the founding. After quoting from an old pamphlet entitled "Address of the Young men of the City of Philadelphia" to which he had responded while president ("We regard our Liberty and Independence, as the richest portion given Us by our Ancestors"), Adams asks Jefferson:

> And who were these Ancestors? Among them were Thomas Jefferson and John Adams. And I very cooly believe that no two Men among those Ancestors did more toward it than those two. . . . The *general Principles*, on which the Fathers achieved Independence, were the only Principles in which that beautiful Assembly of young Gentlemen [representing the numerous religious denominations of the country at the time of the Revolution] could Unite. . . . And what were these *general Principles*? I answer, the general Principles of Christianity, in which all those Sects were United: And the *general Principles* of English and American Liberty, in which all those young Men United, and which had United all Parties in America, in Majorities sufficient to assert and maintain her Independence.
>
> Now I will avow, that I then believed, and now believe, that those general Principles of Christianity, are as eternal and immutable, as the Existence and Attributes of God; and that those Principles of Liberty, are as unalterable as human Nature and our terrestrial, mundane System.[29]

III

Space does not permit a full synopsis of the founders' divine science of politics. Yet it is vital to appreciate the breadth and depth of the vision that their work as lawgivers, philosophers, and statesmen in fact reflects. In discharge of their pragmatic tasks, they moved in full awareness of the Western political tradition and sought to establish, in the wake of the Revolution, the best governments—for the states and through the Constitution for the nation—that the nature of man and the force of circumstance would allow. For this purpose they had full recourse to the differentiated thought of ancient and modern philosophers and the spiritual insight of the Christian faith into the reality of human existence, no less than to the science of government and to extensive experience in practical politics. They knew that the happiness of men is the end of politics and their blessedness the goal of faith: *salus populi suprema lex esto*. They believed the laws of nature and nature's God represented the objective foundation of positive law and of the liberties inherent to themselves as men and, so, inalienable. Blackstone, on the eve of the Revolution, had confirmed the traditional view that the law of nature was "coeval with mankind, and dictated by God himself," and universally obligatory, so that no laws were binding which did not conform to it; in this he was repeating Coke, who had anointed Aristotle "nature's Secretary" in tracing the truth of order. Behind John Locke's powerful rationalistic summary lay the unfolding of the Whig interpretation of politics and history that subtly blended the constitutional order of England and the legacy of the common law back to Magna Carta and immemorial usage with the higher law guaranteed by right reason and "written with the finger of God in the heart of man."[30] At the core of this extensive body of thought lay the notions of government by consent (popular sovereignty) and the sanctity of the fundamental law limiting government's authority, whose kernel of protected liberties unfolded especially from Article 39 of Magna Carta (1215 A.D.). As early as 1646 in America John Winthrop recited the Lockean formula that government primarily exists to protect men's "lives, liberties, and estates, etc., according to their due natural rights, as freeborn English, etc. [*sic*]"[31] This phrase was made famous in 1690 when Locke rendered it as equivalent to "Property," a way station on its long passage from Magna Carta to Declaration to the Fifth and Fourteenth Amendments' Due Process clauses as a part of the supreme law of the land's fundamental liberty. James Madison and the other framers completely understood that their handiwork rested on "the transcendent law of nature and of nature's God, which declares that the safety and happiness of society are the objects at which all political institutions aim, and to which all such institutions must be sacrificed."[32] In the founders' ransacking of the sources of political wisdom to optimally establish a free government of laws and not of men—government dedicated to the good of man through efficacious order and the preservation of individual liberties prized as antecedent to government and enhanced by sound institutional design, yet ultimately dependent upon the people as the supreme human authority—they knew that the virtue of the citizenry was no less essential simply because selfish passion tends to overwhelm ennobling reason and its offspring, law. The sum of all their testimony attests that the founders agreed in principle with the "Judicious" Hooker:

> Two foundations there are which bear up public societies; the one a natural inclination, whereby all men desire sociable life and fellowship; the other, an order expressly or secretly agreed upon touching the manner of their union in living together. The latter is that which we call the Law of a Commonweal, the very soul of a politic body, the parts whereof are by law animated, held together, and set on work in such actions, as the common good requireth. Laws politic, ordained for external order and regiment amongst men, are never framed as they should be, unless presuming the will of man to be inwardly obstinate, rebellious, and averse from all obedience unto the sacred laws of his nature; in a word, unless presuming man to be in regard of his depraved mind little better than a wild beast, they do accordingly provide notwithstanding unto the common good for which societies are instituted; unless they do this, they are not perfect. . . . All men desire to lead in this world a happy life. That life is led most happily, wherein all virtue is exercised without impediment or let.[33]

The theory of the Constitution's most famous innovation, the separation of powers and system of checks and balances, is predicated on the classical and Christian conceptions of man and law succinctly expressed by Hooker. Justice no less than reason is a divine trait of man's nature and not, as in "Hobbes . . . founded in contract solely." Rather it is "instinct, and innate, [imbedded in] the moral sense [that] is as much a part of our constitution as . . . feeling, seeing, or hearing," the gift of "a wise Creator [who] must have seen [it] to be necessary in an animal destined to live in society" virtuously and happily. Because all men enjoy equality of nature, laws—including constitutions—must not only embody justice, but also rest upon the consent of the people. Hence, on the one side, an unjust law is a nullity, and on the other side, "Laws they are not therefore which public approbation hath not made so."[34] In the language of *The Federalist*: "A good government implies two things; first, fidelity to the object of government, which is the happiness of the people; secondly, a knowledge of the means by which that object can be best attained."[35] *Primary* reliance for the securing of a just regime, one conducive to the liberty, well-being and happiness of the country, must ever rest on "the virtue and intelligence of the people of America."[36] Everyone understood, as the debate over the Bill of Rights showed, that if "the great mass of the people shou'd become *Corrupt*! ignorant of their Birthrite—and regardless of their posterity . . . it will not be in the power of Folios of Bills of rights to maintain their Liberties. The rights of Freemen are only to be maintain'd by Freemen."[37] It is essential, however, to cope with the factious, self-serving, passionate inclinations of men (as vividly known to Aristotle and Hooker as to Hobbes) by supplementing the primary "dependence on the people" for good government in a republic with the "auxiliary precautions" of the familiar institutional system of checks and balances resting on rival ambitions (Madison), thereby securing balance and equipoise by managing man's universal desire for emulation (Adams). Therewith, as Dudley Digges quaintly said in 1644, "charity to our neighbor, and love of our selves, doe sweetly kisse each other."[38]

Madison's elegant explanation in *Federalist No. 51* is familiar to all. Adams theorized the problem exhaustively in the *Defence of the Constitutions* and elsewhere, although everyone was familiar with the general theory of the balanced constitution from Blackstone, Montesquieu, and Charles I's classic statement in his *Answer to the XIX Propositions* (1642).[39] The Americans do not view ambition or emulation as utterly depraved *amor sui* (in Augustine's sense), however; and the system of checks and balances upon which it is predicated is at once the most ingenious feature of our government and the rock upon which the Constitution stands. As Adams remarks in discussing this crowning feature of the divine science of politics, the passion of emulation is as central to human institutions as gravity to the motions of the heavenly bodies. Both are rooted in nature, the desire for emulation "implanted in the human heart for the wisest and best purposes [by] God and nature. Democratic and aristocratic states are not in their own nature free. Political liberty is to be found only in moderate governments. . . . It is there only when there is no abuse of power. But constant experience shows us that every man invested with power is apt to abuse it, and to carry his authority as far as it will go. . . . To prevent this abuse, it is necessary from the very nature of things that power should be a check to power." The rule of law and its equivalent, reason, then, is only possible by pitting desire against desire, so "that [the] balance of passions and interests" is achieved "which alone can give authority to reason" in human affairs.

In practice, this requires the separating and checking of "three different orders of men *in equilibrio*." This theory applies the principle of a parallelogram of forces drawn from Newton's second law of motion to the institutionalization of governmental power, government then conceived as operating in analogy to the solar system, ruled by intrinsic psychological forces analogous to the physical forces regulating celestial mechanics.[40]

By such fascinatingly scientific means government can attain moderation and prudence in normal operations, and men more surely progress toward the justice and happiness that are their natural ends. "So far from believing in the total and universal depravity of human Nature," Adams stresses in 1817, "I believe there is no Individual totally depraved. The most abandoned scoundrel who ever existed, never Yet Wholly extinguished his Conscience, and while Conscience remains there is some Religion."[41] With men neither gods nor beasts, capable of virtue but inclined to vice, the means whereby the good polity can be approximated is a properly ordered free government; and "[t]he essence of free government consists in an effectual control of rivalries. . . . The nation which will not adopt an equilibrium of power must adopt a despotism. There is no alternative."[42]

IV

Power and spirit do not polarize in the founders' divine science of politics, despite their great stress on religious liberty and on the division of church and state in the institutional pattern. They never in their wildest flights dreamed of a system so perfect that the people will not need to be good.[43] To the contrary: they knew that good government presupposes good people—good, not perfect. All their aspirations and hopes utterly depend on the maintenance of the integrity of the community as the basis of the intricate constitutional system of their inspired design. Good morals and virtuous people depend, in turn, on true religion. "Patriotism without piety is mere grimace," a minister exclaimed in 1775.[44] In reflecting on the quality of the Constitution and the astonishing unity of the nation in support of its ratification, Madison in *Federalist No. 37* remarks: "It is impossible for the man of pious reflection not to perceive in it, a finger of the Almighty hand which has been so frequently and signally extended to our relief in the critical stages of the revolution."[45] Human affairs are embedded in the natural order conceived on the pattern of creation and Creator. Later expositors of the mind of the founders sometimes share the affliction noted by Jefferson: "They wish it to be believed that he can have no religion who advocates it's [*sic*] freedom."[46]

Indeed, the founders did advocate freedom of conscience, including religious freedom. They did so for several reasons. Most compelling was the one noticed in Adams's letter of June 28, 1813, previously quoted. The common ground of Christianity united the country, but to prefer one sect or denomination over another would have torn the community apart. Religious liberty was the only feasible policy in pragmatic terms, one well-considered when viewed against two centuries of the "madness" of religious strife, civil wars, fanaticism, and persecution.[47] The founders sought to end the dogmatomachy by protecting liberty and institutionalizing separate spheres of action for political and religious communities. This solution ranks without question as one of the very greatest achievements of the entire founding, deserving comparison with the theocratic solutions of Plato in antiquity and of Gelasius' "Doctrine of Two Swords" basic to the *Christianitas* of the Middle Ages.

The force of reason and justice could prevail, by the founders' calculations, only to the degree that passion was minimized in the conduct of public affairs. We have noticed this familiar strand of argumentation in Madison's and Adams's exegesis of the Constitution. The great source of chaos in political life from the sixteenth to the eighteenth century was religious passion. Every political writer of consequence from Bodin and Hooker to Rousseau considered the "madness of enthusiasm" and its cures. Short of Leviathan, no universal orthodoxy was practicable in the modern context and, indeed, there has been no dearth of Leviathans in the twentieth century. But for the founders, solution lay in the espousal of toleration and a tacit minimum dogma. *Either* on the faith that the truth will prevail and that therefore divergent views in religion as in other subjects ought to be allowed full expression (so long as public peace were not disrupted), *or* on the faith that Christ's kingdom is not of this world, that God and Caesar are entitled to their separate due, and that spiritual truth can only be fostered by spiritual means, religious liberty that includes toleration and disestablishment was justified. A man might embrace liberty reasonably on the first grounds and piously on the second. The American mixture of toleration and a minimum dogma at the founding turns on the understanding that basic agreement on the principles of Christianity is an essential element of the moral foundation of the society. That agreement is negatively hedged in by distrust of "popery and prelacy" as defining the outer limit of toleration. Adams and Jefferson profoundly feared the inquisitorial spirit that every denomination was susceptible to, and the great history of opposing Catholicism and establishment of an Anglican bishopric in America powerfully fueled the fears and distrust of these churches and their political schemes in the minds of even the most enlightened Americans of the time.

Americanism itself, then, serves as a kind of commonsense and civil theology based on nonsectarian Christianity and on the reasoned faith that men are more than mere fireflies; that this all is, indeed, not without a father.[48] Into this context step the Argonauts of the Heroic Age of our founding and its myth, reluctantly and rather self-consciously, to be sure; yet step they nonetheless do. The philosopher does not need the dogmas of the public *cultus* to secure his personal order and happiness, but a nation cannot do without them. And it is nobler to secure happiness for a nation than for one or merely a few men. Such is the divine science of politics.

William R. Marty · *The Search for Realism in Politics and Ethics: Reflections by a Political Scientist on a Christian Perspective*

Social Science and Religion

As political or social scientists we ordinarily examine religion to find correlations between religion and political or social behavior. And quite imposing generalizations have sometimes been made. One thinks of Machiavelli, Marx, Weber, and Tawney. But there can be pitfalls in such generalizations. Especially if we examine the more imposing ones, we are quick to find counterexamples. Machiavelli, for instance, held that Christianity made people meek and humble, concerned with the next life rather than infringements of their rights in this one, and that it made them, consequently, poor citizens. And Marx agreed, holding that religion is an opiate of the people, making them docile in the face of oppression. The reformers of the Enlightenment thought much the same, and all these men were correct, for history is full of examples of religion justifying the positions of the mighty while reconciling the poor and the weak to their lot.

Yet religion is not always an opiate. Sometimes it comes as a great storm, calling down the wrath of God upon the unrighteous, who are as likely to be the mighty as the meek. For religion has its prophets who bring the standards of the time and place under the judgment of God and eternity. Thus the prophets of Israel called the mighty, even the Chosen People of God, to judgment. Thus the Cromwellian Roundheads, in the name of God, called down the wrath of the New Model Army upon the Cavaliers of King Charles. Thus the Christian reformers, after centuries of religious justification of slavery, were spearheads in the attack upon it in both England and America. Thus Mohandas K. Gandhi in South Africa and India and Martin Luther King in the United States led mighty movements against colonial oppression and racial injustice. It would seem, then, that it is wise to remember, as

Machiavelli and Marx did not, that those who are weak, and faithful to the injunction to "render unto Caesar what is Caesar's," have standards that are not Caesar's for deciding what that is, and that even the mightiest are not safe when the meek decide that the mark has been exceeded.

Religious people in fact exhibit the most varied behavior. They may be meek; they are sometimes filled with fury. They may be humble; they are sometimes arrogant as only those who think they speak and act for God can be arrogant. They may be submissive, even to monstrous evil; they are sometimes willing to resist to the last person, or to leave nonviolence and nonresistance behind and engage in the most furious crusading. Politically, they may be reactionary, conservative, liberal, radical, passive, or active. They have, in the name of faith, defended monarchy, democracy, and dictatorship. They have defended feudalism, capitalism, and socialism. They have supported social Darwinism, fascism, and Marxism. There is, indeed, hardly a social or political position which has not been defended in the name of God with the fervor of the true believer. If there is but one God, he is nonetheless thought to march with every army.

To contemplate the behavior of the religious is to be brought to wonder if religion is not, after all, merely "sound and fury, signifying nothing." But we must tread warily here, lest we close our minds prematurely. The same type of contradictory behavior and belief which would lead us to dismiss religion and the religious would also lead us to dismiss those who act according to secular systems of thought and belief. Perhaps the point is worth elaboration. In this secular age, science is both our faith and our practice. Yet we should remember that, in the name of science, we have been called upon to adopt the most ruthless form of capitalism (social Darwinism) and the most ruthless form of socialism (the "scientific socialism" of totalitarian Marxism). In the name of science we have been told that the preservation of civilization depends upon repression of the id (Freud) and that a loving and creative society depends upon getting rid of our repressions and inhibitions, especially our sexual inhibitions (various liberation psychologies). With regard to race relations, we have been told that whites are more intelligent than blacks, that Jews are more intelligent than Gentiles, that the Chinese are more intelligent than any of them, and that any use of science to confirm racial differences, as opposed to racial similarities, is racist pseudoscience. With regard to political attitudes, we have been told that conservatism is not a political stance but a personality defect.[1]

This list could go on and on, and in all these cases there have been people willing—all too willing—to shape their behavior accordingly, or, more strictly, to believe what they have wanted to believe and to act accordingly. As in the case of the religious, there is no general political or social agreement among those who claim to be acting according to scientific or secular understanding. Science, then, like religion, has been put in the service of every creed, and, like religion, it is made susceptible to ridicule by the behavior and interpretations of its adherents. If religion, then, is discredited by its adherents, then so are science and secularism by theirs. In either case, that of religion or science, the existence of fallacious interpretations and destructive behavior does not preclude a core of genuine understanding or of behavior appropriate to that understanding. And it is that understanding, not the confusing and contradictory behavior, that may best reward our study.

While the ordinary subject of the scientific investigation of religion is the confusing and contradictory behavior of the religious, a more profitable subject may be the understanding religious people have of certain fundamental human problems, for it is certainly possible that religious perceptions and understandings of the human condition contain truths ignored by our secular age. The subject, then, of this essay will be a consideration of a religious understanding of the root of social evil. The thesis will be that this understanding of social evil explains more, and gives us better predictability and policy guidance, than the dominant secular or modern alternatives, and that we are ill-advised to ignore this understanding simply because of its source.

The Problem Posed: Why Have The Fruits Of The Enlightenment Proved So Unexpectedly Bitter?

We are heirs to the Enlightenment. Until quite recently we still held to its central beliefs (and many of us still do): that suffering and oppression and social evils are not the will of God or rooted in the unchanging nature of things; that by reason we can master nature and put it in the service of man; that by the application of reason to politics and society, we can reduce, enormously and progressively, the age-old evils of hunger, poverty, war, and oppression; that by the application of reason we can produce societies in which men will be free, equal, fraternal, and happy. Condorcet, in the full morning of the Age of Enlightenment, wrote that he would prove

> that no bounds have been fixed to the improvements of human faculties; that the perfectibility of man is absolutely indefinite; that the progress of this perfectibility, henceforth above the control of every power that would impede it, has no other limit than the duration of the globe upon which nature has placed us. The course of this progress may doubtless be more or less rapid, but it can never be retrograde. . . .[2]

Well, we are now nearly three centuries along. How are we doing? Let us look at the Enlightenment in its culmination. If the fruits are not what we expected, it cannot be said that it was for lack of effort. Never has there been such a sustained effort to eliminate social evil as in the last three centuries. We have, in fact, made every effort. We have tried tinkering reforms. We have tried remolding societies from top to bottom. We have tried to remake human nature. How, then, have we fared? Many specific gains have been made, without doubt. Many specific evils have abated. But evil lingers. Nay, it thrives. And it thrives most where some of the greatest and most systematic efforts at its abolition have occurred.

Let us look, for example, at the United States, born of the Enlightenment, confident until quite recently that it was the light of the nations, proud that its institutions had been consciously wrought by man, sure that it was a "New World" that would lead the "Old World" out of the cruel and unenlightened ways of the ages, and that here, at least, men would be free, prosperous, independent, and upright citizens of the new age. And how have things gone? We educate our citizens. We propagandize constantly against bigotry. We attack the institutions and poverty that breed crime. We spend and spend and spend to build the great society—and yet we get the crime and drug-ridden cities of New York and Chicago and Philadelphia. The great society recedes constantly into the future. But let us be specific. Let us look, for example, at the strange persistence of a race problem in the United

States. This was the nation, after all, that proclaimed: "We hold these truths to be self-evident, that all men are created equal, that they are endowed by their Creator with certain unalienable rights, that among these are life, liberty, and the pursuit of happiness." And it was "to secure these rights" that "governments are instituted among men, deriving their just powers from the consent of the governed."

This was an Enlightenment creed. And the founders of this nation shared Enlightenment hopes. Thomas Jefferson, who penned those proud declarations, wrote, shortly before his death: "May it [the Declaration] be to the world what I believe it will be (to some parts sooner, to others later, but finally to all) the signal of arousing men to burst the chains, under which monkish ignorance and superstition had persuaded them to bind themselves, and to assume the blessings and security of self-government."[3] Abraham Lincoln held to the same faith. On his way to be inaugurated president in 1861 he declared that the union had been held together, not only by the separation from Britain but by "something in that Declaration giving liberty, not alone to the people of this country, but hope to the world for all future time. It was that which gave promise that in due time the weights would be lifted from the shoulders of all men, and that *all* should have an equal chance. . . ."[4]

The leaders of this first great movement of the Enlightenment believed, as Jefferson put it, that "the general spread of the light of science has already laid open to every view the palpable truth, that the mass of mankind has not been born with saddles on their backs, nor a favored few, booted and spurred, ready to ride them legitimately, by the grace of God."[5] Brave words, but tragic too, for the founders of the first great modern republic, to their own surprise, were unable to bring that liberty, equality, and government by consent fully into being even in their own nation. Partisans of liberty and democracy, they stood condemned by their own practices, and especially by the practice of slavery. Jefferson himself, who could lead his own slave-holding state of Virginia to give up its western lands from which a number of states were later formed on condition that the Federal Government would ban slavery from those territories forever (a condition accepted in the Northwest Ordinance passed by the first Congress), could not lead Virginia to give up its own slaves. He later mused:

> What a stupendous, what an incomprehensible machine is man! Who can endure toil, famine, strikes, imprisonment, and death itself, in vindication of his own liberty, and, the next moment, be deaf to all those motives whose power supported him through his trial, and inflict on his fellow man a bondage, one hour of which is fraught with more misery than ages of that which he rose in rebellion to oppose.[6]

This tragic failing divided the nation, kept it in a constant sectional turmoil, and finally culminated in the Civil War, sometimes labeled the first modern total war, and gave it its first martyr president, Abraham Lincoln. Surely that was to be the end of the evil. But it was not. Chattel slavery was abolished, but neither peace nor justice ensued. Instead, a system of segregation gradually developed in which black men and women, declared to have unalienable rights, were kept "in their place" by such devices as job ceilings, educational discrimination, legal disabilities, segregation extended even to water fountains and libraries, and outright terror. Black Americans, presumably freed in 1865, living in the nation of the "melting pot," found themselves neither free, nor assimilated, nor equal. Blacks resisted, of course, and by the late 1950s and 1960s this resistance had become a revolt, albeit largely a nonviolent one, and the terror and legal disabilities were largely defeated. Today, in fact, blacks, along with women and certain minorities, are sometimes conferred a privileged position in the law, yet a race problem (as well as a sex problem) remains. Why, after all these years, in this most educated, wealthy, and moralistic of nations, do these problems not go away?

Perhaps the problem was deeper than the Americans realized. Perhaps a greater effort was required. The American Revolution is sometimes referred to as a conservative revolution, and sometimes it is dismissed as merely a war of independence. Let us look, then, to nations that tried harder, more systematically, more radically.

The French Revolution is admitted by all to have been a genuine revolution. It aimed to get rid of the old regime root and branch, and it did. It executed the king. It executed the nobility. It executed its opponents. It opened the jails. It dispossessed the church. It proclaimed the rights of man. It reorganized society from top to bottom. And then it kept on. It turned upon itself. It produced Robespierre, the terror, civil war, the Thermidor,

Napoleon. But it hardly produced liberty, equality, or fraternity. Indeed, if it produced anything, it was not the new age of reason, but a new age of war, blood, turmoil, and nationalism.

The French Revolution did not produce the fruits envisioned by the Enlightenment. But perhaps it, too, misunderstood the problem, or did not go deep enough in its efforts to uproot the old evils. The revolutionary mantle was picked up by the Marxists. If we are honest, we must admit that the Marxists have tried harder, more systematically (and more ruthlessly) to achieve the new society of harmony that was the dream of the Enlightenment than anyone else. How, then, have the Marxists fared?

The Russian Revolution, which stirred the greatest hopes, produced a totalitarian terror unmatched in history—the forced collectivization of peasants at the cost of millions of lives, the Gulag Archipelago of destructive labor camps through which tens of millions of people flowed, most never to return, as well as the great show trials and purges, the abolition of history and freedom, the political insane asylums—but it has not produced the New Socialist Man or the society of uncoerced brotherhood.[7] (We are fond, as Solzhenitsyn says, of thinking of the Spanish Inquisition as one of the horrors of an unenlightened and superstitious age, and so it was. At its height, it killed perhaps ten people a month. At the height of the Soviet terror in our enlightened age, about 40,000 people were executed per month.[8] It is difficult to find the progress, or enlightenment, in this.) Sometimes we attribute this horror to the aberrations of one man, Stalin. But we are wrong to do that, for the terrors of the Soviet regime began before Stalin and continue after. As Alexandr Solzhenitsyn points out, "In 1918 and 1919 the Cheka executed, without trial, more than a thousand persons a month! This was written by the Cheka itself before it understood how this would look to history."[9] The Gulag, too, was begun before Stalin, and continues after him. Raymond Aron estimated in 1978 that there were still one to one and a half million people in the prison camps, and perhaps five to ten thousand dissidents confined to insane asylums.[10] Nor can this aberration be dismissed as merely Russian, for Stalinism has been repeated again and again in the other Marxist states.

China, the largest Marxist state, and for long the most fervent, promised not to repeat the Russian errors. It produced the Great Leap Forward, the Cultural Revolution, and it tried, more strenuously by far, to avoid the New Class, but it produced not only the old terror and forced collectivization, not only the revolutionary justice that killed perhaps five to ten million of its citizens,[11] but its own grey, drab, terrorized repression. It was, after all, virtually the only supporter of the Khmer Rouge Cambodian Revolution, which tried to produce the good society by an unmatched regimentation and cruelty amounting to the genocidal slaughter of its own people.

Cambodia (Kampuchea), the favored of China, whose Communist leaders were trained in France,[12] planned to be totally systematic, and began its reign of reason by driving every single inhabitant out of its capital city, including those in hospitals, in the emergency wards, even on the operating table—an exodus which vast numbers did not survive. And it continued by slaughtering anyone connected with the old regime. It then dealt with the survivors by regimenting them, controlling even the sex and family life of the married, allowing them to cohabit twice a month. The estimates of the deaths range widely, but all are very high. Prince Sihanouk, the former ruler, who acted as Cambodia's spokesman at the United Nations in the debates over the Vietnamese invasion, was content to accept the figure used by the Vietnamese as accurate: three and a half million Cambodians killed in the three and a half years of the Khmer Rouge regime—a million a year, or to compare with Stalin's 40,000 executions a month, 83,333 deaths per month, in a country of perhaps seven million people.[13]

In Vietnam the new order does not preclude imperialism in Laos and Cambodia, and it has included the usual Marxist collectivization of agriculture, destruction of the opposition, destruction or limiting of religious freedom, as well as a special racial element of persecution of people of Chinese origin. People, many of Chinese origin, were forced to flee Vietnam, sometimes at a rate of perhaps twenty to forty thousand per month (the count was made of those who survived the highly dangerous journey through the rough seas).[14] But this is not unusual. While in Vietnam people flee by boat, in Cambodia they flee by land, in China by land and sea, in East Germany by tunneling under the wall, in Cuba by crashing into foreign embassies.[15] What other set of societies has had to build walls, electrified fences, minefields, all patrolled and guarded night and day, to keep its people in? Yet in these societies we have invested our most fervent hopes and we have insisted, as long as they were carefully enough closed off to us, that in them utopia was building—as we so often insisted of Stalinist Russia in the twenties and thirties, and of Fidelist Cuba and Maoist China in the sixties. Dreams die hard. Terror, slaughter, regimentation, indoctrination, cradle-to-grave controls, and thought control—yet no new man. Radical reform, going to the roots, but even greater disaster. Where did we go wrong?

And then there was fascism or nazism, which was for a period one of the main political expressions of the West in the twentieth century. Somehow, out of enlightened Western civilization, the furies have come. There was the attempt to exterminate completely whole peoples—Jews, Gypsies—and, quite literally, to enslave others, with the old and unfit consigned to die. There was the call for a master race and a 1,000 year Reich. Who dreamed that such daemonic fury resided in the depths of modern man?

No, if we gaze on this century, we cannot find in it the culmination of the confident hopes of the Enlightenment. We find instead a century of unparalleled horrors on a global scale with world wars, subversion, strife, slaughter, hatred beyond measure, cruelty, fanaticism, self-righteous fury, will to power cloaked in the garb of reason and virtue, murderous hypocrisy. Yet we have thought now for nearly three centuries that we had grasped the fundamental causes, and cures, of social evil. The empirical evidence suggests that we should reexamine that view. What further horrors must we experience to raise a doubt that we are on the right path?

The question then is posed. Unless we would bury our heads completely, we must consider whether we have been wrong about the causes of evil. Certainly our cures have not cured. What, then, are the views of the Enlightenment, or, if we would be broader, what have been the views of Western man as to the causes, and cures, of social evil?

The Search for the Causes and Cures of Social Evil

Greece is one of the two main sources of Western civilization. Plato, the student of Socrates and the teacher of Aristotle, has a claim to being its preeminent philosopher, and perhaps the preeminent philosopher. So let us begin with Plato. Social evil, according to Plato's Socrates (hereafter referred to simply as Plato), stems from ignorance of our true good. The individual soul, according to

Plato, is composed of three parts: appetites, spirit, and reason. In the well-ordered soul, reason, which knows the good, governs, supported by spirit, with appetites held in proper check. In the disorderly soul either appetite or spirit governs, and the soul is soon at war with itself, producing an individual who is neither happy nor good. As in the individual soul, so in the city. The harmonious city can only be the city ruled by the truly wise, according to their knowledge of the good. Until that happens, the city, like the individual, will be at war with itself, as class competes with class in pursuit of narrow and illusory aims.

The Platonic view has always had its admirers. Early in the Enlightenment there was hope among the philosophers for an enlightened monarch, or at least for one who would listen to the enlightened. But little came of these hopes. The more characteristic development was confident acceptance of Plato's view that ignorance was the cause of evil, but rejection of his view that only the few can know the good. Instead, the faith that evil could be overcome by reason was combined with a much greater faith in the capacity of the common man and a belief in the fundamental equality of men. Ignorance, it was believed, could be dispelled not only in the few, but in the many. The Enlightenment, then, was much more confident than the Greeks, even when the root of evil was similarly assessed. Universal education was to be the answer. The faith of the Age of Reason was expressed by Condorcet "when he declared that universal education and the development of the printing press would inevitably result in an ideal society in which the sun would shine 'on the earth of none but free-men; with no masters save reason; for tyrants and slaves, priests and their hypocritical tools will all have disappeared.'"[16]

In the Platonic view the cure of evil is difficult, for education is arduous, those capable of apprehending the good directly are few, and unless those who know the good rule, which is quite unlikely, then there will be no harmony in soul or state. Even the more optimistic view of one strand of the Enlightenment, that all are capable of knowing the good, still left the difficult task of universal education.

But perhaps the problem is not as difficult as Plato, or even the early Enlightenment, thought. Certainly many of the early (and later) disciples of Rousseau did not think so. Though their interpretations of Rousseau are suspect, that did not prevent them from having a decisive impact on subsequent views of the causes and cures of social evil. The foundations for this view can be found in Rousseau. Thus, according to certain statements by Rousseau, it does not take long and arduous education to produce good men.[17] Quite the contrary, in the *Discourse* that made him famous, Rousseau advanced the idea, said to have come to him in a dream, that "man is naturally good and that our social institutions alone have rendered him evil."[18] As he explained in *Emile*, education is not a matter of teaching virtue or truth, but of preserving a child's natural innocence. "Let us lay it down as an incontrovertible rule that the first impulses of nature are always right."[19]

According to Rousseau, then, man is by nature good; he is only corrupted by bad institutions. The cure for social evil, as his followers saw it, was to get rid of the bad and corrupting institutions. Probably no other analysis of the cause and cure of evil has gained such fervent belief and acceptance in the modern world as this. Certainly it was the theory of the French Revolution with its confident faith that by removing the corrupting institutions of the Old Regime—monarchy, nobility, established church—and replacing them with the uncorrupt institutions which would reflect the will of the people, a society of liberty, equality, and fraternity would come into being. This will, the general will, according to Rousseau, "is always right and tends to the public advantage."[20] No wonder our question is not, Is it right or wrong, but Is it democratic?[21]

But there is one further twist given by Rousseau, with consequences we measure down to our own time. The general will is the test of legitimacy. And "whoever refuses to obey the general will shall be compelled to do so by the whole body." Rousseau added: "This means nothing less than that he will be forced to be free."[22] The Jacobins knew what to make of that. Confident that they embodied the true will and true interests of the people, when their majority failed them, they resorted to terror to cleanse the body politic of its corrupt elements. In the name of virtue and the people they killed even the elected representatives of the people.

Rousseau, it would appear, helped loose that pitiless self-righteous savagery that has marked our enlightened age. Robespierre, who was one of the last persons to visit Rousseau alive at Ermenonville, who "kept the guillotine permanently employed during the Reign of Terror which he dared to call the 'Dictatorship of Virtue,' wrote 'Virtue, apart from which terror is baneful; terror, apart from which virtue is powerless.'"[23] Every modern Jacobin seems to share that sentiment, and puts it into practice when he can. But the terror did not produce virtue then. Why, when the old corrupt institutions and privileges were destroyed, did evil remain?

Marxism, for all its subtle and often compelling historical analysis, is, in its analysis of the cause and cure of social evil, an even simpler version of Rousseau's doctrine. The participants in the French Revolution had at least thought that some care was necessary to replace the corrupting institutions of the Old Regime with an uncorrupt set of institutions giving voice to the general will. But for the early Marxists, at least, the cause and cure of social evil were quite simple indeed. The cause of social evil was the corrupt institution of private ownership of the means of production. This gave rise to all the particular social evils and to class warfare. The cure for social evil was equally simple: get rid of private ownership of the means of production. This would require a revolution, but once it had been accomplished, once the means of production had been socialized, the new age would quickly arrive, men would produce for use, not for profit, there would be plenty, and leisure, and harmony. Men would be free to develop to their potential. Whereas men like Socrates and Goethe had been the peaks before, now that would be the common level. Poverty, oppression, jealousy, war, crime, and theft would disappear. Such was the promise. And private ownership of the means of production has been abolished. Where, then, is that society of brotherhood and harmony? Where is the New Socialist Man who will be like Socrates and Goethe?

There are other theories, similar, or even simpler, than the ones discussed above. Locke's version of man has proved more popular than Rousseau's with non-Marxists. Locke held, not that man was by nature good, but that man was by nature simply a blank page upon which could be written anything at all. Modern sociologists have preferred this. All we need, then, is the right environment, and we can produce any type of person we want. Some psychologists, too, such as B. F. Skinner, have held similar views.

There are, too, the theories that social evils are largely the result of a particular evil race (Hitler preferred Jews, Stokely Carmichael whites) or a type of system (colonialism) and that if they (the population group or system) can be eliminated or ousted, social harmony would return. No empirical evidence has seemed, as yet, to support these theories. The races, isolated or mixed, have not gotten rid of social evils, nor have those evils disappeared with the ousting of the colonials.

There is, of course, something to all these theories. Ignorance does cause evils; so, too, do bad institutions. But why hasn't education or elimination of bad institutions produced the generous and good society? What has gone wrong? Why has this age, given all the tools of science and mass formal education, of revolutions to end monarchy, capitalism, and colonialism, produced so much human suffering, so terrible a new barbarism of mass executions, and despotisms of such horrible intensity and totality as to make a mockery of the horrors of previous ages? Perhaps we had better examine another, and very old, explanation of social evil.

Another View—The Flaw Within

"We have met the enemy and he is us," said the cartoon character Pogo, summarizing one view of our plight. He is expressing a view that derives from Israel, not from Greece; from a religious understanding of man, not from a scientific understanding. But it is a view more in accord with the empirical evidence than the dominant views of this secular and enlightened age. That, at least, is the thesis of this essay.

Man, in the orthodox Christian view, is a sinner. Though that is not his essential nature, for he was not created that way, that has been his nature since Adam, who brought sin into the world, and all man's woe. Science, of course, and philosophy, can make nothing of this. But what do Christians mean when they say these things? What is this original sin, passed from generation to generation? Christians have variously defined the nature of sin. Usually it is defined as pride and self-sufficiency, an attempt by the creature to believe that he can do without the Creator, God, even that he himself can act as God. This might still mean little to scientists and philosophers, though Bertrand Russell seemed to understand the danger. Of John Dewey's call to organize human and social relationships, a call to bring the resources of science to bear on man's societies as they have been brought to bear on the mastery of nature, Russell warned:

> Man, formerly too humble, begins to think of himself as almost a God. The Italian pragmatist Papini urges us to substitute the "Imitation of God" for the "Imitation of Christ."
>
> In all this I feel a grave danger, the danger of what might be called cosmic impiety. . . . When this check upon pride is removed, a further step is taken on the road towards a certain kind of madness—the intoxication of power—. . . to which modern men, whether philosophers or not, are prone. I am persuaded that this intoxication is the greatest danger of our time, and that any philosophy which, however unintentionally, contributes to it is increasing the danger of vast social disaster.[24]

Prescient words, certainly.

One sense of the concept of sin, then, is that man, when he does not recognize his dependency upon God, loses his sense of limits. Thinking himself the center of the universe, he acknowledges no limits on his power, no limits upon the goals he can pursue nor upon the means he may use to obtain these goals. Certainly that loss of a sense of limits is one of the characteristics of the age. With what self-righteous fury, after all, have our Jacobins felt entitled to force millions, against their will, to adopt certain forms of social organization, or even to kill millions, all in the name of man and the creation of universal brotherhood.

Easier, though, to understand are other attributes of man as a sinner. Man, as a sinner, is full of self and self-love; he is concerned first and primarily with himself, and only secondarily and marginally with others or with the common good. He will, consequently, ordinarily work harder for himself than for others, harder for his little group than the larger society. Man can, it is true, break out of this in part, mainly in a one-to-one love relationship within the family or a very small circle; less, but still somewhat within larger groups, but never consistently and reliably on the level of society.

Next, man as a sinner suffers from a defect of will. Even when he knows the good, even when he knows what he ought to do, even when he wants to do it, he often cannot. In the words of St. Paul: "That which I would, I do not, but that which I hate, I do." We are tempted by evil, and often succumb to it, even when we know it is evil. We are tempted to fudge, therefore, on our expense accounts (so common that expense accounts are termed "cheat sheets"), or on our income taxes (about in proportion to what we think we can get away with?), or we are tempted to take advantage of our power or position to use public or corporate property as our own (using copying machines or company cars) or even the power belonging to a public position for private ends (as in the case of the New Class in socialist nations).

Often we succumb to our defects of will and self-centeredness in less obvious ways. Thus in every generation those in positions of power and privilege find it easy to accept theories which justify their positions. No one wants to think ill of himself, and no one wants to give up his privileges either. Thus those on top in a buccaneering capitalist society were all too ready to believe that nature had intended ruthless competition so that "the fittest" would survive, and so improve the race, and this idea was advanced under the umbrella of science, as the social application of Darwinism. Thus every generation or society that interpreted natural law could not avoid incorporating into the universal reason defenses of their particular social structures and privileges.

The Marxists are wise about this, and they have gained a deserved reputation for being able to spot rationalization of self-interest by others, but they too have been naive in at least two respects, for there is self-interest other than the economic self-interest for which they look, and they have failed to realize that this universal tendency to rationalize one's self-interest applies to themselves as well as others. Thus the keen Marxist observer, Rudolf Bahro, was sentenced to eight years in prison by his government, that of East Germany, in 1977 for publishing such observations as "The countries of eastern Europe are ruled by a state machine such as Marx sought to smash in the revolution, and not to let rise again in any form, under any pretext," and that abolition of private property has not meant that it now belongs to the people, rather that now "the whole society 'stands propertyless against its state machine.'"[25] This is acute observation, but having gotten so close to understanding, Bahro can do no better than blame these disasters mainly on Stalin's despotism, and that despotism on Russia's Asiatic backwardness, as though the tendency to abuse nearly unrestrained power could only be a characteristic of backward Asians. Until Marxist analysis moves beyond this, it will never understand why it gives rise to tyrannical regimes wherever it gains power.

Because of the flaw within, even our pursuit of ideal ends tends to be tainted, as every page of history attests, by a parallel if unadmitted pursuit of power, glory, status, wealth, prestige or, at least, self-love and self-esteem. If we are lucky, or, more precisely, if our institutions are correctly designed, the outward results and behavior of such tainted inner motives may still benefit us, as when the politician, seeking gratification of his ego, or fame, fortune, perhaps even glory, bends his efforts to our behalf so that he may retain the public position necessary to gratify his private desires. All too often, though, ideal ends become the vehicle for ruthless self-assertion and will to power. Men, beginning as saviors, end as tyrants.

Curiously, and tragically, the attempt to remain pure can have its own evil effects in politics. Straining to avoid the compromises that involvement in politics inevitably requires, those who would remain pure are often tempted to retreat from politics into isolation. Refusing to dirty their hands in politics, they leave that realm to others less scrupulous, and often leave the relatively innocent to be gobbled up by the aggressors of history. Sometimes this avoidance takes the form of adopting some technique which is then invested with purity, such as pacifism or nonviolence, and holding to it regardless of its consequences for others (Christian nonresistance in the face of Nazis abandons the Jewish neighbor to extinction). Isolationism is another form of this surrender. Individuals, groups, and nations are often tempted to this sacrifice of others in the pursuit of their own purity. United States foreign policy, for example, tends to swing between a refusal to act at all in a futile attempt to remain pure and a crusading self-righteousness once it has assured itself of its purity of motive and its opponent's essential wickedness. Even the search for purity, it seems, can be a temptation, leading us on the one hand to turn our back on our neighbors; leading us, on the other, into terrible self-righteous intervention.

Finally, there are two more aspects of man, according to Christian thought, which are not themselves sinful, but which provide the ground upon which pride, self-centeredness, and the defect of will play. One is man's spiritual nature, which means that in his creativity and freedom, he can never be understood merely as a biological being. Reinhold Niebuhr was speaking of this when he said:

> The expansive character of human ambitions, lusts, fears and desires is the consequence of the indeterminate transcendence

> of man's spirit over the physical, natural and historical processes in which he is involved.
>
> Economic desires are never merely the expression of the hunger or the survival impulse in human life. The desires for "power and glory" are subtly compounded with the more primeval instinct. The lion's desire for food is more easily limited than other human desires; yet the hunger impulse is subject to the endless refinements of the gourmand. Shelter and raiment have much more extensible limits than food. Man's coat is never merely a cloak for his nakedness but a badge of his vocation, or the expression of an artistic impulse, or a method of attracting the other sex, or a proof of social position. Man's house is not merely his shelter but, even more than his raiment, the expression of his personality and the symbol of his power, position, and prestige.[26]

Because of this "spiritualization" of the biological needs and impulses, there is no natural limit to man's needs. There is no point at which one can say that man has enough, that his needs are met, so that there is a natural limit to man's desires for wealth, power, prestige, or goods.

A second aspect of man's nature, not perhaps itself sin, but a ground for sin, is man's deep-rooted anxiety and insecurity, his rebellion against his creatureliness and mortality and inability to control his fate and destiny. Man rebels against this radical insecurity by pretension and pride, by trying to overcome anxiety with power, wealth, prestige, conquest, purity. As his insecurity is radical, his efforts to overcome it tend to be frantic, inordinate, limitless. There is, then, about man a tendency toward excess quite inexplicable in merely natural or biological terms.

What, then, is the primary cause of social evil? It is, in this view, a radical defect in man himself. He is full of inordinate self-love and self-concern, proud, self-righteous, self-centered, arrogant; but suffering, too, from a defect of will, so that even when he knows the good he often does evil; weak, that is, and tending to succumb to temptations to abuse power, or position, or privilege. This defect of will, according to many Christians, taints even the fruits of reason, for it allows us to believe what we want to believe, and what we want to believe is usually something that justifies or enhances our own position or self-esteem. Man is also anxious, worried, insecure, and frantic in his efforts to overcome his anxieties and insecurities, tending, thereby, to excess. He is a creature of spirit, whose biological needs as an animal are always given a spiritual gloss. His needs, then, are not simple or easily met. One age's abundance is another's poverty, and there is always room to have more, always someone with whom one can compete—a creature, then, of inordinate and potentially limitless desires.

In sum, the fundamental causes of man's evil actions are not ignorance of what he ought to do, but lack of will to do it; not bad institutions, though those can be crippling, but the selfishness and self-centeredness that will create and maintain those institutions in pursuit of self-interest, however that self-interest may be rationalized as the common good. Reinhold Niebuhr points to the difficulty inherent in the standard views of modern culture:

> Whenever modern idealists are confronted with the divisive and corrosive effects of man's self-love, they look for some immediate cause of this perennial tendency, usually in some specific form of social organization. One school holds that men would be good if only political institutions would not corrupt them; another believes that they would be good if the prior evil of a faulty economic organization could be eliminated. Or another school thinks of this evil as no more than ignorance, and therefore waits for a more perfect educational process to redeem man from his partial and particular loyalties. But no school asks how it is that an essentially good man could have produced corrupting and tyrannical political organizations or exploiting economic organizations, or fanatical and superstitious religious organizations.[27]

A Religious Critique of Enlightenment Views

Plato and one strand of the Enlightenment agreed that ignorance is the cause of evil, and education its cure. But if such a view is correct then one must wonder why evil has not disappeared in the United States with its universal education, including education to citizenship and education against bigotry. Indeed, if education is the cure, why has not evil disappeared from the Soviet Union, or China, or Cuba, where education is pervasive, even at places of work, and all the virtues of selflessness, the community good, and the brotherhood of the workers are endlessly paraded in lectures, films, and pamphlets? Was Plato's desire to purge society of unworthy thoughts ever more fervently followed? And what of all the products of church and religious education over the ages? With all those sermons, catechisms, and classes in what should be done, why were there so few who managed, consistently, to do it? Why were there so few saints? Was it really ignorance of what should be done? If so, then why were the confessionals full? One surely does not confess unless one knows he did wrong, does one? Why, indeed, do so many steal or engage in shady practices today? Is it ignorance? And why do even the wealthy engage in cheating on income taxes, or corporate fraud and bribery? Are they ignorant that what they are doing is wrong? Can they be explained by their need? Indeed, after all these centuries of ceaseless moral education, what are we to make of the appalling continuance of social evil at every level of society? Why, indeed, can we not simply tell people how they should behave, explain why, and then forget about enforcement of laws enforcing moral behavior?

Consider the record of those going through customs during a strike in Britain. As one customs officer put it, "I doubt whether a penny will have been collected today. We know from our experience of a strike in 1973 that no one uses the 'honesty' boxes."[28] [Honesty boxes are boxes in which you can voluntarily declare what you owe even though you won't be checked]. Why do people stride right past those honesty boxes? Is it really possible that ignorance is the problem? Or isn't it more probable that we would have to have those customs officers even if everyone knew the law and knew he should obey it? Put differently, isn't it more probable that all those sermons, lectures, and indoctrinations failed because of a defect of will rather than an ignorance of what was said? The evidence is overwhelming, after all, that people think they know what they ought to do in a great many circumstances, and still fail, all too often, to do it. There are cases in which we don't know what we ought to do, but there are an enormous number of cases in which we know precisely what we ought to do, and still we don't. Ignorance cannot account for that. A defect of will can.

As long as a defect of will exists, universal education is not the answer to social evil, though it may be an answer to many other things. Neither should we put too much hope in "rule by the wise," or "rule by reason." The idea that the wise and reasonable should rule is unobjectionable, of course, as far as it goes. The difficulty is that those who claim the right to rule in the name of reason are subject, like the rest of us, to the corruptions of self-interest, pride, and will to power. Thinking that they, and not others, represent reason, they all too often think that they are entitled to power and privilege and that they are entitled, in the name of reason (or science, or the people), to command others to obey, and to compel others, even against their will, to do what reason commands. For this reason the old aristocracies quickly became oligarchies and the new Jacobins became tyrants. Again Niebuhr puts it neatly: "Aristotelian and Platonic thought, with all its derivatives, will continue to persuade kings that they are philosophers and philosophers that they are kings; and will tempt them to hide their will to power behind their virtues and to obscure their injustices behind their generosities."[29] The observation applies alike to the kings of old and those modern absolutists who rule in the name of the laws of history and scientific socialism—Lenin, Stalin, Mao, Fidel. Indeed, one of the characteristics of the age is the prevalence of those who claim the right to command us or to kill us in the name of their unique knowledge of what should be done. May God preserve us from these men of reason. And if not God, then an understanding of the temptations and defects of will that plague even philosophers and scientists. This religious view provides that understanding.

Next let us consider the institutional explanation of evil. The Marxists are the most fervent advocates of this view. They hold that evil is the product of private ownership of the means of production, which gives capitalists the power to exploit the proletariat. Moreover, capitalism produces warped, selfish, and alienated men. The solution, then, is to socialize the means of production, whereupon men will produce for use, not profit, harmony and brotherhood will reign, and the New Socialist man will be generous and sharing. Well, they have socialized the means of production, but they have not gotten harmony and the New Socialist Man. They have gotten Stalin and the Gulag Archipelago. Why? Those holding this religious view think they know. Marx was right, they think, about private ownership of the means of production in laissez-faire economies producing some very great evils, but he was naive about the reason. Capitalism produced many great evils because it concentrated very great and largely unrestrained power in a relatively few hands. But that was only a problem because men are sinners and when they have unrestrained power, the temptation to abuse it is well-nigh irresistible. The Marxist solution failed because it took a system in which economic power was vested in relatively few hands, leading to great abuse, and turned it into a system in which virtually every kind of power was concentrated into even fewer hands with even fewer restraints and with the most powerful rationale (and rationalization) for its ruthless use. Stalin is the fruit of putting this nearly absolute power in the hands of one fallible man. Because of man's inordinate self-love and defect of will, no man can safely be given such unrestrained power.

The same explanation accounts for the continued existence of evil in postcolonial and racially homogeneous societies. Colonialism produced abuse because it put great power in the hands of flawed and unrestrained men. But throwing the colonials out is not sufficient to get rid of evil, especially if power then becomes even more concentrated and unrestrained, as it often has. Postcolonial Africa has produced slaughters of enormous magnitude, wars, corruption, tyrannies, all the old evils, because evil is not a characteristic of white men or colonials only, but of man—of man, at least, who has the power to pursue his selfish ends. The Old Adam is alive and well in America, Russia, and Africa, as he is around the globe. And political or social systems which fail to take that into account will continue to produce unanticipated, but catastrophic, results.

Religious Remedies for Social Evil

Since man's sin is his pride, self-sufficiency, and self-centeredness, the ultimate remedy is to break that pride and self-centeredness. This is done through the grace of God, which allows man, to a certain degree, to break out of his self-centeredness by turning his attention upward, in love, to God, and outward toward his fellow man. This requires recognition that one is a sinner, that one requires forgiveness. But God does forgive, that is the Good News of the Gospel, not that Christ came bringing a new moral code (there were plenty of those around), but that He suffered as man has suffered, that He conquered death and sin, and that in forgiveness and mercy, he paid the price for man. The cure for sin, then, is repentance through God's grace. There is dispute among Christians as to how far-reaching this cure is in this life, about whether man can act without sin with the help of God. The Reformation tradition was that man could not, that he remained a sinner, that he could only do the best he could and throw himself on the mercy of God, that there are no guiltless positions in either individual life or politics. The Catholic tradition tends to be more optimistic than the early Reformation tradition, but some modern sects are more optimistic still, seeming to hold that most or nearly all sin can be overcome. It is hard, by observation, to take this optimistic view.

But in addition to the grace and mercy of God, which helps man at least crack his self-centeredness so that he can turn his attention outward away from himself, there are what may be called due recognitions that we must adopt "'dykes' against sin." One such dyke is government itself. Edmund Burke was thoroughly within this tradition when he held that men do have natural rights, and that one of these is the right to be restrained from following one's desires where those would harm another. We shall explore this latter realm, the realm of dykes against sin, as it is of relevance not only to the religious, but also to secularists who can accept the religious estimate of man as empirically valid even if they cannot accept the religion on which it is based.

Before exploring possible applications of the religious view of man to social and political affairs, it is well to notice that Christians do not seem particularly adept at applying the logic of their beliefs to politics, that Christians have not, on the whole, shown more political wisdom than others, and, that, indeed, in the attempt to be relevant, Christians seem to forget how they are different and what resources they have to bring to bear. Instead they seem, too often, to jump on the nearest secular bandwagon, and to add to it mere moral passion—which the age certainly doesn't lack—or, worse, a confident assertion of God's will, which compounds religious fanaticism with secular fanaticism, forgetting, perhaps, that no particular political program of the moment is likely to be the simple expression of God's will. In fact, one of the most typical expressions of sin, in the theological view, is man's confident assumption of the mantle of God for his own projects. We would be wrong, then, to take bearings from whatever happens to be the current expression of Christian enthusiasm. We should, rather, seek out the implications of the enduring view of man. John Hallowell, as a Christian student of political philosophy, speaks of both the limits and contributions of Christian doctrine to social life:

> [Christianity] is not a political philosophy nor an economic program and it provides no short cuts to economic prosperity or social stability. It does not lessen the need to study our political, social and economic institutions or to formulate programs and to institute reforms which may improve our political and social structure but it will, indeed, give us a perspective and provide us with principles in terms of which we may accomplish these tasks better than we would without them. It will save us, moreover, from the illusion that we can establish a system which is perfect or make a reform which is final.[30]

What, then, are some of the political implications of this view of man? If this view is correct, then there will inevitably have to be a considerable degree of coercion in social life to insure that men not only know the good, but do it. This coercion can be the coercion of small groups—intense social pressure—or it can be the coercion of law and threat of punishment through police, courts, or armies. But unless we are to be left free to stride right by those honesty boxes, there will have to be an element of coercion. Man, then, must live according to rules, and these rules will require an element of coercion. To the degree that these rules are fair, and are seen to be fair, the degree of coercion can be reduced, but it can never be eliminated.

And neither will we agree easily on what is fair, for each of us will tend to see the merit of some version of justice that favors ourselves, and fail to see the merit of that which favors others—which is why young white males in the United States now, often and sincerely, see the merit of equal competition for jobs by standard measures while young black males, often and sincerely, see the merit of quotas, affirmative action, and compensatory advantages. There is a rational case to be made for either view, but the taint of self-interest insures that rational men of good will of both races are not randomly distributed on both sides of the question. Because of this, the art of statesmanship, or, less grandiosely, the art of politics, of finding mutually acceptable solutions to problems that divide us, will always be one of the highest and most difficult of human callings.

Man, then, must be ruled. But who can we trust to rule us? The answer, in this view, is that no one can be trusted to rule without restraint on his actions—not philosopher-kings, not priests, not Moslem ayotollahs, not Nixon, or Lenin, or Stalin, or Mao, or Fidel, or Nkrumah, or Nyerere, and not "the people," or "the majority," or "the proletariat," or the "vanguard of the proletariat," or "the master race." No individual or group can be trusted with unrestrained power. James Madison stated the problem well.

> If men were angels, no government would be necessary. If angels were to govern men, neither external nor internal controls on government would be necessary. In framing a government which is to be administered by men over men, the great difficulty lies in this: you must first enable the government to control the governed; and in the next place oblige it to control itself. A dependence on the people is, no doubt, the primary control on government; but experience has taught mankind the necessity of auxiliary precautions.[31]

All this is perfectly commonsensical, one would think, but apparently it is not, for this is the century in which both intellectual elites and common men have fallen over themselves in the scramble to follow and obey and justify charismatic leaders of left and right leading them, they thought, into utopia, but, in fact, into the world of the concentration camps and the Gulag Archipelago. All prudence forgotten, all restraints removed, all decency destroyed, and still we look for that great leader who will lead us into the land of uncoerced harmony, and we suspend disbelief while he stifles freedom, kills his opposition, and enslaves his people as the "necessary" steps in the transition. And Condorcet thought we were becoming brighter.

Given the nature of man, how should we order our political affairs? Perhaps two brief principles may be taken as a starting place. First, "If impulse and the opportunity be suffered to coincide, we well know that neither moral nor religious motives can be relied on as an adequate control."[32] No one, then, can be put in a position where only his internal self-restraint prevents the abuse of power. Second, "the best security for the fidelity of mankind is to make their interest coincide with their duty."[33] This, of course, is a prudent guaranty for right action though it is extremely difficult to achieve. But let us look at constitutional democracy as an attempt to approximate this.

Constitutional democracy is, in the first place, a substitute for unrestrained rule by minorities. The difficulty with rule by minorities, whether religious, scientific, or other, is that because of man's egocentrism, it tends to become rule for them rather than for the common good, even if they genuinely believe they rule for the common good. Monarchy, due to the taint of self-interest, becomes merely tyranny; aristocracy merely oligarchy; rule by the vanguard of the proletariat merely rule by the New Class. Noblesse oblige rarely obliges sufficiently or for long. So we must make it the interest of the rulers to pay attention to the ruled. Revolutions can do that, but only at enormous human cost, at considerable intervals, and with no guaranty of success. Periodic elections, however, with legal oppositions, make it the interest of those who have power to pay at least enough attention to those whom they rule so that they are not replaced in the next election. This does not guarantee good or wise government, but it certainly has a strong tendency to prevent the worst abuses.

Auxiliary precautions are also useful. Since no one can be trusted with absolute power, it is wise to have sufficient separation of powers or checks and balances so that "ambition is pitted against ambition" and power against power. That way it becomes the interest of one group to prevent another from abusing its power, or of men in one branch of government to prevent all power from going to another, and a power base is provided to exercise this restraint. Had the Soviet Union had these institutions—genuine elections and separation of powers—it would not have suffered Stalinism, for in a democratic state with checks and balances no one can get away with a bitterly hated collectivization of agriculture costing millions of lives, or establishment of a system of destructive labor camps containing millions, or blood purges costing up to forty thousand lives per month. No one could even propose such programs without ending his career. Stalin, we must remember, did all these things, and held on to power until he died in bed.

Richard Nixon, too, was labeled a tyrant, by some. Let us consider his career. Shortly after winning an election by the biggest margin in American presidential history, he was forced to resign. What were his tyrannous actions? Was it the death of millions?

The forced collectivization of agriculture? The great show trials? The intervention in Vietnam? No, it was that his lieutenants engaged in "dirty tricks," that they tried to "bug" the Democratic headquarters (apparently without Nixon's prior knowledge), and that Nixon participated in the coverup. He may also have cheated on his income taxes according to one view. Why did Stalin, with the blood of millions on his hands, rule so long and die in bed? Why was Nixon, who did so much less that the comparison is laughable, retired to California? Surely the difference is in the system. In one, man's nature is taken into account. In the other, it is not. Do democratic nations undertake the programs of a Stalin? Obviously not, because it would be political suicide.

Is democracy, then, the sufficient answer? It is not. Majorities, as well as minorities, can be tyrannical when they gain the opportunity. Majorities of whites in the United States exercised tyrannical rule over blacks (and Indians) until very recently. A Greek majority in Cyprus ignored the Turkish minority's claims until Turkey intervened with an army. How, then, protect minorities? There is no certain way. Constitutions and bills of rights which put limits on majorities, as well as minorities, may help, as may independent judiciaries with the power to enforce these rights, but in the long run these require a degree of self-restraint by the majority. Having a society in which there is no permanent majority and no permanent minority helps, but this too is difficult to obtain.

James Madison thought the political system most in accord with man's nature is the large, extended commercial republic.[34] Both its size and its commerce tend to produce a great multiplicity of separate interests, and this multiplicity of interests tends to produce moderate government because no single interest can dominate and simply rule in its own interests. The first impulse of a group is likely to be to gain a distribution of benefits favoring it. But if, because of the multiplicity of groups, it cannot simply impose its will and gain private advantage, then its second impulse is to prevent a distribution that favors any other group. Its first choice, that is, is privilege. Its second choice is a fair distribution. And he hoped the multiplicity of groups and interests would conduce to moderation, which so wise a philosopher as Aristotle held was the closest possible approximation, in political life, to justice. (Religious life provides a case in point. Where one religion is dominant, its followers are tempted to suppress others in the name of defending the true faith. Where there is a multiplicity of sects, none have the power to exclude the others, and the result is likely to be toleration and moderation.) The Madisonian solution does not always work, as the slavery controversy proved, and it is not always possible, for many states may lack the requisite multiplicity of interests, but it is one strategy taking into account the nature of man.

None of this, unfortunately, guarantees success. Where power is concentrated, tyranny is likely to ensue. Where power is divided, stalemate or civil war may ensue. And that is the final answer about political prudence—there is no final answer. A balance must be struggled for in each generation. The acceptable balances of one may not work in the next. Man's nature being what it is, no social or political reform, no revolution, no technique or content of education, no manipulation of man, will finally oust social corruption or evil. Man will never make that utopia about which we dream. Every set of institutions, every technique of social control, will come up against an unsolvable problem—the problem of man's sinful nature, his pride and self-centeredness, his response to a radical anxiety and insecurity. The particular manifestations of that defect of will vary from culture to culture, from age to age, but that defect, always present, will find some expression regardless of the forms through which it must move. So utopia will always beckon, but it will always elude us.

Is this a counsel of despair? It is not. Knowing what man is like, we can devise strategies and institutions to prevent the worst abuses, and frameworks of law in which reforms are possible. None of these strategies or institutions guarantees success, but by their help we can fashion reasonably decent communities for much of mankind much of the time. In an age that has seen millions tortured and murdered in the name of a utopia that will never be, that would be no mean accomplishment.

Finally, economics deserves some discussion. Today two great systems confront each other—capitalism and socialism. Both have promised a natural harmony. Capitalism promised it on this side of the revolution, through the invisible hand of the market. Socialism promised it on the other side of the revolution, through the healing balm of social ownership of the means of production. Neither can deliver what it promised.

There is no natural harmony in the market even if it is self-regulating and self-correcting, which most economists now doubt, because that self-regulating market can produce absolutely enormous disparities of wealth and poverty, and absolutely ruthless economic adjustments, both of which pit man against man, group against group, and class against class and both of which offend man's sense of justice and compassion. If you have nothing the market currently values, you are thrown on a human scrap pile. The market can be cruel and utterly ruthless. Of course the market is supposed to be self-righting. But what does it mean, in human terms, for a fifty-five-year-old man to lose his job in a declining industry and to have to find another job, in competition with the young, in a new and rising industry, possibly in another region? What does it mean for whole communities, dependent on one industry, if that industry leaves, going perhaps to another country? What does it mean to have nothing the market wants for even an interval? The human costs of the "invisible hand" are simply too high to leave the market to itself. Nor can men, in pursuit of profit and self-interest, be counted on to act for the common good, for self-interest and the common good do not always coincide through the market. What is there in self-interest that rewards a company for engaging in expensive treatment of sewage before it is dumped into rivers, or of toxic smoke before it is released into the air, especially if its competitors are not equally scrupulous? For as long as men are self-centered, there will have to be regulation of the market to correct for the worst abuses and cruelties that will arise from it.

Socialism equally fails to deliver what it promises. It has enormous appeal. Everywhere it has capitalism on the defensive. Why? In part because it promises a society which all of us know is what society really should be like. It promises a society in which people are generous, loving, compassionate, willing to produce according to capacity but distribute according to need. It promises a society of brotherhood. And for that reason, it will always attract us more, because we know that is what society should be like. But it cannot deliver. It fails because it is built on what men should be like, not on what they are like. Men will continue, because they are self-centered, to work harder for themselves than for the common good; they will continue to work their private plots of land harder than the collective plots;[35] they will continue to take better care of their own property than of rented or public property; they will continue to produce more when there is a direct and immediate reward than when there is a distant and indirect reward.

There are, of course, other problems with full socialization of the means of production. It concentrates power in a way which almost always leads to serious abuse. It often has pretensions to providing a heaven on earth, and when it fails, as it must, the tendency is to try harder—a little more compulsion, a little more effort to root out the corrupters, a little more thorough education, and heaven will surely come. So the combination of ideology and structure has built into it a strong tendency toward excess, toward totalitarianism, toward ruthless measures to remake man, toward the sacrifice of this generation for the next. Until it is realized that the problem is man himself, it encourages ever more frantic efforts to make it work. But it will never work until there is a new man. And changing property relationships, or teaching moral codes, does not produce a new man.

In actual practice the flaws of each system eventually lead to efforts to reform the system in ways which make it more compatible with man's true nature. Developed capitalism is not laissez-faire capitalism. It is regulated to stop the worst abuses, its distribution according to the market is modified by a considerable amount of redistribution according to need, its cruelty is modified by compassion. And neither is developed socialism the socialism of the presocialist dreams. Government ownership of the means of production has not proved to be specially efficient economically, and neither has it proved specially conducive to liberty or specially humane in its effects. In consequence, developed democratic socialism has retained a large market and private ownership component and has become largely a matter of welfarism rather than a Soviet-type command economy. Labels aside, both advanced capitalist and advanced socialist societies, if democratic, rely in part on the market mechanism and material incentives (even Communist societies retreat to material incentives after moral exhortation and compulsion prove inefficient and ineffective),[36] and both modify the market mechanism by government intervention and planning, as well as by redistribution for the sake of compassion and justice. Both systems, that is, prove more humane, and more efficient, when they take into account the nature of man.

There was, briefly, hope that the limitations of each system were becoming known, and that the passions of ideological struggle were dying in pragmatic or realistic accommodations by both systems. But the trumpeted "end of ideology" died before ideology did, and we were left once again in storms of ideological passion that ignore the nature of man and end by torturing men to compel them to conform to ideological preconceptions. It is a sad culmination to the Age of Reason. Is it not time we take the empirical evidence about man's nature seriously? Is it not time that we admit that the religious were correct about man? Is it not time that we plan on that basis? It almost certainly is not that time, but it surely should be.

Publications of John H. Hallowell

Books

The Decline of Liberalism as an Ideology. 1943. Berkeley, Calif.: University of California Press. Published in the International Library of Sociology and Social Reconstruction, Karl Mannheim, editor (London: Kegan Paul, 1946). Translated into Spanish with an introduction by Salvador M. Dana Montano (Santa Fe, Argentina, 1949). Translated into Japanese and published in Tokyo (1953). Reprinted by Howard Fertig, Inc. (New York, 1971).

Main Currents in Modern Political Thought. 1950. New York: Holt, Rinehart and Winston.

The Moral Foundation of Democracy. 1954. Chicago: University of Chicago Press. Translated into Arabic, Korean, and French.

Books Edited

The Soviet Satellite Nations: A Study of the New Imperialism. 1958. Gainesville, Fla.: Callman.

Development: for What? 1964. Durham, N.C.: Duke University Press.

Eric Voegelin. *From Enlightenment to Revolution*. 1975. Durham, N.C.: Duke University Press.

Prospects for Constitutional Democracy. 1976. Durham, N.C.: Duke University Press.

Books Co-edited

(with R. Taylor Cole) *The Southern Political Scene, 1938–1948*. 1948. Gainesville, Fla.: Callman.

Articles

"The Decline of Liberalism." April 1942. *Ethics* 52: 323–49.
"Compromise as a Political Ideal." April 1944. *Ethics* 54: 157–73.
"Politics and Ethics." Aug. 1944. *American Political Science Review* 38: 639–55.
"Politics and Ethics: A Rejoinder to William F. Whyte." April 1946. *American Political Science Review* 40: 307–12.
"Modern Liberalism: An Invitation to Suicide." Oct. 1947. *South Atlantic Quarterly* 46: 453–66.
"Il liberalismo d'oggi." June 1948. *Il Ponte* 4: 510–17.
"Pacifism—The Way to Peace?" Jan. 1949. *Crozer Quarterly* 26: 30–40.
"Goals for Political Science: A Discussion." Dec. 1951. *American Political Science Review* 45: 1005–10.
"Politics: Art or Science?" Oct. 1952. *Theology Today* 9: 333–47.
"The Meaning of Majority Rule." May 1952. *Commonweal* 56: 167–69.
"Christianity and the Crisis of Our Times." June 1954. Commencement Address. *Bulletin of the General Theological Seminary* 40: 26–33.
"Communism and Christianity." April 1956. *Stetson University Bulletin* 56.
"Natural Rights." 1961. *Encyclopedia Britannica* (Chicago: William Benton) 16: 162C and 162D.
"Political Science Today." March 1961. *Social Order* 11: 107–22.
"The Christian in the University." March 1962. *Motive* 33: 36–43.
"Drei Richtungen in der Amerikanischen Politischen Wissenschaft." Dec. 1963. *Zeitschrift fuer Politik* 10: 346–63.
"Plato and His Critics." May 1965. *Journal of Politics* 27: 273–89.
"Collectivism." 1967. *Encyclopedia Britannica* (Chicago: William Benton), p. 55.
"Liberalism." 1967. *New Catholic Encyclopedia* (New York: McGraw-Hill), 8: 701–6.
"Conservatism," "Democracy," "Liberalism." 1980. *World Book Encyclopedia* (New York: World Book–Childcraft International): 4:734, 5:104–8; 12:204.

Contributor to:

Fairchild, Hoxie N., ed. 1952. *Religious Perspectives in College Teaching.* New York: Ronald Press.

Pike, James A., ed. 1956. *Modern Canterbury Pilgrims.* New York: Morehouse-Gorham Co.

Thorson, Thomas L., ed. 1963. *Plato: Totalitarian or Democrat?* Englewood Cliffs, N.J.: Prentice-Hall.

Keeney, Barnaby C., et al. 1964. *Report of the Commission on the Humanities.* New York: American Council of Learned Societies.

Sharma, S. R., and Tiwari, S. C., eds. 1966. *Political Studies.* Agra, India.

Matthews, Z. K. 1966. *Responsible Government in a Revolutionary Age.* New York: Association Press. World Council of Churches Publication.

Bier, William C., ed. 1971. *Conscience: Its Freedom and Limitations.* New York: Fordham University Press.

Foreword to:

Simon, Yves R. *The Tradition of Natural Law.* 1965. New York: Fordham University Press.

Finlay, James C. 1968. *The Liberal Who Failed.* Washington, D.C.: Corpus Books.

Books published for the Lilly Endowment Research Program in Christianity and Politics to which John Hallowell contributed a Foreword:

Wild, John. 1959. *Human Freedom and Social Order.* Durham, N.C.: Duke University Press.

Thompson, Kenneth W. 1959. *Christian Ethics and the Dilemmas of Foreign Policy.* Durham, N.C.: Duke University Press.

Canavan, Francis P. 1960. *The Political Reason of Edmund Burke.* Durham, N.C.: Duke University Press.

Ramsey, Paul. 1961. *War and the Christian Conscience.* Durham, N.C.: Duke University Press.

Brookes, Edgar H. 1963. *Power, Law, Right and Love.* Durham, N.C.: Duke University Press.

Friedrich, Carl J. 1964. *Transcendent Justice: The Religious Dimension of Constitutionalism.* Durham, N.C.: Duke University Press.

Notes

William C. Havard · *Policy Sciences, the Humanities, and Political Coherence*

1. The following statement characterizes the aims of a number of political scientists who seek a "hard" social scientific basis of knowledge for policy studies: "There is a profound need to enlarge the zone of understanding of human behavior and society. Those of us interested in the intersection of social science and policy do not question the need for fundamental research. We see no competition with those engaged in developing stronger bodies of verified knowledge and firmer theories to explain patterned regularities of behavior. On the contrary, we welcome these efforts. As social science knowledge becomes sturdier, and more predictive, one of the fallouts is that it becomes more trustworthy as a basis for policy advice." Carol H. Weiss, ed., *Using Social Research in Public Policy Making* (Lexington, Mass.: Heath, 1977), p. 1.

2. *The American Science of Politics, Its Origins and Conditions* (London: Routledge and Kegan Paul, 1959).

3. In *The Brazen Face of History* (Baton Rouge: Louisiana State University Press, 1980), Lewis P. Simpson examines (among many other aspects of the literary consciousness in America) the way in which an authoritative "Republic of Letters" emerged out of the development of rationally autonomous, literate man in the eighteenth century and displaced the old authoritative structures of religious and political tradition. This new "estate" was composed originally of men of science, letters, and literature generally, but the advancement of science and its claims to certainty and comprehensiveness of knowledge eventually removed the man of letters and literature from a role in the projected transformation of nature, man, and society, thus leaving the scientists and technologists as the sources of knowledge and power on which this form of "progress" depended.

4. This condition of man's existence is an integral theme in the Voegelin corpus; its extended meaning is explored in considerable detail in several of the essays in *Anamnesis*, trans. and ed. Gerhart Niemeyer (Notre Dame and London: University of Notre Dame Press, 1978), especially part 3.

5. "The Study of Politics in a University," in *Rationalism in Politics and Other Essays* (New York: Basic Books, 1962), p. 321.

6. Ibid.

7. The discussion of the particular instance in which this recurring (or constant) issue developed and spilled beyond the bounds of orderly political resolution was chosen because of its dramatic illustration of the interrelatedness of the components of the practical experience of morals and politics. It has recently been revived in an even older form with the efforts of the religious fundamentalists to secure parity of treatment of "scientific creationism" in the classroom with evolutionary theory. It is not difficult, by the application of dialectical philosophical argument, to establish the lack of relevance of scientific evolutionary theory to the questions of transcendent existence addessed in theology, and vice versa. But the hardening of ideology on both sides (scientism versus religious fundamentalism) has been a constant in this issue since the nineteenth century.

8. The decline (to the point of disappearance in many instances) of the place of classical rhetoric in liberal education is an important, if little noted, contribution to the development of the problems discussed here. We have recently addressed the implications of the connections between the uses of rhetoric and the sciences of ethics and politics in Aristotle for contemporary politics in George J. Graham, Jr. and William C. Havard, "The Language of the Statesman: Philosophy and Rhetoric in Contemporary Politics," paper delivered at the International Seminar for Political Philosophy and Theory, Montebello, Quebec, Canada, May, 1981.

Kenneth W. Thompson · *Ethics and Foreign Policy*

1. Hans J. Morgenthau, *Politics Among Nations: The Struggle for Power and Peace*, 5th ed. rev. (New York: Alfred A. Knopf, 1978), p. 274.
2. Christopher Dawson, *The Making of Europe* (New York: Meridian Books, 1956), pp. 169–238.
3. See the writings of Niebuhr, especially *The Structure of Nations and Empires*, *Moral Man and Immoral Society*, and *The Irony of American History*.

R. Bruce Douglass · *Liberalism as a Threat to Democracy*

The author is indebted to Gary Marfin and Michael Jackson for critical comments on an earlier draft of this paper.

1. The principal works in question are Karl R. Popper, *The Open Society and Its Enemies*, 5th ed., 2 vols. (Princeton, N.J.: Princeton University Press, 1971); Friedrich A. Hayek, *The Constitution of Liberty* (Chicago: University of Chicago Press, 1960). Cf. also Karl R. Popper, *Conjectures and Refutations*, 2d ed. (New York: Basic Books, 1963), and F. A. Hayek, *Studies in Philosophy, Politics and Economics* (Chicago: University of Chicago Press, 1967).
2. In elaboration of his political argument, Locke, e.g., assumes a certain level of sociability, but he does not assume that this just happens spontaneously. As his writings on both education and religion demonstrate, he believed that virtue had to be cultivated. The following passage from his essay "Some Thoughts Concerning Education" illustrates how definite he was on this matter: "That the difference to be found in the Manners and Abilities of Men, is owing more to their *Education* than to anything else; we have Reason to conclude, that great Care is to be had of the forming Children's *Minds*, and giving them that seasoning early, which shall influence their Lives always after. For when they do well or ill, the Praise or Blame will be laid there. And when any thing is done outwardly, the common Saying will pass upon them, That it is suitable to their *Breeding*. As the Strength of the Body lies chiefly in being able to endure *Hardships*, so also does that of the Mind. And the great Principle and Foundation of all Virtue and Worth is placed on this, That a Man is able to deny himself his own Desires, cross his own Inclinations, and purely follow what Reason directs as best, tho the Appetite lean the other way." Cf. James L. Axtell, ed., *The Educational Writings of John Locke* (Cambridge: At the University Press, 1968), p. 138. Not being a democrat, Locke did not confront the problem in the form it assumed in the later development of liberalism. But once liberalism took on a democratic character, there was even more emphasis by liberal theorists on the need to cultivate sociability and self-discipline. A recurring theme of classical utilitarianism, for example, is that good

government requires formal education for the masses, and by education the utilitarians clearly had in mind moral as well as intellectual training. James Mill, e.g., says that "The end of education is to render the individual, as much as possible, an instrument of happiness, first to himself, and next to other beings." He then proceeds to outline a plan of education based on the premise that "the four cardinal virtues of the ancients do pretty completely include all the qualities, to the possession of which it is desirable that the human mind should be trained." "Education" in W. H. Burston, ed., *James Mill on Education* (Cambridge: At the University Press, 1969), pp. 41, 65.

3. Sheldon S. Wolin, *Politics and Vision* (Boston: Little, Brown & Co., 1960), pp. 343 ff.

4. J. S. Mill, "On Liberty" in J. M. Robson, ed., *Essays on Politics and Society* (vol. 18 of the Collected Works) (Toronto: University of Toronto Press, 1977), p. 226.

5. Ibid., p. 261.

6. It is true that Mill did not advocate a single compulsory public, or state-run education system. In *On Liberty* he explicitly rejects such a proposal as a threat to liberty. But his thinking on this topic, like many others, is complex. He was not unaffected by the Benthamite argument for "liberation" of the masses through centrally-administered state educational institutions, and he ended up in the seventh edition of *The Principles of Political Economy* advocating a system of compulsory education and mandatory examinations which has unmistakable paternalistic overtones. Arguing against leaving the availability of formal education up to parental discretion, he says that "the proposition that the consumer is a competent judge of the commodity, can be admitted only with numerous abatements and exceptions. He is generally the best judge (though even this is not true universally) of the material objects produced for his use. These are destined to supply some physical want, or gratify some taste or inclination, respecting which wants or inclinations there is no appeal from the person who feels them; or they are the means and appliances of some occupation, for the use of the persons engaged in it, who may be presumed to be judges of the things required in their own habitual employment. But there are other things, of the worth of which the demand of the market is by no means a test; things of which the utility does not consist in ministering to inclinations, nor in serving the daily uses of life, and the want of which is least felt where the need is greatest. This is peculiarly true of those things which are chiefly useful as tending to raise the character of human beings. The uncultivated cannot be competent judges of cultivation. Those who most need to be made wiser and better, usually desire it least, and, if they desired it, would be incapable of finding the way to it by their own lights. It will continually happen, on the voluntary system, that, the end not being desired, the means will not be provided at all, or, that, the persons requiring improvement having an imperfect and altogether erroneous conception of what they want, the supply called forth by the demand of the market will be anything but what is really required. Now any well-intentioned and tolerably civilized government may think, without presumption, that it does or ought to possess a degree of cultivation above the average of the community which it rules, and that it should therefore be capable of offering better education and better instruction to the people, than the greater number of them would spontaneously demand. Education, therefore, is one of those things which it is admissible in principle that a government should provide for the people. The case is one to which the reasons of the non-interference principle do not necessarily or universally extend." J. S. Mill, *Principles of Political Economy*, bk. 5 (vol. 3 of the Collected Works) (Toronto: University of Toronto Press, 1965), pp. 947–48. For the back-

ground, cf. E. G. West, "Liberty and Education: John Stuart Mill's Dilemma," *Philosophy* 40 (1965): 129–42.

7. Cf. J. S. Mill, "Utilitarianism," in J. M. Robson, ed., *Essays on Ethics, Religion and Society* (vol. 10 of the Collected Works) (Toronto: University of Toronto Press, 1969), pp. 227–33.

8. Hayek, *Constitution of Liberty*, p. 35.

9. Ibid., p. 36.

10. Hayek observes that "a successful free society will always in large measure be a tradition-bound society" (*Constitution of Liberty*, p. 61). In a similar vein Popper comments that "among the traditions we must count as the most important is what we may call the 'moral framework' (corresponding to the institutional 'legal framework') of a society. This incorporates the society's traditional sense of justice or fairness, or the degree of moral sensitivity it has reached. This moral framework serves as the basis which makes it possible to reach a fair or equitable compromise between conflicting interests when this is necessary. It is, of course, itself not unchangeable, but it changes comparatively slowly. Nothing is more dangerous than the destruction of this traditional framework. . . . In the end its destruction will lead to cynicism and nihilism, i.e., to the disregard and the dissolution of all human values." (*Conjectures and Refutations*, pp. 351–52). Precisely. As descriptions of how actual historic "free" societies have functioned, these statements are excellent. As descriptions of how an open society in the liberal individualist sense would function, however, they are very misleading. For neither Hayek nor Popper is willing to countenance the measures that are necessary to maintain and preserve the traditions they value.

11. Popper, *Conjectures and Refutations*, p. 374.

12. Cf. the discussion of this theme in the work of Hayek in Anthony de Crespigny, "F. A. Hayek: Freedom for Progress," ed. Anthony de Crespigny and Kenneth Minogue, *Contemporary Political Philosophers* (New York: Dodd, Mead & Co., 1975), p. 54.

13. Hayek, *Constitution of Liberty*, p. 61.

14. Reinhold Niebuhr, *The Children of Light and the Children of Darkness* (New York: Charles Scribner's Sons, 1944), p. 7.

15. Hayek, *Studies in Philosophy, Politics and Economics*, p. 162.

16. Cf. Carl J. Friedrich, *Transcendent Justice* (Durham, N.C.: Duke University Press, 1964).

17. Aristotle, *The Politics*, 1280b.

Francis Canavan · *Liberalism in Root and Flower*

1. University of California Publications in Political Science (1943), reprinted New York: Howard Fertig, 1971.

2. Ibid., pp. 5, 35–36, 9.

3. Ibid., pp. 10, 50.

4. See Frederick Vaughan, *The Tradition of Political Hedonism* (New York: Fordham University Press, 1982).

5. For an exposition of this view see Frank M. Coleman, "The Hobbesian Basis of American Constitutionalism," *Polity* 7 (1974): 67–74, with further references in n. 27.

6. *Politics and Vision* (Boston and Toronto: Little Brown & Co., 1969), p. 293.

7. *Leviathan*, ed. with intro. by Michael Oakeshott (Oxford: Blackwell, n.d.), chap. 15, p. 104.

8. *Essay concerning Human Understanding*, bk. 2, chap. 20, sect. 2, in *The Works of John Locke*, 10 vols. (London: Thomas Tegg et al., 1823, reprinted by Scientia Verlag Aalen, Germany, 1963), 1:231.
9. *An Introduction to the Principles of Morals and Legislation* in *The Works of Jeremy Bentham*, 11 vols., reproduced from the Bowring Edition of 1838–43 (New York: Russell & Russell, 1962), 1:1.
10. Ed. Oskar Piest (Indianapolis and New York: The Library of Liberal Arts, Bobbs-Merrill Co., 1957), pp. 45, 48, 49.
11. *Leviathan*, chap. 15, p. 104.
12. See John Dunn, *The Political Thought of John Locke* (Cambridge: At the University Press, 1969), p. 187.
13. *Anarchical Fallacies*, in *Works*, 2:501.
14. *A Preface to Democratic Theory* (Chicago and London: University of Chicago Press, 1956), pp. 45, 32.
15. Hobbes, *Leviathan*, intro., p. lv. The second of the nominalist doctrines, that will is precedent to reason in both God and man, is a consequence of the first doctrine, that the reality of a thing is its individuality.
16. Locke says all of this so often that it is almost otiose to give references, but see bk. 4, chap. 3, sect. 23, in *Works*, 2:374; 2, 1, 2, in 1:83; 4, 6, 11, in 3:7; 2, 23, 32, in 2:30; 2, 31, 6–13, in 2:129–35; 3, 3, 20, in 2:185; 3, 3, 11, in 2:72.
17. *English Political Thought in the 19th Century* (New York: Harper & Bros., 1962), p. 16.
18. *The Philosophy of J. S. Mill* (Oxford: Clarendon Press, 1953), pp. 119–21, 181–82, 173.
19. *Preliminary Discourse to the Encyclopedia of Diderot*, trans. and ed. Richard N. Schwab (Indianapolis and New York: The Library of Liberal Arts, Bobbs-Merrill Co., 1963), p. 22.
20. *Personal Knowledge* (New York and Evanston: Harper & Row, 1964), pp. 139–40.
21. Ibid., p. 141.
22. It is of course questionable whether we can explain living, organic matter by a blind, mechanical development of its chemical composition. Be that as it may, all we need insist upon here is that an organism cannot be understood as a mere sum of its parts. It is intelligible only as a composite but single, living whole.
23. *The Ruler: a Modern Translation of Il Principe* (Chicago: Henry Regnery Co., 1955), chap. 25, p. 123.
24. *Leviathan*, chap. 11, p. 64.
25. *Political Philosophy and the Issues of Politics* (Chicago and London: University of Chicago Press, 1977), p. 316.

James L. Wiser · *The Force of Reason: On Reading Plato's* Gorgias

1. Plato, *Gorgias*, trans. W. C. Helmbold (Indianapolis: Bobbs-Merrill, 1952), p. 79.
2. Ibid., p. 95.
3. Ibid., p. 100.
4. "The transfer of authority from Athens to Plato is the climax of the *Gorgias*. . . . The transfer of authority means that the authority of Athens, as the public organization of a people in history, is invalidated and superseded by a new public authority manifest in the person of Plato. That is revolution." Eric Voegelin, *Plato and Aristotle* (Baton Rouge: Louisiana State University Press, 1957), p. 39.

5. Plato, *Gorgias,* pp. 81–82.
6. ". . . everyone who has learned an art [acquires] that character which is imparted to him by the knowledge of it." Ibid., p. 20.
7. Cf. ibid., p. 10.
8. Ibid., p. 31.
9. Ibid., p. 49.
10. Ibid., p. 51.
11. Cf. ibid., p. 62.
12. Ibid., p. 54.
13. Ibid., p. 86.
14. Cf. ibid., p. 83.
15. Ibid., p. 26.
16. Cf. ibid., p. 35.
17. Ibid., p. 48.
18. Ibid., p. 49.
19. Cf. ibid., p. 10.
20. Cf. ibid., p. 31.
21. Cf. ibid., p. 90.
22. Ibid., p. 90.
23. This is Callicles' analysis of the mistakes of Gorgias and Polus. He himself makes a similar error for the same reasons later when he admits that he is arguing only to please Gorgias. Cf. ibid., pp. 50, 80.

Walter B. Mead · *Will as Moral Faculty*

1. It is for this reason that, in the present context, I have some preference for the term "autoinductive" over "autonomous." "Autonomous will" has sometimes been taken to suggest volition operating within an axiologically vacuous universe.
2. *Republic* 440b-d.
3. Ibid. 441a; Aristotle, *Politics* 1334b 22–25.
4. *Republic* 519a; Aristotle, *Nicomachean Ethics* 1111b 13–15, 1145b 21 ff., 1179b 4–31.
5. Therefore Plato suggests that the proper therapy for a wrongly oriented intellect is *periagoge*, or a turning around. Both Plato and Aristotle seem to agree that, on the other hand, proper treatment for the spirited and appetitive faculties is, in most instances, the correcting of excess or deficiency. Unlike ignorance, even hunger, in proper proportion, has a proper function. *Republic* 518e; *Nicomachean Ethics* 1106b 15-1109b 27.
6. *Republic* 519a-b; 619c-d.
7. Ibid. 375ff.; *Nicomachean Ethics* 1149a 25 ff.
8. *Nicomachean Ethics* 1095b 2–13.
9. Ibid. 1113a 10–12, 1139a 23-1139b 5; *De Anima*, bk. 3, chaps. 9–12.
10. *Nicomachean Ethics* 1145b 21 ff.
11. *Republic* 540c-541a.
12. Ibid. 514 ff.
13. Ibid. 515c, 515e. Emphasis added.
14. Ibid. 202a, 479d, 509 ff.
15. Ibid. 500c.
16. Ibid. 518d-e.
17. *Phaedrus* 246a-250c.
18. *Republic* 520a.

19. *What Is Called Thinking?*, trans. F. Wieck and J. Gray (New York: Harper and Row, 1968).

20. Hereafter I shall use "nilling" to refer to negative willing (willing that something not be), thereby distinguishing it from not-willing.

21. Hannah Arendt, *The Life of the Mind*, 2 vols. (New York: Harcourt Brace Jovanovich, 1977–78), 2 : 135. Here Arendt is representing the position of Duns Scotus.

22. Ibid., 2 : 69.

23. We are not speaking here of moral authority, which cannot be said to transcend reason. Rather, at present we speak of authority only in terms of capacities that man finds are "permitted," or available, to him.

24. Except when not-willing occurs, which—as we shall see—leaves us with no arbiter.

25. *Nietzsche*, 2 vols. (Pfullingen, 1961), 1 : 63–64, 161, quoted in Arendt, *Life of the Mind*, 2 : 176.

26. Arendt, *Life of the Mind*, 2 : 195.

27. *Nietzsche*, 1 : 63–64, quoted in Arendt, *Life of the Mind*, 2 : 177.

J. M. Porter · *Democracy and Autonomy in Rousseau*

1. Carl Cohen, *Democracy* (Athens: University of Georgia Press, 1971), p. 269.

2. In a seminal article Stephen G. Salkever has said that in modern political thought there seem to be two choices: "the life of individual liberty (of economic man liberated from unnecessary political control) versus the life of the autonomous citizen in the free community (political man liberated from the impurities of economic life)." Each choice depends upon some idea of a self-determining or autonomous individual. Salkever's thesis, however, is that neither choice is made from an adequate political perspective. "Virtue, Obligation and Politics," *American Political Science Review* 68 (1974): 91.

3. Chicago: University of Chicago Press, 1954.

4. Ibid., p. 69.

5. Ibid., p. 74.

6. Ibid., pp. 80–81.

7. For Rousseau's influence on Kant, Hegel, and Marx, see: John Plamenatz and Nathan Rotenstreich, *Basic Problems of Marx's Philosophy* (New York: Bobbs-Merrill, 1965); Andrew Levine, *The Politics of Autonomy* (Amherst: University of Massachusetts Press, 1976); Louis Althusser, *Politics and History: Montesquieu, Rousseau, Hegel and Marx*, trans. Ben Brewster (NLB, 1972); G. D. H. Cole, "Introduction," Jean Jacques Rousseau, *The Social Contract and Discourses* (London: Everyman's Library, 1950); Ernst Cassirer, *Rousseau, Kant, Goethe* (Princeton: Princeton University Press, 1944).

8. Levine, *Politics of Autonomy*, p. 14. Levine is quoting from *Social Contract*, bk. 1, ch. 4. The exact words are: "Renoncer à sa liberté, c'est renouncer à sa qualité d'homme, aux droits de l'humanité, même à ses devoirs. Il n'y a nul dédommagement possible pour quiconque renonce à tout. Une telle renonciation est incompatible avec la nature de l'homme; et c'est ôter toute moralité à ses actions que d'ôter toute liberté à sa volonté." C. E. Vaughan, *The Political Writings of Jean Jacques Rousseau* (Cambridge: At the University Press, 1915), 2 : 28.

9. Ibid., 149–50.

10. Quoted in Cole, "Introduction," p. xlix.

11. Vaughan, *Political Writings*, 1 : 168.

12. Cole, "Introduction," p. xxxviii.
13. "Games, Justice and the General Will," *Mind* 74 (1965): 554.
14. Ibid., 556. Quotations are from *Social Contract.*
15. Cole, "Introduction," p. xlii.
16. Levine, *Politics of Autonomy*, p. 43.
17. This delineation of the relationship between autonomy and the General Will is, of course, deficient in its treatment of the psychological or experiential dimension. So much has been written on Rousseau and alienation that it seems necessary to correct an imbalance by stressing the structural and rational coherence of Rousseau's program.
18. Stephen Salkever has argued that happiness, not freedom, is Rousseau's goal. Freedom, though, describes the "mode of existence" and entails happiness. See "Freedom, Participation and Happiness," *Political Theory* 5 (1977): 391–413; "Rousseau and the Concept of Happiness," *Polity* (1978): 27–45.
19. Levine, p. 56.
20. *Participation and Democratic Theory* (Cambridge: At the University Press, 1970), pp. 25–27.
21. "Rousseau's Images of Authority," *American Political Science Review* 58 (Dec. 1964): 931.
22. Ibid., p. 923.
23. *Moral Man and Immoral Society*, p. 4. Quoted in Dorothy Emmet, *The Moral Prism* (New York: St. Martin's Press, 1979), p. 29.
24. Stuart Hampshire, *Thought and Action* (London: Chatto and Windus, 1959), p. 262.

Claes G. Ryn · *History and the Moral Order*

1. The epistemological aspect of historicism is discussed in Claes G. Ryn, "Knowledge and History," *The Journal of Politics* 44 (May 1982): 394–408. For a more comprehensive treatment of the subject, see Benedetto Croce, *Logic* (London: Macmillan, 1917; this translation is not without flaws).
2. Leo Strauss, *Natural Right and History* (Chicago: University of Chicago Press, 1953), p. 97.
3. Strauss does not identify the particular passage, but he is undoubtedly referring to bk. 5, vii (1134b18–1135a6) of *Nicomachean Ethics.*
4. Strauss, *Natural Right and History*, p. 157.
5. Ibid., p. 158. (emphasis added).
6. Ibid., p. 159.
7. Ibid. (emphasis added).
8. Ibid., pp. 159–61. Strauss is aware of the apparent proximity of his line of argument to some Machiavellian ideas. He suggests that unlike Machiavelli Aristotle does not deny natural right, for he does not take his bearings by "the extreme situations." (Ibid., p. 162.) This would appear to blur the distinction between Machiavellianism and natural right as interpreted by Strauss, for although it is true, as Strauss points out, that Machiavelli is not very reluctant to see normally respected moral rules broken, he explicitly states that such rules are applicable and indispensable in ordinary situations.
9. Ibid., pp. 163–64.
10. Ibid., p. 162 (emphasis added).
11. Ibid., p. 159 (emphasis added).

12. If Strauss is not so much expressing his own view as trying to explicate Aristotle, he does not take exception to the view attributed to Aristotle or indicate how it should be improved.

13. Heinrich Rommen, *The State in Catholic Thought* (New York: Greenwood Press, 1969), pp. 166–67.

14. For a more extensive discussion of the moral imperative as will, see Claes G. Ryn, *Democracy and the Ethical Life* (Baton Rouge: Louisiana State University Press, 1978), esp. pt. 2.

15. Irving Babbitt, *Democracy and Leadership* (Boston: Houghton Mifflin, 1962), pp. 171–72.

16. The relationship of will to reason and imagination is treated in depth in Croce, *Logic*. See also Benedetto Croce, *The Philosophy of the Practical* (New York: Biblo and Tannen, 1967; reprint of the original, partly unreliable, English translation), esp. pp. 86–93. This section discusses the relationship between reason and will in general (not specifically moral will). Close attention to the many valuable elements in Croce's philosophy should be combined with caution against his highly questionable monistic assumptions which betray his only partial liberation from Hegelian metaphysics.

17. Strauss, *Natural Right and History*, p. 159. For an account in the work of Croce of the relationship between rules of conduct and will, see, in particular, *The Philosophy of the Practical*, first pt., vii, and third pt.

18. Walter Lippmann, *The Good Society* (New York: Grosset and Dunlap, 1943), p. 347.

19. Strauss, *Natural Right and History*, p. 313.

20. Strauss notes (ibid., pp. 312–13) that Burke's criticism of abstract plans in politics has a parallel in his earlier work on aesthetics. This might have alerted Strauss to the fact that the discovery of history was not, as Strauss believes, something "peculiar to eighteenth-century political philosophy." (Ibid., p. 34.) Developments in the arts and in aesthetics were at least as important and even primary. The notion of society as an organic whole was developed earlier in these areas than in political thought. The revolt against the artificial confinement of abstract rules, formulated by a French-classicistic reason increasingly imbued with Cartesianism, was a widespread cultural phenomenon by no means restricted to political thought. One might mention the reaction against mercantilistic planning in the area of economics.

21. Ibid., p. 161.

22. Strauss interprets Burke's insistence that abstract speculation cannot guide political action as in part a salutary return to the "prudence" of Aristotle. But Burke is pointing the way to, if not himself developing, a new conception of reason. One of the central achievements of historicism was to be its refutation of the ancient principle *de individuis nulla scientia* which denies the possibility of knowledge of the historical particular. Contributions to this refutation were given by Windelband and Rickert, but it was carried to greater maturity in the work of Croce. Arguing that phenomena can be known only insofar as the universal can be recognized in them, Aristotle never satisfactorily explains how the individual as such can enter into the "practical syllogism." In his criticism of "abstract" rationality and attention to the concrete particular, Burke is not so much returning to Aristotle as anticipating the later unification of history and reason and the eventual refutation of the existence of a "practical reason." For a brief summary of that refutation, see Benedetto Croce, *Aesthetic* (New York: Macmillan, 1922; this translation is not without flaws), p. 49.

A systematic and extensive treatment of the epistemological issues only briefly touched upon here is found in Folke Leander and Claes G. Ryn, *Will, Imagination and Reason* (forthcoming).

23. Strauss, *Natural Right and History*, p. 33.

Thomas A. Spragens, Jr. · *David Hume's "Experimental" Science of Morals and the Natural Law Tradition*

1. *A Treatise of Human Nature*, 3, 1.1.
2. *An Enquiry Concerning the Priciples of Morals*, sect. 1.
3. *Principles of Morals*, sect. 1.
4. *Treatise*, 3, 1.1.
5. *Principles of Morals*, sect. 1.
6. *Treatise*, 3, 1.1.
7. Ibid.
8. *An Enquiry Concerning Human Understanding*, sect. 8, pt. 1.
9. *Treatise*, 3, 3.1.
10. *Principles of Morals*, sect. 5, pt. 2.
11. *Treatise*, 3, 1.2.
12. *Principles of Morals*, sect. 5, pt. 2. (Emphasis added.)
13. *Treatise*, 3, 1, 2.
14. Ibid.
15. *Principles of Morals*, appendix 3.
16. *Treatise*, 3, 3, 6.
17. Ibid., 3, 2, 2. (Emphasis in original.)
18. *Principles of Morals*, appendix 4.
19. Ibid.
20. *Principles of Morals*, appendix 1.
21. Compare *Principles of Morals*, appendix 1, with *The Republic*, chap. 14.
22. *The Republic*, chap. 33.
23. Ibid., chap. 21.
24. *Principles of Morals*, sect. 9, pt. 2.
25. Ibid.
26. *Principles of Morals*, sect. 9, pt. 1.
27. *Principles of Morals*, sect. 1.
28. Ibid.
29. *Principles of Morals*, sect. 9, pt. 1.
30. Ibid., sect. 9, pt. 2.
31. *Principles of Morals*, sect. 9, pt. 1.
32. "A Dialogue," appendix to the second edition of *Principles of Morals*.
33. *Treatise*, 3, 2, 2.
34. *Treatise*, 3, 3, 6.
35. L. A. Selby-Bigge, "Introduction" to Hume's *Enquiries*.
36. The phrase is Robert Dahl's, arising in the context of his dismissal of the "operational" meaningfulness of natural right. *A Preface to Democratic Theory* (Chicago: University of Chicago Press, 1956), p. 45.
37. See his appendix, "Illustrations of the Tao," to *The Abolition of Man* (New York: Macmillan Co., 1947).
38. *Principles of Morals*, sect. 2, pt. 2.
39. Walter Lippmann, *The Public Philosophy* (New York: New American Li-

brary, 1956), p. 40. Lippmann, I think, would clearly have approved of the general strategic orientation of this essay, since he felt that "the poignant question is whether, and, if so, how modern men could make vital contact with the lost traditions of civility." (Ibid., p. 80.)

Fred H. Willhoite, Jr. · *Biocultural Evolution and Political Ethics*

1. G. W. F. Hegel, *Reason in History: A General Introduction to the Philosophy of History*, trans. Robert S. Hartman (Indianapolis and New York: The Library of Liberal Arts, Bobbs-Merrill Co., 1953), p. 27.

2. Edward O. Wilson, *Sociobiology: The New Synthesis* (Cambridge, Mass.: Harvard University Press, 1975).

3. The literature is much too copious to cite, but see Thomas C. Wiegele, ed., *Biology and the Social Sciences: An Emerging Revolution* (Boulder: Westview Press, 1981). A provocative introduction to natural selectionist reasoning is Richard Dawkins, *The Selfish Gene* (New York: Oxford University Press, 1976). Perhaps the most substantial collection of theoretical and empirical studies is Napoleon Chagnon and William Irons, eds., *Evolutionary Biology and Human Social Behavior* (North Scituate, Mass.: Duxbury Press, 1979), and the most intellectually impressive overview thus far is Richard D. Alexander, *Darwinism and Human Affairs* (Seattle: University of Washington Press, 1979).

4. See Fred H. Willhoite, Jr., "Reciprocity, Political Origins, and Legitimacy," paper presented at the 1980 annual meeting of the American Political Science Association, Washington, D.C.

5. This key concept was developed by W. D. Hamilton, in "The Genetical Evolution of Social Behavior, I, II," *Journal of Theoretical Biology* 7 (1964): 1–52.

6. R. D. Alexander, *Darwinism*, pp. 48–55.

7. Ibid., pp. 17, 237.

8. See, e.g., Sarah Blaffer Hrdy, "Infanticide Among Animals: A Review, Classification and Examination of the Implications for the Reproductive Strategies of Females," *Ethology and Sociobiology* 1 (1980): 13–40; Jane Goodall, "Life and Death at Gombe," *National Geographic* 155 (1979): 592–621.

9. This point is still controversial. The best summary of the argument for it is in Alexander, *Darwinism*, pp. 208–33.

10. Ibid., p. 222.

11. "Population pressure" as the primary impetus for the "agricultural revolution" is trenchantly argued and supported with much evidence in Mark N. Cohen, *The Food Crisis in Prehistory: Overpopulation and the Origins of Agriculture* (New Haven, Conn.: Yale University Press, 1977).

12. This bald assertion summarizes an enormous area of anthropological study and controversy. My interpretation follows Pierre van den Berghe, *Human Family Systems: An Evolutionary View* (New York: Elsevier, 1979), passim, esp. pp. 86–102.

13. "A Theory of the Origins of the State," *Science* 169 (1970): 734.

14. The political significance of this primeval tactic of emigration is persuasively stressed by Ronald Cohen, in "State Origins: A Reappraisal," in *The Early State*, ed. Henri J. M. Claessen and Peter Skalnik (The Hague: Mouton, 1978), pp. 31–76.

15. This is a schematic summary of Carneiro's theory. See n. 13, above.

16. See Elman R. Service, *Origins of the State and Civilization: The Process of Cultural Evolution* (New York: W. W. Norton, 1975), pp. 79–93.

17. Ibid., p. 86; see also E. Adamson Hoebel, *The Law of Primitive Man: A Study in Comparative Legal Dynamics* (New York, Atheneum, 1979 [1954]), p. 322.

18. Marshall Sahlins, *Tribesmen* (Englewood Cliffs, N.J.: Prentice-Hall, 1968), pp. 92–93.

19. van den Berghe, *Human Family Systems*, p. 216.

20. Carneiro, "Theory," p. 733.

21. Most of my discussion of "early" states is based upon an excellent recent compendium of case studies and interpretative essays, Claessen and Skalnik, eds., *The Early State*. See n. 14, above.

22. Ibid., p. 639.

23. Dennis H. Wrong, *Power: Its Forms, Bases and Uses* (New York: Harper & Row, 1979), p. 2.

24. See Walter D. Connor, *Socialism, Politics, and Equality: Hierarchy and Change in Eastern Europe and the USSR* (New York: Columbia University Press, 1979).

25. Alexander, *Darwinism*, p. 17.

26. Hallowell, *Moral Foundation*, p. 108.

27. Ibid., p. 126.

28. William Irons, "Natural Selection, Adaptation, and Human Social Behavior," *Evolutionary Biology*, p. 9.

29. *Rationalism in Politics* (London: Methuen, 1962), pp. 187, 194.

Barry Cooper · *Ideology, Technology, and Truth*

1. *In Defence of Politics* (Penguin ed., 1968). Hannah Arendt made the same point in "What is Freedom?" in *Between Past & Future* (New York: Viking, 1968).

2. *Introduction à la lecture de Hegel*. (Paris: Gallimard, 1947). I have discussed Kojève's interpretation at some length in *The End of History* (Toronto: University of Toronto Press, forthcoming).

3. My interpretation of technology relies on the insights of Jacques Ellul, and especially on his two books, *The Technological Society*, trans. John Wilkinson (New York: Vintage, 1964) and *The Technological System*, trans. Joachim Neugroschel (New York: Continuum, 1980). See also George Grant, "Knowing and Making," *Transactions of the Royal Society of Canada*, 4th series, no. 12 (1974): 59–67.

4. Consider Grant's remarks regarding abortion in *English-Speaking Justice* (Sackville, N.B.: Mount Allison University, 1978).

5. Emmet Kennedy, *Destutt de Tracy and the Origins of "Ideology"* (Philadelphia: American Philosophical Society, 1978), pp. 36–37.

6. See *Philosophy of Right*, para. 5 and addition. The remark about cabbage and *ein Schluck Wassers* is from the *Phänomenologie des Geistes* (Hamburg: Meiner, 1952), p. 419.

7. Kennedy, *Destutt de Tracy*, pp. 79–84.

8. "Ideology in Modern Empires," in *Perspectives of Empire: Essays Presented to Gerald S. Graham*, ed. John E. Flint and Glyndwr Williams (London: Longmans, 1973), pp. 189–97.

9. See his remarks in *Technology and Empire: Perspectives on North America* (Toronto: Anansi, 1969), p. 132.

10. I have in mind particularly *A Clockwork Orange* and *1985* but one should not neglect his *Napoleon Symphony*.

11. *Technology and Empire*, p. 143.

12. An entire hermeneutic strategy is implied in Leavis' remark. See F. R.

Leavis, *Nor Shall My Sword: Discourses on Pluralism, Compassion and Social Hope* (London: Chatto and Windus, 1972), p. 62.

13. "'The computer does not impose upon us the ways it should be used,'" in *Beyond Industrial Growth*, ed. Abraham Rotstein (Toronto: University of Toronto Press, 1976), pp. 117–31.

14. Quoted by Kennedy, *Destutt de Tracy*, p. 167.

15. Servan quoted by Michel Foucault, *Discipline and Punish: The Birth of the Prison*, trans. Alan Sheridan (New York: Pantheon, 1977), p. 103.

16. See Foucault, "Truth and Power," in *Power/Knowledge: Selected Interviews and Other Writings, 1972–1977*, ed. Colin Gordon (New York: Pantheon, 1980), pp. 109–33. A more complete account is in Alan Sheridan, *Michel Foucault, The Will to Truth* (London: Tavistock, 1980) or my *Michel Foucault, An Introduction to his Thought* (Toronto: Mellen, 1982).

17. This is the burden of Foucault's inaugural lecture at the Collège de France, *L'Ordre du Discours* (Paris: Gallimard, 1971). A not entirely reliable transation by Rupert Swyer is available in the Appendix to Foucault, *The Archaeology of Knowledge*, trans. A. M. Sheridan Smith (New York: Harper, 1972), pp. 215–37.

18. Foucault, "Intellectuals and Power," in *Language, Counter-Memory, Practice*, ed. Donald F. Bouchard, trans. Bouchard and Sherry Simon (Ithaca: Cornell University Press, 1977), pp. 205–17.

19. Foucault, "Revolutionary Action: 'Until Now,'" in *Language, Counter-Memory, Practice*, pp. 218 ff.

20. Foucault, "Nietzsche, Genealogy, History," in *Language, Counter-Memory, Practice*, pp. 139 ff.

Gerhart Niemeyer · *Communism and the Notion of the Good*

1. Lloyd D. Easton and Kurt H. Guddat, eds. and trans., *Writings of the Young Marx on Philosophy and Society* (Garden City, N.Y.: Doubleday & Co., Anchor Books, 1967), pp. 206–14.

2. Ibid., p. 260.

3. Karl Marx and Friedrich Engels, *The Communist Manifesto*, sect. 3, in *Essential Works of Marxism*, ed. Arthur P. Mendel (New York: Bantam Books, 1965), p. 41.

4. Easton and Guddat, *Young Marx*, pp. 262 ff., slightly modified.

5. *The Rebel* (New York: Random House, Vintage Books, 1956), p. 135.

6. *The Two Sources of Morality and Religion* (Garden City, N.Y.: Doubleday & Co., Anchor Books, 1954), p. 38.

7. New York: Oxford University Press, 1973.

James W. Skillen · *Societal Pluralism: Blessing or Curse for the Public Good?*

1. For the purpose of this essay "societal pluralism" or "structural pluralism" will be used broadly to refer to both larger cultural/group differences and the differentiated institutional and organizational entities of family, church, business enterprise, school, voluntary association, the state, etc. My concern is primarily with the variety of social structures rather than with the variety of interest groups viewed from the standpoint of political influence. See Kenneth D. McRae, "The Plural Society and the Western Political Tradition," *Canadian Journal of Political*

Science 12 (Dec. 1979): 675–88, esp. 677–78. See also McRae's *Consociational Democracy: Political Accommodation in Segmented Societies* (Toronto: McClelland Stewart, 1974); D. Nicholls, *Three Varieties of Pluralism* (London: Macmillan, 1974); and R. McCarthy, et al., *Society, State, and Schools: A Case for Structural and Confessional Pluralism* (Grand Rapids, Mich.: Eerdmans, 1981), pp. 15–50.

2. See the two chapters on unity and diversity among states in my book: *International Politics and the Demand for Global Justice* (Sioux Center, Iowa: Dordt College Press; and Burlington, Ontario: G. R. Welch Co., 1981). And note the renewal of reflection on ethics and justice among students of international politics: for example, Stanley Hoffmann, *Duties Beyond Borders: On the Limits and Possibilities of Ethical International Politics* (Syracuse, N.Y.: Syracuse University Press, 1981); Hedley Bull, *The Anarchical Society: A Study of Order in World Politics* (New York: Columbia University Press, 1977).

3. John Hallowell, *Main Currents in Modern Political Thought* (New York: Holt, Rinehart and Winston, 1950), p. 65.

4. Volumes have been written in defense and in criticism of Constantine, the crusades, Puritanism, Christian socialism, and many other expressions of "Christian" politics. Several important contemporary historical studies that I have found especially helpful include: John Howard Yoder, *The Politics of Jesus* (Grand Rapids, Mich.: Eerdmans, 1972); Walter Ullmann, *Medieval Political Thought* (Baltimore: Penguin Books, 1975); Quentin Skinner, *The Foundations of Modern Political Thought*, vol. 2: *The Age of Reformation* (New York: Cambridge University Press, 1978); and Arthur F. McGovern, *Marxism: An American Christian Perspective* (Maryknoll, N.Y.: Orbis Books, 1980). Also see my article: "Augustine and Contemporary Evangelical Social Thought," *The Reformed Journal* (Jan. 1979): 19–24.

5. Commenting on the influence of Judeo-Christian monotheism, McRae underestimates the importance of God's transcendence in biblical revelation. He notes that monotheistic universalism was used by church and emperor to reach for universality of earthly dominion at the expense of cultural pluralism. McRae, "The Plural Society," p. 680. But the biblical testimony to God's sovereignty is a constant warning and judgment against unjust kings and kingdoms, especially when they claim too much and fail to do justice.

6. For further development of this idea, see Alan Storkey, *A Christian Social Perspective* (Leicester, England: Inter-Varsity Press, 1979); James Skillen, "Politics, Pluralism, and the Ordinances of God," ed. Henry Vander Goot, *Life is Religion: Essays in Honor of H. Evan Runner* (St. Catharines, Ontario: Paideia Press, 1981), pp. 195–206.

7. One of the most important early modern thinkers who contributed to legal and political reflection on societal pluralism was Johannes Althusius. Otto von Gierke rediscovered the obscure sixteenth-century Calvinist in the last century. Carl Friedrich, Frederick Carney, and others began to look at Althusius with new seriousness a few decades ago. And now there is a considerable revival of interest in his work. See Althusius. *The Politics of Johannes Althusius*, trans. Frederick S. Carney (Boston: Beacon Press, 1964); James Skillen, "The Political Theory of Johannes Althusius," *Philosophia Reformata* (Amsterdam), 39th year (1974): 170–90; and Thomas O. Hueglin, "Covenant and Federalism in the Politics of Althusius" (forthcoming in a volume produced by the "Workshop on Covenant and Politics," Center for the Study of Federalism, Temple University, Philadelphia).

8. Jean Jacques Rousseau, *The Social Contract*, ed. and trans. Charles Frankel (New York: Hafner Pub. Co., 1947), bk. 2, chap. 3, p. 27.

9. Herman Dooyeweerd, *Roots of Western Culture: Pagan, Secular, and Christian Options*, trans. John Kraay, ed. Mark VanderVennen, and Bernard Zylstra (Toronto: Wedge Pub. Foundation, 1979), p. 170.

10. Ibid., pp. 170–71. Dante Germino's response to Rousseau at this juncture is too superficial, suggesting simply that Rousseau "would have little sympathy with what has since come to be called interest-group politics." Germino, *Machiavelli to Marx: Modern Western Political Thought* (Chicago: University of Chicago Press, 1972), p. 193. The more serious charge that needs to be leveled at Rousseau concerns the lack of public legal standing not of interest groups but of associations and institutions such as families, schools, churches, etc.

11. Dooyeweerd, *Roots*, p. 170. The words "sphere sovereignty" in this quotation are a translation of the Dutch "*souvereiniteit in eigen kring*," coming from the circles of Dutch Calvinists active in nineteenth- and twentieth-century culture and politics. It refers to the sovereignty of each social entity in its own sphere and thus reflects what I have called the structural diversity of the creation and its orderliness under God. See my article, "Politics, Pluralism, and the Ordinances of God," n. 6 above. For an introduction to Dooyeweerd's philosophy in which the concept of sphere sovereignty is developed in detail, see L. Kalsbeek, *Contours of a Christian Philosophy*, ed. and trans. Bernard and Josina Zylstra (Toronto: Wedge Pub. Foundation, 1975). The historical development of the idea is pursued in my dissertation, written under John Hallowell at Duke University: "The Development of Calvinistic Political Theory in the Netherlands, with Special Reference to the Thought of Herman Dooyeweerd" (1974). Dooyeweerd's analysis of Rousseau's thinking is developed in further detail in his *A New Critique of Theoretical Thought*, vol. 1, trans. David H. Freeman and William S. Young (Philadelphia: Presbyterian and Reformed Pub. Co., 1953), pp. 313–24.

12. Hallowell, *Main Currents*, p. 178.

Mulford Q. Sibley · *The Problem of Coercion*

1. Francis J. McConnell, *Christianity and Coercion* (Nashville: Cokesbury, 1933), p. 1.

2. Isa. 31:1–3.

3. Jer. 24–29.

4. Zech. 4.6.

5. *Republic*, bk. 1, 335.

6. Matt. 5:44.

7. Matt. 4:8–10.

8. Matt. 26:52.

9. Adolf Harnack, *The Mission and Expansion of Christianity* (Eng. trans., New York: Williams and Norgate, 1908, 2 vols.) and *Militia Christi* (Tübingen: J. C. B. Mohr, 1905); and C. J. Cadoux, *The Early Church and the World* (Edinburgh: Clark, 1925).

10. Rom. 13:1.

11. *Contra Celsum*, chaps. 8, 68. Cadoux, *Early Church*, discusses his and other church fathers' attitudes.

12. The record of Maximilianus' trial is reprinted in Harnack's *Militia Christi*, pp. 115–17.

13. Luther's position is vigorously criticized in Jean Lasserre, *War and the Gospel*, trans. Oliver Coburn (Scottdale, Pa.: Herald Press, 1962), pp. 133–41.

14. Pacifists like William Penn supported a non-Augustinian emphasis.

15. See Leo Tolstoy, *The Kingdom of God Is Within You* and *Peace Essays* (London: Oxford, 1935). See also his novel *Resurrection.*

16. Ursula LeGuin, *The Dispossessed* (New York: Harper and Row, 1974).

17. See, for example, Heinrich Rommen, *The State in Catholic Thought* (St. Louis: Herder, 1945), pp. 665–67.

18. Thomas Gilby, *Between Community and Society* (London: Longmans, 1953).

19. C. M. Case, *Non-Violent Coercion* (New York: Century, 1923).

20. *The Quiet Battle* (New York: Doubleday Anchor, 1963).

21. Richard Gregg, *The Power of Non-Violence*, rev. ed. (Nyack, N.Y.: Fellowship Pub., 1959).

22. St. John of the Cross, *Subida del Monte Carmelo*, bk. 1, chap. 13.

23. Rom. 13:3–5:8.

24. Paul Tillich, *Love, Power, and Justice* (New York: Oxford, 1954), passim.

25. Wincenty Lutoslawski, *The World of Souls* (London: Allen and Unwin, 1924), pp. 161–62.

26. Walter Millis, "The Uselessness of Military Power," in *America Armed*, ed. R. A. Goldwin (Chicago: Rand-McNally, 1963), pp. 22–42.

27. Epictetus, *Discourses*, bk. 3, chap. 22.

Clarke E. Cochran · *The Radical Gospel and Christian Prudence*

1. These themes may conveniently be found in *A Reader in Political Theology*, ed. Alistair Kee (Philadelphia: The Westminster Press, 1974). For a relatively superficial acceptance, see Richard J. Cassidy, *Jesus, Politics, and Society* (Maryknoll, N.Y.: Orbis Books, 1978). For an uncritical rejection, see Ernest W. Lefever, *Amsterdam to Nairobi* (Washington, D.C.: Ethics and Public Policy Center, 1979).

2. All Scripture quotations are from the Revised Standard Version, as published in *The New Oxford Annotated Bible with the Apocrypha* (New York: Oxford University Press, 1977).

3. I am grateful to my student, Rob Swanton, for suggesting some of these ways. Such responses are also discussed in John H. Yoder, *The Politics of Jesus* (Grand Rapids, Mich.: Eerdmans, 1972), pp. 16–18 et passim.

4. *Christ and Culture* (New York: Harper Colophon Books, 1975) esp. chaps. 2 and 6.

5. See A. James Reimer, "German Theology and National Socialism," *The Ecumenist* 19 (Nov.–Dec. 1980): 1–8, for a discussion of how this happened in Germany during the 1920s and 1930s. Many claim that Marxism and theology have made such a marriage today. See David Martin, "Revs and Revolutionaries: Church Trends and Theological Fashions," *Encounter*, Jan. 1979, pp. 10–19, and Lefever, *Amsterdam to Nairobi.*

6. Jim Wallis, *Agenda for Biblical People* (New York: Harper & Row, 1976), for example, criticizes the ideological gospels of the left and right while hewing to a radical line.

7. See *Baker's Dictionary of Theology* (Grand Rapids, Mich.: Baker Book House, 1960), s.v. "prudence," and *Interpreter's Dictionary of the Bible* (New York: Abingdon, 1962), s.v. "discretion and prudence."

8. "Politicizing Christianity: Focus on South Africa," Ethics and Public Policy Reprint #17 (Washington, D.C.: Ethics and Public Policy Center, 1979), pp. 10, 11.

9. Aquinas considers prudence especially in *Summa Theologica*, IIa-IIae, q. 47–56.

10. I have developed these themes extensively in *Character, Community, and Politics* (University, Ala: University of Alabama Press, 1982).

11. *The Moral Foundation of Democracy* (Chicago: University of Chicago Press, 1954), p. 126.

12. Ibid., pp. 128, 57.

13. *Christ and Culture*, p. 83.

14. See Donald D. Wall, "The Confessing Church and the Second World War," *Journal of Church and State* 23 (Winter 1981): 15–34.

15. *New Catholic Encyclopedia* (New York: McGraw-Hill, 1967), 11:928, col. 2.

16. St. Thomas Aquinas, *Philosophical Texts*, select. and trans. by Thomas Gilby (New York: Oxford University Press, 1951), p. 357.

17. Peter H. Davids, "God and Caesar, II," *Sojourners*, May 1981, pp. 24–26.

Ellis Sandoz · *Power and Spirit in the Founding: Thoughts on the Genesis of Americanism*

1. Adams to James Warren, June 17, 1782, in *Works of John Adams*, ed. Charles F. Adams, 10 vols. (Boston: Charles C. Little and James Brown, 1851–54), 9:512; cf. John to Abigail Adams ("Portia"), "early 1780," in *Letters of John Adams*, ed. Charles F. Adams, 2 vols. (Boston: Charles C. Little and James Brown, 1841), 2:68; Jefferson to Edward Rutledge, June 24, 1797, in *Writings of Thomas Jefferson*, ed. A. A. Lipscomb and A. E. Bergh, 20 vols. in 10 (Washington, D.C.: Thomas Jefferson Memorial Association, 1905), 9:409; cf. Adams to Benjamin Rush, July 7, 1805, in Adams, *Old Family Letters, Copied from the Originals for Alexander Biddle* (Philadelphia, 1892), 70.

2. Raoul de Roussy de Sales, "What Makes an American?" *Atlantic Monthly*, March 1939; quoted from Dixon Wector, *The Hero In America: A Chronicle of Hero Worship* (1941; repr. ed. Ann Arbor, Mich.: Ann Arbor Paperbacks, 1963), p. 81.

3. W. F. Craven, *The Legend of the Founding Fathers* (1956; repr. ed. Ithaca, N.Y.: Cornell University Press, 1965), pp. 87–88.

4. Jefferson to Adams, Aug. 30, 1787, in *The Adams-Jefferson Letters*, ed. Lester J. Cappon, 2 vols. in 1 (1959; repr. ed. New York: Simon and Schuster, Clarion Books, 1971), 1:196; Adams to John Jay, Sept. 22, 1787, in *Works*, 8:452. Cf. Max Farrand, *The Framing of the Constitution* (New Haven, Conn.: Yale University Press, 1913), pp. 39–41; Jefferson to Adams, Mar. 25, 1826, *Adams-Jefferson Letters*, 2:614.

5. Adams to John Penn, Jan. 1776, in *Works*, 4:203.

6. Adams to William Cushing, June 9, 1776, ibid., 9:391; Adams to Abigail Adams, Oct. 26, 1777, in *Letters of John Adams*, 2:14. Rush's account of Adams's views is given ibid., pp. 15–16.

7. Jürgen Gebhardt, *Die Krise des Amerikanismus: Revolutionäre Ordnung und gesellschaftliches Selbstverständnis in der amerikanischen Republik* (Stuttgart: Ernst Klett Verlag, 1976), p. 46. This German work is the best study of Americanism I have found, resting on an exhaustive examination of John Adams's published and manuscript writings and a large portion of the relevant secondary literature.

8. *Letters of John Adams*, 2:16n.

9. *Works*, 4:291–92. Cf. *Federalist no. 38*.

10. Adams, *Works*, 4:292, and Gebhardt, *Amerikanismus*, pp. 45–46.

11. Adams to James Warren, June 17, 1782, *Works*, 9:512.

12. Adams to Benjamin Rush, April 4, 1790, quoted from Gebhardt, *Amerikanismus*, p. 22.

13. Adams to Benjamin Rush, Feb. 25, 1808, and Adams to Benjamin Waterhouse, Aug. 16, 1812, quoted from ibid., p. 21.

14. Adams to Cunningham, April 24, 1809, quoted from ibid., p. 9.

15. Stiles's sermon runs to over a hundred printed pages in its second edition, published in Worcester, Mass., by Isaiah Thomas in 1785. For convenience I have quoted principally from the selections given in Conrad Cherry, ed., *God's New Israel: Religious Interpretations of American Destiny* (Englewood Cliffs, N.J.: Prentice-Hall, Inc., 1971), pp. 82–92 at 83–84.

16. Ibid., p. 85.

17. Ibid., pp. 87, 90, 91, 92. Additional material interpolated and quoted from the text of the sermon as printed in John W. Thornton, ed., *The Pulpit of the American Revolution; Or, the Political Sermons of the Period of 1776* (Boston: Gould and Lincoln, 1860), pp. 453–65. See Edmund S. Morgan, *The Gentle Puritan: A Life of Ezra Stiles, 1727–1795* (New Haven & London: Yale University Press, 1962), pp. 453–55 (for the quoted sermon), p. 447 (as a student of mysticism).

18. Perry Miller, "From Covenant to Revival," in *Religion in American Life*, ed. J. W. Smith and A. L. Jamison, 4 vols. (Princeton, N.J.: Princeton University Press, 1961), 1:342–43. I make no attempt to cite here the large related literature.

19. Quotations from official reports dated August 20, 1776, and June 20, 1782, in Gaillard Hunt, *The History of the Seal of the United States* (Washington, D.C.: Department of State, 1909), pp. 11, 41–42. See the dollar bill! The reverse of the seal is in disuse for any other purpose, uncut since 1884, as "spiritless, prosaic, heavy, and inappropriate."

20. Ibid., p. 42. The mottoes are from Virgil: "Audacibus annue coeptis" (favor my daring undertaking), *Aeneid*, 9, ver. 625; cf. *Georgics* 1.40; and "Magnus ab integro seclorum nascitur ordo" (the great series of ages begins anew) from the fourth *Eclogue*, ver. 5 (ibid., p. 34).

21. *Christian Science Monitor*, Oct. 16, 1952.

22. Aristotle, *Nicomachean Ethics* 1095b23–1096a6. See the exchange of letters between the second and third presidents of the United States during the summer and fall of 1813 in *Adams-Jefferson Letters*, 2:335–413. Cf. Douglass Adair, *Fame and the Founding Fathers*, ed. Trevor Colbourn (New York: W. W. Norton & Co., 1974).

23. Cf. Eric Voegelin, *The New Science of Politics* (Chicago: University of Chicago Press, 1952), chaps. 2–3; cf. the analysis in Sandoz, *The Voegelinian Revolution: A Biographical Introduction* (Baton Rouge: Louisiana State University Press, 1982), pp. 90–115. Related to the argument of the present paper is my "Classical and Christian Dimensions of American Political Thought," *Modern Age* 25 (1981): 14–25, and the literature cited therein. Cf. my "Political Obligation and the Brutish in Man," *Review of Politics* 33 (1971): 95–121; and "The Civil Theology of Liberal Democracy: Locke and His Predecessors," *Journal of Politics* 34 (1972): 2–36, whose arguments are presupposed here.

24. John H. Hallowell, *The Moral Foundation of Democracy* (Chicago: University of Chicago Press, 1954), pp. 98–100.

25. Adams to James Warren, Aug. 4, 1778, quoted from Gebhardt, *Amerikanismus*, p. 37.

26. Adams, *Works*, 4:293.

27. *The Federalist*, ed. Jacob E. Cooke (Middletown, Conn.: Wesleyan Univer-

sity Press, 1961), pp. 9 (*no. 2*) and 88 (*no. 14*). Jefferson to Henry Lee, May 8, 1825, in *The Life and Selected Writings of Thomas Jefferson*, ed. Adrienne Koch and William Peden (New York: Modern Library, 1944), p. 719.

28. Adams, *Works*, 3:463.

29. Adams to Jefferson, June 28, 1813, in *Adams-Jefferson Letters*, 2:339–40. Cf. Adams, *Works*, 9:187–88 for the response to the Philadelphians, dated May 7, 1798.

30. William Blackstone, *Commentaries*, 1:40–41; Edward Coke, 7 *Reports*, at 12a–12b, *Calvin's Case* (1610), the latter quoted from Edward S. Corwin, *The "Higher Law" Background of American Constitutional Law* (1928, 1929; repr. ed. Ithaca, N.Y.: Cornell University Press, Great Seal Books, 1955), p. 46.

31. Not with approval, however. See *Winthrop's Journal: "History of New England," 1630–1649*, ed. James K. Hosmer, 2 vols. (New York: Charles Scribner's Sons, 1908), 2:301: quoted by Winthrop as the claim of one Dr. Robert Child, with whom the colony was in serious conflict. Cf. John Locke, *Second Treatise of Government*, sec. 123, where he calls the three terms together *Property*. The earliest use of the formula "lives, liberties, and estates" that I have found occurs in the unfortunate notice from Charles I of the impeachment of Lord Kimbolton and the five members of the House of Commons (Hampden, Pym, et al.) of Jan. 3, 1642; see S. R. Gardiner, ed., *Constitutional Documents of the Puritan Revolution, 1625–1660* (3rd ed., rev. Oxford: At the Clarendon Press, 1906), p. 236; J. W. Gough, *Fundamental Law In English Constitutional History* (cor. ed. Oxford: At the Clarendon Press, 1961), p. 78.

32. *Federalist*, ed. Cooke, p. 297 (*no. 43*), a view confirmed forty years later and, again, at the very end of his life. Cf. Madison to N. P. Trist, April 1827, Madison to C. Caldwell, Sept. 20, Nov. 23, 1826, in Irving Brandt, *James Madison*, 6 vols. (Indianapolis and New York: Bobbs-Merrill Co., 1941–61), 6:445–46; "The Nature of the Union: A Final Reckoning," (1835–36) in *The Mind of the Founder: Sources of the Political Thought of James Madison*, ed. Marvin Meyers (Indianapolis and New York: Bobbs-Merrill Co., 1973), p. 567. On the role of "higher law" jurisprudence in American constitutional law generally, and through the development of such doctrines as substantive due process (Old and New), nationalization of the Bill of Rights through the Due Process Clause of the Fourteenth Amendment, emergence of fundamental rights as a privileged sphere, some of them plainly extra-constitutional or "penumbral," and emergence of substantive Equal Protection, see my discussion in *Conceived In Liberty: American Individual Rights Today* (North Scituate, Mass.: Duxbury Press, 1978).

33. Richard Hooker, *Of the Laws of Ecclesiastical Polity*, intro. Christopher Morris, 2 vols. (London: J. M. Dent & Sons, Ltd.; New York: E. P. Dutton & Co., Everyman's Library, 1907), 1:188; bk. 1, chap. 10, par. 1, published in 1593. Cf. Aristotle, *Politics* 1.2 (1253a2–18); 3.16 (1287a29–35).

34. Jefferson to Adams, Oct. 14, and Adams to Jefferson, Nov. 4, 1816, in *Adams-Jefferson Letters*, 2:492, 494. Hooker, *Ecclesiastical Polity*, p. 194; quoted by Locke, *Second Treatise of Government*, sec. 134n.

35. Madison, *Federalist*, ed. Cooke, p. 419 (*no. 62*); cf. Adams, "Thoughts on Government" (1776), *Works*, 4:193: "We ought to consider what is the end of government, before we determine which is the best form. Upon this point all speculative politicians will agree, that the happiness of society is the end of government, as all divines and moral philosophers will agree that the happiness of the individual is the end of man." A similar passage in Adams to John Penn that same year is followed by this, inter alia: "for the true idea of a republic is an

empire of laws, and not of men; and, therefore, as a republic is the best of governments, so that particular combination of power which is best contrived for a faithful execution of the laws, is the best of republics." Ibid., p. 204.

36. *Federalist*, ed. Cooke, p. 341 (*no. 49*); cf. p. 315 and editor's note (*no. 46*), and p. 349 (*no. 51*).

37. George Lee Turberville to James Madison, April 6, 1788, in *The Papers of James Madison*, ed. R. A. Rutland and C. F. Hobson (Charlottesville: University Press of Virginia, 1977), 11:24.

38. *Federalist*, ed. Cooke, p. 349 (*no. 51*); Adams, *Works*, 6:279 and passim. Digges quoted from Richard Tuck, *Natural Rights Theories: Their Origin and Development* (Cambridge: Cambridge University Press, 1979), p. 106.

39. Cf. Charles de Secondat de Montesquieu, *Spirit of Laws*, bk. 9; William Blackstone, *Commentaries*, 1:154–55; C. C. Weston, "Beginnings of the Classical Theory of the English Constitution," *Proceedings of the American Philosophical Society* 100 (1956): 133–44.

40. *Works*, 6:234–98, 397–99; 5:10, 40, 488; 4:391, 408, 436. Cf. the discussion in Correa M. Walsh, *The Political Science of John Adams: A Study in the Theory of Mixed Government and the Bicameral System* (New York and London: G. P. Putnam's Sons, 1915), p. 233 and passim. On the *amor sui* and *amor Dei* in Augustine, see *The City of God* 14.28, 15.1–8.

41. Adams to Jefferson, April 19, 1817, in *Adams-Jefferson Letters*, 2:509.

42. Adams, "Discourses on Davila" (1790), in *Works*, 6:280. Cf. Zoltan Haraszti, *John Adams and the Prophets of Progress* (1952; repr. ed. New York: Grosset & Dunlap, Universal Library, 1964), pp. 165–79; John R. Howe, Jr., *The Changing Political Thought of John Adams* (Princeton, N.J.: Princeton University Press, 1966), pp. 28–58.

43. Cf. T. S. Eliot, "Choruses from 'The Rock,'" in *The Complete Poems and Plays, 1909–1950* (New York: Harcourt, Brace & World, 1971), p. 106.

44. Reverend Thomas Coombe, quoted in Miller, "From Covenant to Revival," p. 329.

45. *Federalist*, ed. Cooke, p. 238.

46. Jefferson to Adams, June 15, 1813, in *Adams-Jefferson Letters*, 2:331. On Jefferson's religion see the useful survey in Charles B. Sanford, *Thomas Jefferson and His Library* (Hamden, Conn.: Shoe String Press, Archon Books, 1977), chap. 4.

47. Cf. the material cited in n. 29 above. For a characteristic view of the "religious madness called enthusiasm" see *Cato's Letters: or, Essays on Liberty, Civil and Religious*, 4 vols. in 2 (6th ed., 1755; repr. ed. New York: Da Capo Press, 1971), 4:143–52 and passim. Originally published in England in the early 1720s, these essays by John Trenchard and Thomas Gordon were widely circulated in America as staples of Old Whig politics.

48. Cf. Adams, *Works*, 6:281. See also Sandoz, "Civil Theology of Liberal Democracy," esp. pp. 31–36.

William R. Marty · *The Search for Realism in Politics and Ethics: Reflections by a Political Scientist on a Christian Perspective*

The major thesis and many of the arguments of this essay are borrowed from John Hallowell, as those familiar with his work will recognize. J. Harvey Lomax and Barbara Meissner Campbell made useful criticisms of an earlier version which appeared in *Logos*, 1 (1980), pp. 93–124.

1. There may be a type of personality peculiarly susceptible to fanaticism or authoritarianism, but in a world full of left-wing authoritarians, it is obvious that it is not restricted to the political right. For a classic statement of the view that conservatives are conservative in their politics because of defects in their personality structures (though there may be individual exceptions) see Herbert McClosky, "Conservatism and Personality," *American Political Science Review* 52 (1958): 27–45, esp. 36–43.

2. From *Outlines of an Historical View of the Progress of the Human Mind*, cited in Hallowell, *Main Currents in Modern Political Thought* (New York: Holt, Rinehart and Winston, 1950), p. 132.

3. Cited in Harry V. Jaffa, *How to Think About the American Revolution: A Bicentennial Celebration* (Durham, N.C.: Carolina Academic Press, 1978), p. 60.

4. Ibid., pp. 60–61.

5. Ibid., pp. 106–7.

6. Ibid., p. 66.

7. Alexandr Solzhenitsyn estimated a few years ago that the Soviet Regime had annihilated sixty million people altogether. *The Listener* (London), 22 Feb. 1979, p. 271.

8. Solzhenitsyn, *Solzhenitsyn: The Voice of Freedom* (Washington, D.C.: AFL-CIO, 1975), p. 9.

9. Ibid. Solzhenitsyn notes that the Cheka apologized because its data were not complete.

10. Cited in a syndicated column by George Will, May 22, 1978. Vladimir Bukovsky, an inmate of the Soviet prison camps for much of his life, says: "According to our most accurate estimates, the number of prisoners in the Soviet Union is never less than two-and-a-half-million." He adds that "almost a third of the Soviet population has passed through the camps." *Sunday Telegraph* (London), Oct. 22, 1978.

11. See Peter L. Berger, *Pyramids of Sacrifice: Political Ethics and Social Change* (Garden City, N.Y.: Doubleday and Co., Anchor Books, 1976), p. 169.

12. William Shawcross, *Commercial Appeal* (Memphis), Nov. 19, 1978. Shawcross covered Indochina for the *Sunday Times* (London).

13. *The Economist* (London), Feb. 17, 1979, p. 61.

14. The flight of the "boat people" slowed after international pressures on Vietnam, but a new exodus began in 1981.

15. In April 1980 some 10,000 people crowded into the Peruvian embassy in Havana seeking asylum. A furious Fidel Castro offered free exit to any Cuban who wanted to leave. More than 125,000 responded, but this exodus ended when the United States refused to accept more Cuban refugees.

16. Cited in Reinhold Niebuhr, *Moral Man and Immoral Society* (New York: Charles Scribner's Sons, Lyceum Edition, 1932, 1960), p. 24.

17. In *Emile*, of course, Rousseau describes a long and careful education, though its purpose is to avoid corrupting the natural impulses of man.

18. Cited in Hallowell, *Main Currents*, p. 168.

19. From the Barbara Foxley translation of *Emile*, cited in Romain Rolland, *The Living Thoughts of Rousseau* (New York: Longmans, Green and Co., 1939), pp. 88–89. Compare Allen Bloom's translation, "Let us set down as an incontestable maxim that the first movements of nature are always right. There is no original perversity in the human heart." Jean Jacques Rousseau, *Emile: or On Education* (New York: Basic Books, 1979), p. 92.

20. Rousseau, *Social Contract and Discourses*, trans. G. D. H. Cole (New York: E. P. Dutton and Co., Everyman's Library, 1950), p. 26.

21. This question represents the popularized, not the strict, understanding of Rousseau's General Will.

22. Rousseau, *Social Contract,* p. 18.

23. Cited in Hallowell, *Main Currents,* p. 182.

24. Bertrand Russell, *A History of Western Philosophy* (New York: Simon and Schuster, 1945), p. 828.

25. Cited in *The Economist* (London), Oct. 22, 1978, p. 123.

26. Niebuhr, *The Children of Light and the Children of Darkness: A Vindication of Democracy and a Critique of its Traditional Defense* (New York: Charles Scribner's Sons, Lyceum Edition, 1944, 1972), pp. 61–62.

27. Ibid., p. 17.

28. Cited by Christopher Bramwell, *Daily Telegraph* (London), Feb. 24, 1979.

29. Niebuhr, *The Nature and Destiny of Man: A Christian Interpretation,* 2 vols. (New York: Charles Scribner's Sons, 1941, 1964), 1:227.

30. Hallowell, *Main Currents,* p. 692.

31. Alexander Hamilton, James Madison, and John Jay, *The Federalist Papers* (New York: The New American Library, Mentor Books, 1961), no. 51, p. 322.

32. Ibid., no. 10, p. 81.

33. Ibid., no. 72, p. 437.

34. Ibid., nos. 10 and 51.

35. As an example, in spite of half a century of socialist education and exhortation, "private plots account for only 3 percent of the farmland in the Soviet Union but produce an astonishing 30 percent of the food, according to official [Soviet] statistics." Associated Press release, *Commercial Appeal* (Memphis), Nov. 23.

36. The Soviet use of private plots and bonuses and the whole tenor of recent economic policy in the Peoples Republic of China illustrate this point. But the best illustration is, perhaps, the complete failure of the Cuban attempt to downplay material incentives between 1966 and the early 1970s and the return, as a matter of governmental policy, to material incentives by 1973–74. See Jorge I. Dominguez, "Socialism in Cuba," in *Socialism in the Third World,* ed. Helen Desfosses and Jacques Levesque (New York: Praeger Publishers, 1975), pp. 41–45.

Index

Contributors

Francis Canavan, professor of political science at Fordham University, is the author of *The Political Reason of Edmund Burke*, *Freedom of Expression: Purpose as Limit* (forthcoming) and of articles in professional and other journals.

Clarke Edward Cochran, professor of political science at Texas Tech University, is the author of articles on contemporary political theory and of *Character, Community and Politics*, as well as coauthor of *American Public Policy: An Introduction.*

Barry Cooper is professor of political science at the University of Calgary and is the author of *Merleau-Ponty and Marxism*, *Michel Foucault*, *The End of History*, and several articles on Canadian political thought.

R. Bruce Douglass is associate professor of government at Georgetown University and has been a visiting professor in the Department of Government and Foreign Affairs at the University of Virginia. He has published in *The Journal of Politics*, *The Review of Politics*, *Political Theory*, *The Political Science Reviewer*, and other journals.

William C. Havard is professor and chairman of the Department of Political Science at Vanderbilt University. A graduate of Louisiana State University and holder of a Ph.D. degree from the University of London, he is a former editor of *The Journal of Politics* and the author of numerous articles and books. His most recent work is *Band of Prophets: The Vanderbilt Agrarians after Fifty Years*, coedited with Walter Sullivan.

William R. Marty, associate professor of political science at Memphis State University, is the author of a number of essays, which include "Nonviolence, Violence, and Reason," and "Rawls and the Harried Mother."

Walter B. Mead, professor of political science at Illinois State University, is the author of *Extremism and Cognition: Styles of Irresponsibility in American Society* and of articles in normative theory and political philosophy.

Gerhart Niemeyer, emeritus professor of government in the University of Notre Dame, is the author of *Law Without Force, Deceitful Peace, Between Nothingness and Paradise,* and a host of articles in intellectual journals. In 1980 he was ordained a priest in the Episcopal Church.

J. M. Porter is professor of political science at the University of Saskatchewan. He has edited *Martin Luther: Selected Political Writings* and *Sophia and Praxis: The Boundaries of Politics.* His articles have appeared in *Marxist Perspective, The American Journal of Jurisprudence, The Denver Quarterly, The Journal of the History of Ideas,* and elsewhere.

Claes G. Ryn is chairman of the Department of Politics at The Catholic University of America. He has written a book on American intellectual conservatism published in Sweden, *Democracy and the Ethical Life*, and, with Folk Leander, *Will, Imagination and Reason* (forthcoming). Articles by him have appeared in *The Journal of Politics, The Political Science Reviewer, Modern Age, Thought,* and other journals.

Ellis Sandoz is professor of political science at Louisiana State University and a member of the National Council on the Humanities. He is the author of *Political Apocalypse: A Study of Dostoevsky's Grand Inquisitor, Conceived in Liberty: American Individual Rights Today,* and *The Voegelinian Revolution: A Biographical Introduction.* He edited *Eric Voegelin's Thought: A Critical Appraisal* and, with Cecil V. Crabb, Jr., *A Tide of Discontent: The 1980 Elections and Their Meaning.* Currently he is at work on *A Government of Laws: Essays on the American Founding.*

Mulford Q. Sibley is professor emeritus of political science and American studies at the University of Minnesota. He has written articles and books on such themes as pacifism, conscientious objection, civil rights, and the history of political ideas. A recent book is *Nature and Civilization: Some Implications for Politics.*

James W. Skillen, executive director of the Association for Public Justice in Washington, D.C., is the author of *International Politics and the Demand for Global Justice* and *Christians Organizing for Political Service*, and coauthor of *Disestablishment a Second Time: Genuine Pluralism for American Schools*.

Thomas A. Spragens, Jr., professor of political science at Duke University, is the author of several books and articles on modern and contemporary political theory. His most recent book is *The Irony of Liberal Reason*.

Kenneth W. Thompson, director of the Miller Center of Public Affairs and Commonwealth Professor at the University of Virginia, is the author of numerous writings, which include *Morality and Foreign Policy*, *Masters of International Thought*, *Cold War Theories* (vol. 1), and *Political Realism*.

Fred H. Willhoite, Jr., professor of political science at Coe College, is the author of articles on political theory and evolution and of *Beyond Nihilism: Albert Camus's Contribution to Political Thought*.

James L. Wiser, professor and chairman of the Political Science Department at Loyola University of Chicago, is the author of articles on classical and contemporary political theory and of *Political Philosophy: A History of the Search for Order*.

Books of related interest

From Enlightenment to Revolution

Eric Voegelin, *edited by* John H. Hallowell

Eric Voegelin's Thought

A Critical Appraisal

Edited by Ellis Sandoz

Development: For What?

Edited by John H. Hallowell

Prospects for Constitutional Democracy

Essays in Honor of R. Taylor Cole

Edited by John H. Hallowell

The Recollections of R. Taylor Cole

Educator, Emissary, Development Planner

R. Taylor Cole

The Principles of Social Order

Selected Essays of Lon L. Fuller

Edited by Kenneth I. Winston